S0-DPP-680

Women, Minorities, and Employment Discrimination

Women, Minorities, and Employment Discrimination

Edited by

Phyllis A. Wallace
Massachusetts Institute of Technology

Annette M. LaMond
Yale University

Lexington Books
D.C. Heath and Company
Lexington, Massachusetts
Toronto

Chapter 4, Barbara R. Bergmann, "Towards More Useful Modes of Research on Discrimination in Employment and Pay," *Sloan Management Review* Spring 1974, vol. 15, no. 3, pp. 43-45, has been reprinted in this volume by permission of the *Sloan Management Review.*

Chapter 7, Solomon W. Polachek, "Differences in Expected Post-School Investment as a Determinant of Market Wage Differentials," *International Economic Review* June 1975, pp. 451-470, has been reprinted in this volume by permission. Copyright 1975 by the Wharton School of Finance and Commerce, University of Pennsylvania and the Osaka University Institute of Social and Economic Research.

Library of Congress Cataloging in Publication Data

Main entry under title:
 Women, minorities, and employment discrimination.

 "Papers . . . prepared for research workshops . . . held at M.I.T. during 1974 . . . [by] the Industrial Relations Section of the Alfred P. Sloan School of Management."
 1. Discrimination in employment—United States—Congresses. 2. Wages—United States—Congresses. I. Wallace, Phyllis Ann. II. LaMond, Annette M. III. Massachusetts Institute of Technology. Industrial Relations Section.
HD4903.5.U58W65   331.1'33'0973   76-53903
ISBN 0-669-01282-3

Copyright © 1977 by Massachusetts Institute of Technology

Reproduction in whole or in part permitted for any purpose of the United States Government, including reproduction by National Technical Information Service in microfiche only.

All rights reserved. No part of this publication may be reproduced or transmitted in any form or by any means, electronic or mechanical, including photocopy, recording, or any information storage or retrieval system, without permission in writing from the publisher. The provision of the United States Government constitutes the only exception to this prohibition. This book was prepared with the support of NSF Grant ERPA 73-02721. However, any opinions, findings, conclusions or recommendations herein are those of the authors and do not necessarily reflect the views of NSF.

Published simultaneously in Canada.

Printed in the United States of America.

International Standard Book Number: 0-669-01282-3

Library of Congress Catalog Card Number: 76-53903

Contents

HD
4903
.5
.U58
W65

211982

Acknowledgments

A grant from the National Science Foundation, Research Applied to National Needs (RANN), provided the initial funding for the research workshops on equal employment opportunity that were held at the Massachusetts Institute of Technology in 1974. Significant support for the completion of this effort and the preparation of the manuscript from the papers and proceedings of the conference was provided by the Industrial Relations Section of the Alfred P. Sloan School of Management at M.I.T. We are indebted to Professor Charles A. Myers, director of this section.

We are exceedingly grateful to the authors represented in this collection. For more than a year, while we sought permission to publish these materials, they waited patiently. Others who contributed to this project are: Gladys Handy, program manager for the NSF grant; Lorraine Goldstein and Carole La Mond, skillful editors; Frances M. Chan, administrative assistant on the NSF project, and Joyce Yearwood who supervised the final typing.

We hope that we have encouraged some social scientists to be more willing to explore the methodologies of other disciplines. If any of the analytic techniques discussed in this book can help to reduce the differential treatment of women and minorities in the labor market, this volume will have been a labor of love.

Phyllis A. Wallace
Annette M. La Mond

Introduction

Phyllis A. Wallace and
Annette M. LaMond

The papers in this book were prepared for research workshops on equal employment opportunity that were held at the Massachusetts Institute of Technology during 1974. The Industrial Relations Section of the Alfred P. Sloan School of Management invited economists, psychologists, and sociologists to assess the scope of research on employment discrimination. Their papers and comments provide not only an overview of the status of research on employment discrimination but also a prospectus that defines common dimensions for future research. The final recommendations reflect the views of both academic researchers and decision makers from business, labor unions, government, and organizations concerned with equal employment opportunity.

The opening paper by Annette La Mond traces the development of the economic literature on employment discrimination. From 1957, when Gary Becker published his pioneering theoretical work, *The Economics of Discrimination*, until the present, economists have attempted to explain persistent race and sex wage differentials through the neoclassical model. Such studies have failed to consider the manner in which economic variables feed back on social and psychological conditioning of individual workers. The impact of economic variables on the formation of discriminatory tastes has remained outside the neoclassical model. Unfortunately, the insights offered by alternative models, for example, statistical discrimination, dual labor market, and bargaining models, have not been incorporated into the mainstream of economic thought on employment discrimination.

La Mond notes that the limited exchange between institutional and neoclassical economists, as well as the lack of communication between economists and other social scientists, have resulted in economic models of labor discrimination that are naive in terms of psychological and social insights. An approach that integrates the various perspectives would help to shape a more comprehensive and robust theory of employment discrimination. Glenn Loury's paper takes an important step in this direction by extending the neoclassical model to include the effects of family and community background on racial income differences.

Patricia Gurin's paper, "The Role of Worker Expectancies in the Study of Employment Discrimination," reviews the economic literature on employment discrimination from the psychologist's perspective, and offers new ideas about how social psychological research could be used by economists to understand employment discrimination. Traditional research strategies in both economics and psychology have emphasized personal deficiencies of workers as the source of sex and race differentials in employment and wages. Gurin suggests that the focus be shifted to factors on the demand side of the market—to employer beliefs, personnel practices and policies, and organizational and structural characteristics of firms, which may explain productivity differentials. Gurin argues that perceptions of the market, beliefs about opportunities, and awareness of channeling processes may affect expectancies of success, and hence, motivation, productivity, and supply elasticities. Thus, a strong case is made for collaboration between economists and psychologists on research that examines the impact of expectancies on employment behavior as well as the sensitivity of expectancies to changes in market opportunities.

In her comment on Gurin's paper, Carolyn Shaw Bell seconds the call for further research on the psychological parameters of labor supply functions, and points out that psychological research on the beliefs and perceptions of women and minorities about markets and opportunities will be vital in two major respects. First, incorporation of the notion of expectancies into the theory of choice may yield new insights into the individual's decision to supply labor. Bell suggests that by viewing a particular job or employment opportunity in the context of life or career experience, economists may build a "permanent employment theory" where jobs are recognized to contain permanent and transitory elements. A significant question is, thus, whether jobs held by men and women differ in the ratio of transitory to permanent elements. Bell also notes that this approach to the labor supply decision requires a reconsideration of assumptions regarding the income unit, including its size and composition over time, as well as its permanence. Second, recognition of the full range of information conveyed by market feedback mechanisms may be expected to enrich economic theory. Bell argues that unless economists recognize the psychological dimension of market operations, they will become increasingly handicapped in offering policy programs.

Lotte Bailyn recommends that the Gurin paper should be closely read not only by economists but also by psychologists. Bailyn points out that psychologists have traditionally viewed career development in a sequence flowing from individual motives and aspirations to job-related behavior and finally to experiences in the labor market. Bailyn notes that Gurin's contribution is to reorder the career development sequence by recognizing that experiences in the labor market shape aspirations and job-related behavior in turn. Bailyn suggests that in subsequent elaborations of Gurin's model psychological research focus on the ways careers actually develop in specific people. Research of this nature will be critical to furthering our understanding of how experiences are translated into expectations and subsequent market behavior.

In her paper, "What Psychological Research on the Labor Force Participation of Women is Needed?," Judith Long Laws proposes an organizing framework for psychological research on the labor force participation of women. These research questions might be placed in one of three major categories. The first focus would be on the development and change of work orientations and the labor force attachment of women in a life cycle context. Such a framework of the female life cycle, defining key decision points and stages, is essential if research on the labor force participation of women is to be conducted in a coherent manner. The second research area would encompass experimentally oriented studies of the sex composition of the work force within the firm. Research at this level might explore both the effectiveness of female and male leaders, given task structure, group climate, and legitimacy of the leadership position, and the differential effects of mixed-sex versus same-sex work groups. Research studies in the third area would examine employer attitudes and behavior. Questions here would be directed to the situation that the female worker confronts, especially the behavior and attitudes of those responsible for the implementation of equal opportunity policy.

A major concern of the participants at the research workshops was how to facilitate research on employment discrimination. Barbara Bergmann's essay, "Towards More Useful Modes of Research on Discrimination in Employment and Pay," addresses this question and asks why economic research has failed to have a major impact on the process of ending discrimination. Bergmann states that the issue is not the direction of national policy, but the speed at which policy is implemented. Economists, however, have focused almost exclusively on explaining and measuring the effect of discrimination on the wages and employment of particular groups and hardly at all on the difficult economic issues raised by the implementation of equal employment and affirmative action policy. Bergmann calls for new, *useful* modes of research to remedy this imbalance, and suggests that such research might take two directions. First, at the industry level, economists can work to identify and document discriminatory employment patterns in different industries. Second, at the firm or establishment level, economists can contribute to the implementation of policy by assisting in the planning process through the formulation of affirmative action goals, timetables, incentive schemes, and so forth.

An example of the policy-oriented research recommended by Bergmann is provided by Ray Marshall's paper, "Black Employment in the South," which summarizes the major findings of his study of black employment patterns in thirteen southern states. The specific questions raised were: (1) What are the black employment patterns and trends?, (2) What are the main explanations for the patterns and trends?, and (3) What kinds of public policies are most effective in improving black employment opportunities? Rural and nonmetropolitan places as well as metropolitan areas were studied. Detailed field surveys and analyses were made in Atlanta, Birmingham, Houston, Louisville, Memphis, Miami, and New Orleans. Employment patterns in both the private and public sectors were analyzed, and comparisons were made with the non-South. An important by-product of this study was a critique of existing theories of the economics of racial discrimination.

Michael Piore commends Marshall for combining his study of employment practices in particular industries with theory and data in an "eclectic" approach to policy problems, and notes that it is important to question whether there is a single pattern underlying discriminatory practices in specific industries. If a single pattern is detected, is the pattern in the South different from that in the North? Given the answers to these questions, policies may be designed to bring an end to discrimination not only in specific industries but also in its underlying systemic form.

Questions were raised by some participants about whether labor market studies could expand our knowledge of employment discrimination. In "Modeling a Segmented Labor Market," Charles Holt discusses labor market processes and structural relationships and alternatives for formalizing their quantitative and dynamic characteristics in a systems model. A description of a model of a demographically segmented labor market is presented, including a review of model formulation, data issues, econometric problems, and strategy for progressing from simple to successively more complex system models and applications. Holt notes that in modeling labor markets it is essential to recognize that workers are highly differentiated by skill ability, experience, location, preferences, race, and sex. Similarly, jobs are differentiated by skill requirements, inducements, location, and perhaps extraneous restrictions. Behavior interactions in the labor market that are influenced by these factors have the effect of segmenting the market. The group-transition model selected by Holt groups similar workers and firms and carries out the system simulation in terms of the sizes of particular groups in various states and the probabilities of individual transfers between them. Holt points out that the group-transition model captures much of the heterogeneous behavior between groups, yet offers simplicity of modeling derived from relative homogeneity within groups. By developing a sequence of group-transition simulation models, Holt hopes to contribute to our understanding of the operation of labor markets in validated, quantitative terms.

Following the Holt paper are comments by James Annable and Bennett Harrison. Annable admits to reservations about Holt's model in two general areas: first, whether the model is successful in capturing the structure of the labor market, and second, whether it contributes to our knowledge of employment opportunity. In the first area, Annable points out several problems, including data limitations (particularly on the supply side) and insufficient detail in the specification of the model structure. In the second area, Annable questions whether the Holt model adds to our understanding of the factors that cause impediments to equal opportunity. For example, given Holt's reliance on a simple neoclassical specification of individual objective functions, the model can neither explain why particular groups experience different probabilities with respect to employment, and unemployment, nor analyze the causes of job-access barriers. As such, Annable suggests that unless Holt incorporates factors not presently considered, for instance, the development of labor market expectations, the model is unlikely to explain the nature of, or provide solutions to, the problem of unequal employment opportunity.

Harrison is optimistic that the techniques developed by Holt, though not the current model, will provide decision makers with a significant equal employment policy tool. Harrison argues that if Holt's techniques are to be successfully applied to the problem of labor market discrimination, he must address several issues. The Holt model cannot capture feedback effects arising from the response of different groups of workers or producers to changes in the circumstances of others. Second, in the Holt model, the transition of individuals from one state to another, for example, from employment to unemployment, is determined almost exclusively by the supply characteristics of workers. Labor demand variables—employer profits, market concentration, et cetera—receive little attention. Third, the Holt model overlooks the interactions between the labor market and other income-bearing activities, such as welfare dependency, criminal activities, and quasi-legal "hustling."

Another body of literature, the human capital investment school, can also be more closely linked to studies on employment discrimination. In "Differences in Expected Post-School Investment as a Determinant of Market Wage Differentials," Solomon Polachek outlines a theory of post-school investment, or on-the-job training, when labor force participation over the life cycle is expected to be intermittent. Given the assumption that an individual's labor force participation may be intermittent, Polachek demonstrates that both the quantity of investment and its rate of accumulation differ with the degree of attachment to the labor force. Post-school investment functions thus differ according to sex and marital status. Polachek uses measurements of expected human capital investment to explain male-female and married-single wage differentials.

Ronald Oaxaca notes that Polachek implicitly assumes that differences in post-schooling investment between males and females, or blacks and whites, are mainly voluntary in the absence of discrimination. The policy recommendation that follows from Polachek's analysis is that women should be encouraged to form stronger attachments to the labor force if they are to narrow male-female earnings differentials. Oaxaca observes, however, that in spite of the rising labor force participation rate of females over the 1955-1971 period, there was no dramatic narrowing of the male-female earnings differential among year-round, full-time workers. In light of the increasing labor force participation of women, Oaxaca suggests the interesting question is not whether differences in on-the-job training exist, but why the differentials have not been narrowed.

The social environment within which economic activity takes place is explicitly incorporated within the economic model developed by Glenn Loury. In "A Dynamic Theory of Racial Income Differences," Loury investigates the mechanism by which *past* discrimination against blacks impacts the earning potential of current and future generations of black workers. Loury argues that traditional neoclassical theory does not adequately reflect either the impact of an individual's family and community background on his ability to acquire skills valued in the labor market or the influence of social relations between racial groups on market processes and outcomes. Loury analyzes the effects of socioeconomic factors on the skill acquisition process in a racially stratified society and demonstrates that racial income differences may persist if the low relative educational and earning status of blacks in one generation inhibits the ability of succeeding generations to acquire human capital. One may thus question whether an equal opportunity policy that guarantees that persons with identical qualifications will be treated equally in the labor market is a sufficient tool for assuring the elimination of racial income differentials in the long run.

Loury suggests that economists analyze the impact of "social" human capital investments in individuals. Lester Thurow raises several questions to be addressed in future extensions of the Loury model and the social capital concept. For example, to what extent are educational investments joint products, that is, products that are partially investment goods and partially superior consumption goods with a high income elasticity of demand? To what extent is the market for human capital atrophied so that individuals must internally generate their own funds for human capital investments? The answers to these questions will further strengthen Loury's conclusion that equal opportunity in the labor market will not be sufficient to eliminate racial income differences even in the long run.

In the final paper, Phyllis Wallace summarizes the themes and recommendations from the several research workshops on equal employment opportunity. The participants at these sessions generated a full set of questions that in their view constituted a feasible research agenda. The discussions were focused on employment discrimination in both the public and private sectors and the relationship of equal employment opportunity to the development and management of human resources. We believe that the papers and proceedings from the research workshop provide a framework for both more rigorous analysis and a better formulation of policy on the progress of minorities and women in achieving equality in the work force.

1 Economic Theories of Employment Discrimination

Annette M. LaMond

As social scientists, economists have been slow in identifying discrimination in the labor market as a problem for analysis. The pioneering work in developing an economic theory of discrimination to explain racial wage differentials was published by Gary Becker less than twenty years ago, yet received little attention until the late 1960s. Analytical interest in the problem of sex discrimination is of still more recent vintage, and is regarded by some economists as the parochial reserve of women economists. This review attempts to place the contributions of the last twenty years in perspective, and in doing so, to preface the papers contained in this volume.

The neoclassical model offered by Becker in *The Economics of Discrimination* is directed primarily to the problem of racial discrimination, but has been applied to the case of sex discrimination as well.[1] Based on utility maximization principles and the usual neoclassical assumption of a perfectly competitive economy, the Becker model traces the economic consequences of a "taste for discrimination" by employers, employees, or consumers against otherwise equally productive black or women workers. According to Becker, "If an individual has a 'taste for discrimination,' he must act *as if* he·were willing to pay something either directly or in the form of reduced income, to be associated with some persons instead of others."[2] Becker uses discrimination coefficients that correspond to tariffs in international trade to measure the monetary premium paid by different factors of production, employers, or consumers for not associating with particular groups.

Becker's definition of discrimination as a "taste" provided an explanation of the presence of racial wage differentials that seemed to fit neatly into the tradition of neoclassical economics. In addition, the policy implications of the Becker model were comforting ones. Specifically, the model predicts that employers with no discrimination coefficients would respond to the differential in black-white or male-female wages by hiring blacks and women, forcing competitors to do the same, so that, in the long run, wage differentials would disappear. Thus, from the Becker perspective, economic discrimination is essentially a reflection of market imperfections or monopoly power on the part of employers, a problem to be attacked largely through enforcement of the antitrust laws.

On the supply side of the labor market, Becker and other neoclassical economists have pointed out that a portion of racial and sexual wage differentials is due to differential productivity.[3] The so-called human capital school

1

argues that the lower relative wage received by blacks and women reflects their lower relative investment in human capital, including both formal education and on-the-job training. Moreover, the human capital theorists argue that women have different expectations from men with respect to labor force participation over their lifetime and that these expectations lead to a differential investment in human capital. Following Becker's lead, human capital theorists recognized the importance of nonmarket activities within the household in addition to the traditional work–leisure dichotomy in women's labor supply decisions.[4] From this perspective, women's decision not to acquire the requisite human capital for continuous labor force participation is a rational one. Moreover, the concentration of women in a limited number of occupations that are suitable for discontinuous employment appears to be the product of wholly rational behavior rather than of labor market discrimination.

While supply factors unquestionably contribute to racial and sexual differentials in income and occupational segregation, the factors underlying the individual's accumulation of human capital are considered to be exogenous by the human capital theorists. That is, interactions between economic variables on the one hand, and the individual's socialization and psychological conditioning on the other, are left outside of the model. Indeed, by looking at supply factors in isolation from demand factors, the human capital school fails to consider whether blacks' and women's human capital decisions are either partially or wholly a response to employer discrimination.

Only after economists had been jolted by the events of the 1960s did they seriously begin to examine the Becker contribution to a definition of discrimination.[5] The first such work addressed the difficulty of explaining a "taste for discrimination" on the part of white "capitalists" who do not associate physically with black workers. For example, Ann Krueger attempts to bring the Becker model into closer correspondence with reality by hypothesizing that employers' racial interests, rather than their physical distaste for contact with blacks, may modify strict profit maximization calculations.[6] In Krueger's elaboration of the Becker model, white capitalists seek to maximize the income of all whites rather than their own income. From a different perspective, Marcus Alexis postulates that "envy-malice" on the part of white employers or foremen may motivate them to attempt to maximize the relative share of wage income received by white workers.[7]

Although the contributions of Krueger and Alexis are significant in terms of their recognition that group interests may go beyond the self-interested decision making assumed in the Becker model, they do not model the economic forces that cause the development of such group interests, whether founded in an altruistic desire to aid the members of one's own race or in a feeling of envy-malice on the part of whites against blacks. Thus, like Becker, Krueger and Alexis fail to consider the manner in which economic variables feed back on exogenous factors.

Focusing on employee "tastes" for discrimination, Finis Welch argues that the most serious economic consequences of discrimination stem less from employers' discriminatory behavior than from white workers' preference for working with members of their own race.[8] In Welch's elaboration of the Becker model, a worker's wage is a decreasing function of the proportion of that worker's race in the firm's work force. Given this assumption, cost minimization leads to a racially segregated work force. This result stands in contrast to the Becker model's prediction of an integrated work force where white workers receive a premium to cover the disutility derived from the association with black coworkers. Welch points out, however, that if black and white workers are complementary rather than perfect substitutes, racial wage differentials will result in his formulation of the model as well. While Welch's analysis provides new insights, like Krueger's or Alexis's, it does not resolve the questions posed by the exogenous treatment of tastes.

Also in the neoclassical tradition is Barbara Bergmann's attempt to reconcile the predictions of the Becker model with the reality of a persistent racial and sexual segregation in the labor market.[9] Bergmann distinguishes the occurrence of discriminatory wage differentials *within* an occupation from wage differentials *between* equal-skill occupations. Bergmann's model assumes the existence of two occupations, both requiring identical skills, but one prestigious and one menial. Blacks and women, who differ from white males only in ascriptive characteristics, are restricted by demand factors to the low-status occupation. Employers with discriminatory preferences will hire blacks or women into the prestigious occupation when their marginal productivity in the high-status occupation exceeds that in the low-status one by more than a given critical wage differential. Given the restriction of blacks and women into low-status occupations, such occupations are characterized by a relatively large supply of workers, and hence, by lower worker marginal productivity and wages than would be the case in the absence of discrimination. Conversely, white males in the prestigious occupation exhibit higher marginal productivity and wages than if constraints to occupational hiring did not exist.

While Bergmann's model yields important insights into the consequences of occupational segregation, the complete occupational segregation that follows from her assumptions depends on an extreme distribution of employer tastes, especially where men and women and blacks and whites are perfect substitutes. Moreover, while Bergmann's grounding of "tastes" in status considerations is more satisfactory than a distaste for physical association, the impact of economic variables on the formation of such status-based discriminatory tastes remains outside the model.

A further variation in the neoclassical approach departs from the assumption of a competitive labor market in order to focus on the wage implications of monopsony, that is, monopoly power in the hands of employers. In contrast to a perfectly competitive labor market where a worker's wage is equal to the value of his or her marginal product, in a monopsonistic labor market, wages are less than value marginal product. While the presence of racial or sexual wage differentials in a competitive labor market reflect differing productivities arising out of either demand factors (taste for discrimination) or supply factors (lower investment in human capital), wage differentials in the monopsonistic labor market reflect the degree of monopsony in the market or the wage elasticity of supply of labor.

The monopsony model first developed by Joan Robinson has recently been applied to the problem of sex discrimination in employment by Janice Madden.[10] Central to her model is the relationship between the elasticity of supply and wages. Given a monopsonistic employer and an upward supply curve of labor, women workers will receive a lower wage than men to the extent that their labor supply curve is less elastic than that of men. Madden argues that such differential elasticity is caused by women's relative immobility in the labor market. This immobility may be related to familial constraints on women's participation in the work force or to restricted demand for women workers. Although Madden's model is an interesting one, her approach requires further development, especially in explaining why women's relative immobility outweighs other factors that might be expected to render women's labor supply more wage-elastic than men's.

The results of these varied neoclassical elaborations of the original Becker model represent partial equilibrium solutions. Given the shortcomings of a partial analysis, Kenneth Arrow attempts to remedy the deficiency of the Becker model in explaining the persistence of racial discrimination in employment by considering the general equilibrium aspects of discrimination, that is, the compensating behavior stimulated by racial or sexual wage differentials.[11] In the long run, the partial equilibrium formulation of the competitive model implies that simple calculations of self-interest will cause some employers to take advantage of the gap between black and white wages by demanding black workers. Such profit-minded bidding for black workers by less discriminatory employers will drive more discriminatory employers out of business, or, at least, eliminate racial wage differentials.[12] Focusing on the long-run adjustment processes, Arrow notes that real world nonconvexities of indifference surfaces may render marginal hiring and wage changes by nondiscriminatory employers uneconomic. Yet, sudden and complete transitions may also be rejected by the employer without discriminatory tastes on the basis of the information and personnel costs associated with hiring, training, and firing. These labor turnover costs may thus prevent, or, at least, slow adjustments that would reduce racial wage differentials. Accordingly, Arrow's analysis suggests that the key to reconciling the intergenerational persistence of racial and sexual wage differentials within the Becker model lies in a fuller development of the theory of the firm. As such, Arrow implicitly rejects the possibility that racial and sexual employment discrimination that is systemic in nature, that is, rooted in institutional practices and customs, may explain the existence of continuing racial wage differentials.

Recognizing the possibility of "still other factors" grounded in employer perceptions and personnel investment costs, Arrow has offered an alternative to the "central" neoclassical model. In Arrow's alternative model, the employer's actions are based not on a taste for discrimination but on "perceptions of reality." Arrow and E.S. Phelps in independent efforts introduced the concept of "statistical discrimination."[13] That is, where the employer must incur some cost to determine a potential employee's true productivity, the employer's assessment of the job applicant is based on preconsidered ideas about the average characteristics of the group or groups to which the applicant belongs rather than the individual's characteristics. If the probability that a random black or woman worker is qualified is less than the probability that a random white male is qualified, it follows that the white male worker's wage will be greater than the black or woman worker's wage. Phelps notes in his comment on the statistical theory of racial and sexual discrimination that "the employer who seeks to maximize expected profit will discriminate against blacks or women if he believes them to be less qualified, reliable, etc., on the average than whites and men, respectively, and if the costs of gaining information about the individual applicant is excessive."[14] The difficulty with the statistical model is that beliefs, unlike tastes, presumably will change as further information becomes available.

In an earlier review of the Becker model, Lester Thurow argues that such an approach does not adequately describe discrimination in all its forms in a society that is not only segregated, but also white (male) supremacist.[15] Thurow identifies seven broad types of discrimination: employment (differential incidence of unemployment); wage (differential pay for equal work); occupation (differential entry); human capital (differential investment); capital (differential access to capital markets); monopoly (differential enjoyment of monopoly returns); and price (differential prices in goods markets). Thurow points out that within and between the various types of discrimination there are conflicts among whites. Thus, when one type of discrimination is viewed apart from others, economic forces might be predicted to break down the discriminatory behavior in question. However, when the various types of discrimination are viewed together, not only are such forces attenuated, but each form of discrimination may be seen to support others. Thus, in contrast to the passive government policy indicated by the Becker model, the Thurow analysis recommends government actions directed to end white (male) monopoly power in all of its forms—employment, wage, occupation, human capital, and monopoly.

Dissatisfaction with the mechanical deductive reasoning of the neoclassical model has led some economists to take an institutional approach to the problem of employment discrimination. In a recent survey article, Ray Marshall has noted that the neoclassical theory of discrimination fails to distinguish between specific overt acts of discrimination and institutionalized discrimination. "When discrimination becomes institutionalized, as it has for blacks, overt discrimination becomes a relatively less important cause of the disadvantages of discriminatees, because inadequate education, segregated labor market institutions, and other forces which deny equal access to jobs, training, and information greatly reduce the probability that those discriminated against will aspire to, prepare for, or seek to enter the status occupations."[16]

Institutional approaches to the problems posed by employment discrimination received their impetus from the manpower programs of the late 1960s and the concurrent growth of interest in "internal labor markets."[17] Briefly, the internal labor market may be defined as the complex of rules and networks, both formal and informal, that determine the movement of job classifications within administrative units. Essentially, jobs are classified according to recruitment sources. Jobs filled from sources external to the firm are generally lower-level positions, while higher-level jobs are filled from internal sources, that is, through promotion of presently employed workers.

Thus, while the wages of lower-level or entry jobs may be governed by the operation of competitive market forces, promotion ladders to upper-level jobs are subject to formal administrative roles and informal information networks. Because potential for advancement is largely determined by the original entry-level job, the economic consequences of discrimination against blacks and women in key entry positions, whether due to "tastes" or "statistical" perceptions, may be compounded by differential access up promotion ladders. Advocates of the internal labor market approach argue that occupational differences between men and women and blacks and whites may reflect employer decisions to exclude blacks and women from certain entry-level slots, for example, management training programs, and associated promotion ladders, or to promote and upgrade women and blacks more slowly than white men given statistical perceptions of average group characteristics. Indeed, women's and blacks' restricted access to jobs with good promotion ladders may mean not only that they receive lower wages, but also that they are less productive due to differential on-the-job training.[18]

One outgrowth of the internal labor market analysis is the "dual labor market" hypothesis formulated by Peter Doeringer and Michael Piore.[19] According to the proponents of this hypothesis, the labor market is essentially divided into primary and secondary sectors. Primary sector jobs are characterized by high wages, good working conditions, stability, opportunity for advancement, and so on, while secondary jobs are described by low wages, poor working conditions, little security or possibility of advancement. Given this distinction, discrimination in the labor market is said to exist where blacks or women are restricted to secondary jobs on statistical or other grounds. That is, discrimination exists where blacks and women are not assessed in terms of their individual characteristics, but in terms of statistical characteristics associated with their group.

Although the recognition of institutional job distinctions represents an important contribution to the work on discrimination, the origins of labor market segmentation on the primary-secondary dichotomy are not specified in the dual labor market hypothesis. Nor does the hypothesis explain occupational segregation or wage differentials within the primary and secondary sectors of the labor market. Presumably, future work by dual labor market economists will address these questions.

Economists writing from a modern Marxist perspective have also contributed insights into the forces producing labor market segmentation.[20] The "radical" economists argue that capitalists have worked to harness preexisting forces of racism and sexism to divide workers in primary and secondary markets, thereby preventing the development of a class consciousness unifying all workers. The motivating factor in the radical model is the capitalists' desire to maximize surplus value extracted from the work force. Radical as well as other economists have pointed out that racial and sexual segmentation of the labor market effectively sets up a zero-sum game situation, where the affirmative action gains of blacks and women are derived at the expense of white males. The radical contribution to date is a significant one, but requires further elaboration, especially with respect to employer motivations.

In an attempt to define racial discrimination in a system that incorporates the labor union, Ray Marshall has recently proposed an industrial relations or bargaining model.[21] In Marshall's formulation, emphasis is placed on job control that is composed of a constellation of factors, including job status, working conditions, stability, opportunity for advancement, extent to which workers participate in the formulation of job rules, as well as wage rates. Critical environmental features include economic and labor market conditions, community race relations, the distribution of power in the larger community, industry structure and growth potential, labor market skills and education of the black and white populations relative to the labor requirements of various companies and industries and the operation of labor market institutions. Given the environmental setting, each group of economic agents (employers, white workers, black workers, unions) develops "mechanisms" to improve its power position relative to others. Specifically, employers are assumed to be motivated by profit maximization and status considerations, white workers by job control motivations, and white-controlled unions by a desire to preserve and ration job opportunities. The power of black workers to overcome racial discrimination is assumed to depend on the available supply of labor. The Marshall bargaining framework thus emphasizes group processes, especially as they relate to white workers' control of jobs.

A significant flaw in the Marshall framework is the incomplete specification of the dynamics of the system, that is, the central economic purpose served by discrimination. Moreover, the Marshall formulation may overemphasize the importance of labor unions in an economy in which less than 25 percent of the work force is unionized. Finally, unlike other attempts to model the economics of racial discrimination, Marshall's framework cannot be applied to the case of sexual discrimination in employment, in spite of common elements underlying them both.

In conclusion, no one theoretical approach to the problem of discrimination in employment has been wholly satisfactory. Neoclassical theory has not been successful in explaining the basic causal factors underlying discrimination as evidenced by racial and sexual differentials in wages, employment, and occupational patterns, and human capital. Rather, by defining discrimination as an exogenously given "taste," neoclassical economists have merely traced the economic consequences of discriminatory preferences. This approach ignores the interrelation between market outcomes and the formulation of individual attitudes, and thus adds little to our understanding of the process of ending discrimination. As a result, the policy suggestions of neoclassical models have been something less than inspired. Moreover, while institutional analysis has provided valuable insights, particularly in describing the rigidities stemming from the division of the labor market into primary and secondary sectors, the institutional perspective has not been shaped into a theory of discrimination. Nor have the insights of the institutional approach been incorporated into the neoclassical analysis.

Just as there has been only limited commerce between institutional and neoclassical economists, so there has been little exchange between economists on the one hand and psychologists and sociologists on the other. This lack of communication among social scientists has resulted in economic models that are unnecessarily naive in psychological and sociological terms. Incorporation of psychological findings regarding the employment expectations of black and white and male and female workers into economic theory promises to yield more powerful analyses of employment discrimination. (See Gurin, Bell, and Laws in this volume.) Similarly, building sociological insights into economic models should strengthen economists' analyses. (See Loury in this volume.)

Although a sizable body of theoretical work on the economics of discrimination has accumulated over the past decade, it is in many respects a fragmented one. *The* theory of discrimination, explaining racial and sexual differentials in wages, employment, and so forth, has yet to be written. It is clear, however, that *the* theory must integrate not only the neoclassical and institutional economic approaches, but also the findings of sociological and psychological research. In short, the economics of employment discrimination is at a critical stage, where the insights of economists, psychologists, and sociologists must be integrated and shaped into a comprehensive and robust theory.

Notes

1. Gary Becker, *The Economics of Discrimination*, 2nd ed. (Chicago: University of Chicago Press, 1971).

2. Ibid., p. 14.

3. See, for example, Gary Becker, *Human Capital: A Theoretical and Empirical Analysis* (New York: National Bureau of Economic Research, 1964); Jacob Mincer, "Labor Force Participation of Married Women: A Study of Labor Supply," in *Aspects of Labor Economics*, National Bureau of Economic Research (Princeton, N.J.: Princeton University Press, 1962): 63-105; Jacob Mincer and Solomon Polachek, "Family Investments in Human Capital: Earnings of Women," *Journal of Political Economy* 82 (March/April 1974): 76-111; Finis Welch, "Labor Market Discrimination: An Interpretation of Income Differences in the Rural South," *Journal of Political Economy* 75 (June 1967): 225-240.

4. Gary Becker, "A Theory of the Allocation of Time," *Economic Journal* 75 (September 1965): 493-517. For a compilation of recent work in this area, see Cynthia B. Lloyd, ed., *Sex, Discrimination, and the Division of Labor* (New York: Columbia University Press, 1975).

5. The empirical literature on black-white and female-male differentials in employment and income also grew significantly after 1966. Several reviews of this work have appeared in recent years. See, for example, R.B. Freeman, "Labor Market Discrimination: Analysis, Findings, and Problems," in *Frontiers of Quantitative Economics*, Vol. 2, M.D. Intriligator and D.A. Kendrick, eds. (New York: North-Holland Publishing Company, 1974): 501-555; and Hilda Kahne, "Economic Perspectives on the Roles of Women in the American Economy," *Journal of Economic Literature* 13, 4 (December 1975): 1249-1292.

6. Ann Krueger, "The Economics of Discrimination," *Journal of Political Economy* 71 (October 1963): 481-486.

7. Marcus Alexis, "The Political Economy of Labor Market Discrimination: Synthesis and Exploration," in *Patterns of Discrimination*, Vol. II, A. Horowitz and G. von Furstenberg, eds. (Lexington, Mass.: D.C. Heath, 1974).

8. Finis Welch, "Labor Market Discrimination: An Interpretation of Income Differences in the Rural South," *Journal of Political Economy* 75 (June 1967): 225-240.

9. See Barbara Bergmann, "The Effect on White Incomes of Discrimination in Employment," *Journal of Political Economy* 79 (March/April 1971): 294-313; and Barbara Bergmann, "Occupational Segregation, Wages and Profits when Employers Discriminate by Race or Sex," *Eastern Economic Journal* 1 (April/July 1974): 103-110.

10. Janice Madden, *The Economics of Sex Discrimination* (Lexington, Mass.: D.C. Heath, 1973).

11. See Kenneth Arrow, "Models of Job Discrimination" and "Some Models of Race in the Labor Market," in *Racial Discrimination in Economic Life*, A. Pascal, ed. (Lexington, Mass.: D.C. Heath, 1972); Kenneth Arrow, "The Theory of Discrimination," in *Discrimination in Labor Markets*, O. Ashenfelter and A. Rees, eds. (Princeton, N.J.: Princeton University Press, 1974): 3-33.

12. R.B. Freeman, "Labor Market Discrimination: Analysis, Findings and

Problems," in *Frontiers of Quantitative Economics, Vol. II*, M.D. Intriligator and D.A. Kendrick, eds. (New York: North-Holland Publishing Company, 1974): 501-555. Freeman hypothesizes that discriminatory employers may survive due to a limited supply of nondiscriminating employers whose ability to expand is constrained by U-shaped cost curves. This explanation, however, appears to be strained, especially in the long run.

13. Kenneth Arrow, "Models of Job Discrimination" and "Some Models of Race in the Labor Market" in *Racial Discrimination in Economic Life*, A. Pascal, ed. (Lexington, Mass.: D.C. Heath, 1972), and E.S. Phelps, "The Statistical Theory of Racism and Sexism," *American Economic Review* 62 (September 1972): 661.

14. E.S. Phelps, "The Statistical Theory of Racism and Sexism," *American Economic Review* 62 (September 1972): 659-661.

15. Lester Thurow, *Poverty and Discrimination* (Washington: The Brookings Institution, 1969), Chapter 7.

16. Ray Marshall, "The Economics of Racial Discrimination: A Survey," *Journal of Economic Literature* 12, 3 (September 1974): 861.

17. Peter Doeringer and Michael Piore, *Internal Labor Markets and Manpower Analysis* (Lexington, Mass.: D.C. Heath, 1971).

18. Francine Blau and Carol Jusenius, "Economists' Approaches to Sex Segregation in the Labor Market: An Appraisal," *Signs* 1, 3, ii (Spring 1976): 181-199.

19. Doeringer and Piore, *Internal Labor Markets.*

20. For example, see F.J. Franklin and S. Resnik, *The Political Economy of Racism* (New York: Holt, Rinehart, Winston, 1974) and Samuel Bowles and Herbert Gintis, "The Problem with Human Capital Theory—A Marxian Critique," *American Economic Review, Papers and Proceedings* 65 (May 1975): 74-82.

21. Marshall, "Economics of Racial Discrimination."

Bibliography

Alexis, Marcus. "The Political Economy of Labor Market Discrimination: Synthesis and Exploration." In *Patterns of Discrimination*, Vol. II, A. Horowitz and G. von Furstenberg, eds., Lexington, Mass.: D.C. Heath, 1974.

Arrow, Kenneth. "Models of Job Discrimination" and "Some Models of Race in the Labor Market." In *Racial Discrimination in Economic Life*, A. Pascal, ed., Lexington, Mass.: D.C. Heath, 1972.

Arrow, Kenneth. "The Theory of Discrimination." In *Discrimination in Labor Markets*, O. Ashenfelter and A. Rees, eds., Princeton, N.J.: Princeton University Press, 1974.

Becker, Gary. *Human Capital: A Theoretical and Empirical Analysis.* New York: National Bureau of Economic Research, 1964.

Becker, Gary. "A Theory of the Allocation of Time." *Economic Journal* 75 (September 1965): 493-517.

Becker, Gary. *The Economics of Discrimination.* 2nd ed. Chicago: University of Chicago Press, 1971.

Bergmann, Barbara. "The Effect on White Incomes of Discrimination in Employment." *Journal of Political Economy* 79 (March/April 1971): 294-313.

Bergmann, Barbara. "Occupational Segregation, Wages and Profits When Employers Discriminate by Race or Sex." *Eastern Economic Journal* 1 (April/July 1974): 103-110.

Blau, Francine, and Carol Jusenius. "Economists' Approaches to Sex Segregation in the Labor Market: An Appraisal." *Signs* 1, 3, ii (Spring 1976): 181-199.

Doeringer, Peter, and Michael Piore. *Internal Labor Markets and Manpower Analysis.* Lexington, Mass.: D.C. Heath, 1971.

Franklin, R.J., and S. Resnik. *The Political Economy of Racism.* New York: Holt, Rinehart, Winston, 1974.

Freeman, R.B. "Labor Market Discrimination: Analysis, Findings, and Problems." In *Frontiers of Quantitative Economics,* Vol. 2, M.D. Intriligator and D.A. Kendrick, eds., New York: North-Holland Publishing Company, 1974.

Kahne, Hilda. "Economic Perspectives on the Roles of Women in the American Economy." *Journal of Economic Literature* 13, 4 (December 1975): 1249-1292.

Krueger, Ann. "The Economics of Discrimination." *Journal of Political Economy* 71 (October 1963): 481-486.

Lloyd, Cynthia B., ed., *Sex, Discrimination, and the Division of Labor.* New York: Columbia University Press, 1975.

Madden, Janice. *The Economics of Sex Discrimination.* Lexington, Mass.: D.C. Heath, 1973.

Marshall, Ray. "The Economics of Racial Discrimination: A Survey." *Journal of Economic Literature* 12, 3 (September 1974): 849-871.

Mincer, Jacob. "Labor Force Participation of Married Women: A Study of Labor Supply." In *Aspects of Labor Economics,* National Bureau of Economic Research. Princeton, N.J.: Princeton University Press, 1962.

Mincer, Jacob, and Solomon Polachek. "Family Investments in Human Capital: Earnings of Women." *Journal of Political Economy* 82 (March/April 1974): 76-111.

Phelps, E.S. "The Statistical Theory of Racism and Sexism." *American Economic Review* 62 (September 1972): 659-661.

Thurow, Lester. *Poverty and Discrimination.* Washington: The Brookings Institution, 1969.

Welch, Finis. "Labor Market Discrimination: An Interpretation of Income Differences in the Rural South." *Journal of Political Economy* 75 (June 1967): 225-240.

2

The Role of Worker Expectancies in the Study of Employment Discrimination

Patricia Gurin

Introduction

The recent emergence of models and empirical work on *current* discrimination as a source of race, ethnic, and sex differentials in employment status, job classification, and wages is an exciting development in labor market economics. The standard position as recently as the mid-1960s argued that race and sex differentials simply could not be sustained by employer discrimination in a competitive labor market.[1] The continuing differentials in unemployment, occupational classification, and wages were generally viewed as the result of productivity differences, admittedly perhaps the residue of previous racial inequalities rather than labor market discrimination. Paying unequal wages to equally qualified workers would threaten the profits of discriminating employers in a rational, competitive marketplace.

This traditional picture of the market has led to the development of a standard research strategy in the study of race and sex differentials. Most research has focused on wage differentials and most studies have depended on regression techniques to assess how much these differentials would be reduced by adjusting for race and sex differences in pertinent productivity proxies—schooling, age, marital status, number of children, full-time versus part-time work, length and continuity of labor force participation, occupational classification, and so forth. The size of the reduction obviously depends on how many and which productivity proxies are included in the analyses. The orthodox are never convinced that the residual represents wage discrimination in any case, since additional productivity proxies can always be suggested. This is why psychological variables have occasionally been invoked. When discussed at all, motivational characteristics of workers have been advanced as additional explanatory variables that might further reduce the residual not accounted for by the standard productivity proxies suggested by labor market economists. This traditional approach suggests, for example, that women earn less than comparably educated men of the same age because they may be less career motivated and thus work less continuously. Or women who approximate the participation of men may still earn less because they may not be motivated to enter the high-demand, high-paying jobs that often attract men.

Whether stressing obvious job behavior proxies or motivational characteristics, supply analyses of wage differentials are the economic "victim deficit" analog to personality deficit approaches in psychological research on sex and

13

race. Productivity differences are but part of the explanation. That traditional research has looked almost exclusively to the personal deficiencies of workers as the source of sex and race differentials in employment is yet another instance of the bias in social science to look for individualistic explanations of behavior. The disproportionate focus on supply characteristics reflects a bias in both economists and psychologists to look primarily for problems *in* people.

Recent challenges to traditional concepts of a competitive market offered by various exponents of monopsonistic models suggest that different issues need to be studied. By showing conditions under which employers can profit from sex and race discrimination, these monopsonistic models should encourage serious attention to the demand side of the market. The new models of monopsony now legitimate the need for research on the impact of employer beliefs, personnel practices and policies, organizational and structural characteristics of firms, firm market power, type of industry, and so on. The experience of organizational psychologists and sociologists will likely be more useful than the experience of labor market economists as studies of job channeling procedures and organizational responses to nondiscriminatory and affirmative action laws and judicial agreements are undertaken.

More research also needs to be done on the processes by which worker monopolies, whether unions or professional associations, may exclude women and minorities and thereby influence supply functions. Moreover, some supply questions still need further clarification in light of these discussions of monopsony, although they are not those traditionally raised in supply analyses. The market does have characteristics that workers see and evaluate. It is largely sex segregated. It is also a dual market in which some jobs are relatively more regular and protected than others. Blacks work disproportionately in the less protected, less regular jobs, and they know this. It is possible that their knowledge and perceptions of the market may influence their behavior in it.

This paper will argue that the psychological research that will provide the information we still need on supply characteristics must focus on the market experiences and perceptions of women and minorities instead of on their presumed personality deficits that further justify employment inequities. It will review evidence from the traditional research on supply characteristics—both the obvious productivity proxies, suggested particularly by economists and demographers, and the motivational variables, suggested by psychologists—in accounting for sex and race differentials in employment.

The evidence shows that we must distinguish supply characteristics which represent personal deficiencies that may lower productivity from those which reflect the realities of the current situations faced by women and minorities. It is women's and minorities' perceptions of the market, beliefs about opportunities, and awareness of channeling processes that may indeed affect their expectancies of success, expectancies that are an important aspect of motivation but in no way imply productivity deficiencies in the old, traditional sense. Expectancies may in turn influence supply elasticities that can be exaggerated by biased employers.

The stress on the continued need for study of certain supply characteristics is not intended to minimize the greater need for research on the demand side, especially on the effects of legal efforts to require nondiscriminatory and affirmative action in both the public and private sectors. One paper could not do justice to the role of expectancies as supply characteristics and to the issues of conducting impact studies and research on compliance and resistance processes in various types of work organizations.

Sex and Race Differentials in Employment

Sex and race income differentials are sizable. Black women are the most disadvantaged in terms of income. In 1970 black women in the nation earned $552 less than white women who earned $2,237 less than black men who earned $3,439 less than white men.[2] Race differentials in income are largest in the South and are smallest in the West for both men and women.[3] Occupational differentiation by sex and race likewise continues. A paper prepared by Ashenfelter and Heckman in 1973 for the Equal Employment Opportunity Commission (EEOC) treats occupational position thoroughly.[4] Their index of occupational positions[5] shows that the occupations held by black women in 1970 represented only 45 percent of the occupational positions of white men; occupations held by white women represented 50 percent of those of white men; occupations held by black men represented 80 percent of those of white men. Ashenfelter documents regional variations in these sex and race differences. Race disparities are greatest in the South where the underrepresentation of black women in clerical positions, and of black men in all six of the top-paying occupations, are greatest.[6]

Analyses of shifts in both wage differentials and occupational classification confirm that the status of white women workers has improved very little since the mid-1960s and much more slowly than that of other workers since the early 1950s.[7] At the present time this means that race discrimination is more pronounced against black men than black women. Black women have been able to move into clerical jobs from which they have been particularly excluded, and thereby have improved their earnings, more quickly than black men have been able to break into the highest paying occupations that white men have held disproportionately. However, because the market is so severely sex segregated, this should not imply that black women are doing well in an absolute sense and certainly not when compared to either group of men. Black women are only beginning to reach parity with white women, and then in only certain regions of the country and largely because the job status and income of white women have changed so little.

Sex Differentials

Productivity proxies reduce sex differentials, but not nearly as much as was once considered definitive. Sanborn's early research in the 1950s estimated that 90 percent of the sex differential in wages could be attributed to differences in education, residence, occupation, job turnover, absenteeism, and experience.[8] Most of the studies done in the last five to eight years, however, show sizable disparities, even after adjusting for such factors. Fuchs's data show that women earn only 66 percent of the male wage even after marital status, classification of job, length of work trip, schooling, age, and city size are taken into account.[9]

In a somewhat different approach to estimating discrimination, Levitan, Quinn, and Staines used achievement-productivity factors, such as education, tenure with the employer, tenure on a specific job, number of hours worked, amount of supervisory experience, and occupational status of the job, as dependent variables in a regression equation explaining male earnings.[10] Using the weights from that equation to predict women's wages from these same factors, women in Levitan's 1969 sample earned $3,458 less than their predicted wage while men (a second random half) earned only $27 less than the prediction.

Most studies agree that the lower, less continuous, and more part-time participation of women in the labor market in large part explains wage differentials. It is argued that if women were to develop "career commitments" more like the commitments of men, their wages would become commensurate. Available evidence suggests that the differential would at least be sizably reduced. The income differential of all black women to all black men in 1970 was reduced by $1,042 among year-round, full-time workers. The differential between all white women and white men workers was reduced by $1,604 when full-time workers were compared.[11] The differences did not disappear, however. Oaxaca estimates that only 22 percent of the sex differences in income for whites and just 6 percent for blacks are attributable to the effects of children, marital status, and part-time employment.[12] Suter and Miller also show wage differentials, even after controlling for intermittent work force behavior.[13] Their study includes a sample of women who have worked at least six months in every year since leaving school, which they considered as approximating continuing career commitments. Women who worked continually earned 73 percent as much as men of the same age, and 75 percent of what they would have earned by working full time throughout those years. In contrast, women who worked in only half the years earned only 23 percent as much as men of the same age and 49 percent of what they would have earned if they had worked full time when they worked. Thus, the results show that the differential was much less when there was career commitment, but it did not disappear even within a group of women who did not represent the more typical woman's work pattern.

Most research agrees that occupational differentiation by sex, through which women and men end up in different jobs and become reasonably separate labor pools, is the *most* important productivity characteristic in accounting for wage differentials. Research that has managed to equate job classifications for men and women generally shows much closer earnings.[14] Nonetheless, the studies that control for census classifications of jobs continue to demonstrate sex differentials in earnings. For the four occupations she studied, Hamilton estimates that 8 percent to 18 percent of the male wage is the discrimination figure.[15] Suter and Miller report that women teachers earn $2,800 less than men; women sales persons, $3,800 less than men; and women operatives in nondurable goods manufacturing industries, $3,000 less than men.[16] Levitan's research shows that the proportion of women earning $3,500 or more below what they should have been earning, given their productive characteristics, varied by occupational group from only 12 percent operatives up to 70 percent among the professions.[17] Of course, these occupational classifications are gross. In a case study of a single employer with 272 professional employees, Malkiel and Malkiel show that men and women with the same characteristics at truly equal job levels earn equal pay.[18] The problem, as they saw it, is that men and women with Ph.D.s and working in a research organization are generally not assigned to the same job levels.

These studies indicate that wage differentials remain significant, even when gross job classifications are controlled; that wage differentials become insignificant when men and women *in exactly the same job* are compared; and, thus, that occupational differentiation continues to be the mechanism through which sex discrimination occurs. Indeed, Madden observes that what surprises her in all these studies, given their restriction to wage differentials, is that they generally show some evidence of discrimination in what may *not* be the most likely expression of sex discrimination.[19] We need much more research on "access" or "employment" discrimination, the processes by which women enter and stay in different job categories, especially in the lower end of the spectrum.

Race Differentials

Previous studies generally agree that race differentials in both employment access (or classification) and wages continue to be sizable, especially among men, even after adjusting for obvious productivity characteristics. Blacks are generally in lower-paid occupations. Among men the picture is consistent—they are always disproportionately in the lowest-paid occupations and underrepresented in the highest-paid occupations. Among women, blacks are primarily underrepresented in clerical occupations.[20] This occupational differential is *not* largely attributable to productivity characteristics. Most studies generally agree that educational differences explain only a moderate amount of the variance in occupational classification. Ashenfelter estimated that relative educational attainments could explain no more than one third of the difference between the occupational positions of blacks and whites.[21] This was true of both men and women. Fogel similarly estimated that only 30 percent to 40 percent of the variance in occupational position is accounted for by differences in educational attainment.[22] Duncan's path analytic results showed that educational attainment, as measured by years of schooling, explained only one fifth of the variance in occupational status of blacks and whites (men only).[23]

Income differentials by race persist even after adjusting for productivity characteristics. Black men and black women earn less, even after adjusting for work experience and type of work—private nonagricultural, self-employed nonagricultural, and government work.[24] Even with controls for occupational classification and level of education, the incomes of black men continue to be lower than those of white men.[25] Among women, only those blacks whose educational level is below that of high school graduate earn less than whites.[26]

Equating occupational classifications reduces income differentials between black and white women. In many occupations black women in the nation have attained income parity with white women. Wallace has pointed out, however, that this conclusion needs more careful scrutiny since it may depend greatly on the region involved and on particular local labor markets.[27] For example, in the South black teachers do not earn as much as white teachers. Moreover, none of the analyses that show income parity between black and white women control for length and continuity of labor force participation.

Many commentators suggest that the more continuous employment of black women may largely account for income parity despite the continuation of race discrimination. Conservatively, it may be concluded that race differentials are greater among men than women and are not reduced as much by the obvious productivity proxies thus far analyzed. Race discrimination among women simply requires more complicated analyses. Wallace has highlighted the special need to further disaggregate data if the possible misinterpretation that black women no longer face market discrimination because of race is to be avoided.[28]

Previous studies, admittedly most conducted only with data on men, also agree that the regression slope that predicts income from educational attainments and occupational status is much lower for blacks than for whites.[29] Duncan's presentation of the issue dramatizes the problem. The path coefficient from education to income is actually higher for black men than for white men, but the compound path (education to occupation to income) works out to be much lower.[30] Duncan comments that exponents of the human capital theory have not explained how blacks will realize the "returns to education" as they are urged to "learn, baby, learn."

Motivational Characteristics of Workers

Motivational variables have been viewed as plausible productivity proxies because it is widely believed that blacks and whites, and women and men, differ in patterns of work motivation, job preferences, and reward incentives. What is the evidence to show that sex and race differences determine work-related motivation?

The Motivations of Blacks and Whites

Research on motivation and performance issues that might be construed as productivity proxies in the labor market is further along vis-à-vis race than sex. The somewhat earlier, albeit very late, concern about race discrimination promoted attention to possible productivity differences stemming from motivation and/or performance. More of the evidence is now in. There is no support for the contention that black and white youngsters *want* different types of jobs or that black youngsters desire less education.[31] With a controlled socioeconomic background, black and white high school students express much the same future job preferences. Black youngsters hold higher educational aspirations than whites of comparable social status. At the college level the career aspirations of black men and white men are almost exactly the same. The only exception is the somewhat greater preference among blacks for professional jobs and the somewhat lower preference for careers in business.[32] Likewise, black women and white women attending college aspire to much the same occupations.[33] Moreover, the sex differential in career aspirations is almost exactly the same among black and white college students.[34]

Conclusions from most of the studies on achievement-related motivation show very similar patterns of motivation among black and white samples. In comparisons of black and white youngsters from similar class backgrounds, both achievement motives have turned out much the same.[35] A recent study of a national sample of adults explored whether traditional measures of motives and values would be structured differently by black and white adults. Factor analysis showed very much the same motivation clusters for these two groups.[36]

Some investigators have suggested that black workers differ from white workers in challenge-related job attributes, either in terms of the salience to them of intrinsic motivations[37] or in terms of other aspects of their need structures.[38] These differences are somehow presumed to moderate the responses of blacks to the challenge of their work. Their satisfaction with challenge is therefore not presumed to reflect the realities of how much challenge their jobs actually offer. Research on the working conditions of a national sample of black and white workers suggest otherwise.[39] Blacks were in jobs offering less challenge and were correspondingly less satisfied with them. Moreover, the quality of employment or the amount of challenge offered explained approximately the same amount of variance in job satisfaction for blacks and whites.

The one way in which black and white achievement motivation may differ is in a reality-based perception among blacks that their chances for success are relatively poor. For example, while blacks adhere as strongly as whites to Protestant ethic values that attribute success to hard work, talent, and perseverance, they believe less often that such virtues will pay off for them. Their sense of personal efficacy and expectancies of success are somewhat lower, despite equally strong commitments to achievement values and motives. Gurin and several colleagues have documented this pattern of racial similarity in values and motives but dissimilarity in expectancies and sense of personal control in a variety of samples[40]: a national sample of adults participating in manpower retraining programs; a sample of high school dropouts participating in a JOBS project; and, most recently, a national probability sample of adults eighteen years old and older. The national data were collected during the 1972 election study by the Survey Research Center at the University of Michigan. The Internal-External Control Scale[41] was included in the interview, providing the first national data on this measure that has become so popular in psychological research. Several results from the analyses of responses by blacks and whites to the questions on this scale are pertinent to this discussion.

First, the factor analyses of the individual items comprising the scale resulted in almost exactly the same factors for blacks and whites. Both groups distinguished values from a sense of personal control and produced the same two general value factors. One group included six items that referred to the relative importance of internal virtues and fate in accounting for success in the culture at large. This factor is called a measure of Protestant ethic ideology. Those people who expressed a conventional value position felt, for example, that "Some people just don't use the breaks that come their way; if they don't do well, it's their own fault," and rejected the idea that "People who don't do well in life often work hard, but the breaks just don't come their way."

The second factor that measured values referred more specifically to job success. This is termed a measure of success mobility ideology. Those people who held conventional achievement values believed, for example, that "Becoming a success is a matter of hard work; luck has little or nothing to do with it," and rejected the notion that "Getting a good job depends mainly on being in the right place at the right time."

Separate factor analyses of the responses of blacks and whites also produced the same five-item measure of personal control consistently found in previous work with the Internal-External Control Scale. All five of these items were cast in the first person. Those people who showed a strong sense of personal control said, for example, that "What happens to me is my own doing," and disagreed with the statement that "Sometimes I feel I don't have enough control over the direction my life is taking." Racial similarity went beyond the respondents' common conceptions of control.

The average scores of blacks and whites on the two value measures, Protestant ethic ideology and success mobility ideology, were also much the same. Thus, blacks and whites shared the same structure of beliefs about the determinants of success in the culture at large and were equally committed to the same work ethic values. By contrast, they did not feel equally effective about their own lives. Whites expressed a significantly greater personal control.

The aspirations of black and white college students for advanced education show much the same contrast between desire and expectancy. While black students just as frequently aspire to enter graduate and professional education, they are considerably less certain they will actually be able to pursue higher degrees.[42] With five times as many black students as white students from poverty backgrounds in college, the uncertain expectations of black students about actually pursuing advanced degrees reflect reality constraints,[43] *not* different values or motives. A study of graduating seniors in 1964 found that 62 percent of the graduates of black colleges, as compared to 36 percent of a national sample of white students, owed money for college expenses at the time they graduated.[44] Close to half of the black graduates but only 17 percent of the white graduates cited finances as a major reason why they might not attend graduate school. It is thus impossible to argue that occupational differentiation by race in any way represents different aspirations or even different patterns of motivation except as motivation refers to situationally defined expectancies.

The Motivations of Women and Men

The evidence from previous research on sex differences is far more complicated. Women not only attain less education but also express lower educational aspirations. The longitudinal follow-up of the post-high school educational experiences of 9,000 students conducted by Sewell and his associates[45] showed that the lower educational aspirations of women while in high school played an important role in accounting for sex differential in educational attainment in subsequent years. Women were also disadvantaged by having had less educational encouragement from teachers and parents while in high school. Likewise, national data on college seniors show that women at that level express lower educational aspirations for the future. Men were three times as likely to aspire to enter professional or graduate schools.[46] These aspiration differences undoubtedly account in part for the continued male advantage in enrollment at the graduate level. Sewell estimates that men from the bottom socioeconomic category had a 250 percent advantage, and those from the top socioeconomic category had a 120 percentage advantage, over women in attending a graduate or professional school.[47]

Men at both the high school and college levels also express aspirations for high-paying and more prestigious jobs. Women predominantly aspire to those jobs that at the present time are held mostly by women—teaching, nursing, social work, and clerical jobs.[48] Astin and Panos concluded from research on students attending a national sample of colleges and universities that the sex of the student was more important than any other personal predictor in explaining the choice of a major field, graduate school plans, and occupational preferences.[49] Women attending college make their occupational decisions earlier than men, enter college with lower aspirations, and when they shift during college, change to a lower rather than a higher level of aspiration. One of the most reliable facts about change among college students is the accentuation of sex differences in preferences for academic field, occupation, and number of years of desired education. Sex differences increase during college because men do not change in a "feminine" direction while women become increasingly traditionally feminine.[50]

These first-order sex differences, however, are considerably reduced, and sometimes even disappear, when the levels of expectancy of men and women are equated. Among women who judge their chances for getting "masculine" jobs as positively as do men, preference and desire are also equivalent.[51] Of course, such results do not tell what causes what—whether women who hold high expectations of success in nontraditional fields develop preferences for them, or the reverse. It is also known that women who aspire for nontraditional women's careers do so because of much the same motivational dynamics that correlate with men's aspirations for the same high-level prestige professions. Heightened expectancies and self-confidence are among these motivational correlates for both sex groups.[52] The issue is how women can develop both the motivations and aspirations if they counter the cultural norms of appropriate and acceptable goals and motivations for women. In a study of students in historically black colleges, Epps and Gurin found that women who attended colleges where faculty-student interaction was unusually high (especially the women at such colleges who themselves reported frequent contact with faculty), and where the press of academic values was unusually strong in the student culture, more often aspired to nontraditional jobs for women.[53] Freshmen women in such colleges showed stronger aspiration for such careers at the end than at the beginning of the first year. Thus, colleges do not always reduce the occupational aspirations of women. Some kinds of colleges do; some kinds serve to counteract sex role constraints on women.

The evidence on work motivation shows that level of expectancy is almost equally important in accounting for sex differentials. The stereotype says that men are motivated in their choice of jobs by opportunities for advancement, independence, and challenge, while women are motivated by desire for good interpersonal relations, good supervision, and pleasant work conditions. Crowley, Levitan, and Quinn point out that very few studies report sex differences larger than 10 percent on any one of these work motivations.[54] Moreover, there is increasing evidence that sex differences in preferences or desire disappear when expectations are controlled. As an example, take the issue of job challenge. Data from a national study of working men and women show that when the jobs men and women currently hold provide them with a challenge, they equally often value challenge as an important work element. When their current jobs are unchallenging, women value work challenge less than men.[55] Earlier socialization of work preferences continues if the current experience does not provide opportunity to express, if not discover, the forms of gratification that result as "natural" preferences among men. Data from the same national study make the same argument about the desires of men and women to be promoted. In response to the question of when they would like to take on a job at a higher level, more women than men said they never wanted to be promoted. Women also expressed lower expectations of being given a chance to take on a job at a higher level. However, once the expectations of whether promotion was likely to occur were controlled, the sex difference in desire for promotion disappeared. When women believe they can be promoted, they want to be promoted as much as men.[56]

This brief review indicates that women and men do express genuinely different aspirations. In this way the research on sex shows greater differences than does that on race. These sex differences in aspirations also seem to account, at least partially, for the lower educational and job attainments of women, and thus would have to be altered if the status of men and women were to be equalized. By contrast, educational and job aspirations cannot account for race differentials in employment because blacks and whites express many of the same aspirations. Previous studies on sex and race agree, however, in suggesting that expectancies of success serve as important motivational influences for both blacks and women. For women, expectancies probably influence educational and job status directly as well as through their role in reducing aspirations. For blacks, expectancies seem to operate independently of aspirations. Future research needs to focus on the ways in which current discrimination and experiences in the market influence these expectancies and encourage some female and black workers to take jobs that are inappropriate for their training or that discourage them from filing for promotion, training programs, job transfers, or complaints of discrimination. This is not to imply that these behaviors substitute for the direct impact of race and sex discrimination in employment, but that discrimination also influences the subsequent behavior of workers through its effects on their beliefs and expectancies. This may make for different supply elasticities for women and minorities.

Future research also needs to explore the impact of these current experiences on expectancies and their role in changing job behaviors, rather than looking so exclusively to personal deficiencies and to early family socialization, especially in the case of women, as sources of deficient work motivation. Sewell notes, for example, that a model that included the education of the parents and the role of the parents, teachers, and friends during the high school years was much less effective in explaining sex differentials than social class differences in post-high school educational attainments. He concludes that much more attention needs to be given to influences on women in the months and years immediately following high school.[57]

Race and Sex: The Myth of the Black Woman's Dominance

The search for motivational variables to explain income and occupational differentials takes a somewhat strange direction in analyses of the economic status of black women. Because black women experience the dual burden of race and sex discrimination, one might be expected to stress particularly personality deficits and motivational limitations. Actually, just the opposite occurs. Although black women earn the least of the four sex and race groups, income statistics have been shown and interpreted so as to present black women as doing relatively well. This has been accomplished by presenting race differentials, controlling for sex, and demonstrating that while black women do not earn as much as white women, the race differential among women and men is less striking than it is in the comparison of white men and black men.[58] These relative comparisons of the race differentials among women and men have generally *not* been interpreted as indicating that black women suffer some *additional* race discrimination beyond the discrimination they face as women. Rather, the fact that the additional variance contributed by race discrimination is less than the variance it accounts for in the income of men has been interpreted, in a strange process of reasoning, as somehow indicating that black women have done relatively better than black men.

In the same vein, the fact that sex discrimination is less among blacks than among whites, at least on some economic indicators, has been interpreted as indicating that black women have done relatively better than white women. Motivational analyses have therefore tended to search for "strengths" rather than "weaknesses" in black women, particularly when compared to black men. At first glance, this focus on strengths may seem to contradict the contention that motivational analyses of sex and race differences tend to follow a "victim deficit" model. It is not a contradiction, however, within the general context of our literature on race in which the strengths of black women have been discussed invidiously within a framework of the "black matriarchy," "female dominance," and the weaknesses of black men. The economic and motivational analyses of the economic position of black women dramatically illustrate the influence of group status differentials.

Much previous research has drawn a picture of black women that makes them appear more effective than both black men and white women. Losing sight of the fact that black women face a double source of discrimination, many commentators conclude that they must be more appropriately motivated for the world of work than black men because race differentials are smaller among women than men, and they must be more effectively motivated than white women because sex differentials are smaller among blacks than among whites. An example of this kind of motivational argument appears in a recent analysis of the success of black professional women. Epstein[59] argues that black professional women have achieved unusual success, at least in high-prestige professions such as law and medicine, because of personal strengths they possess in greater abundance than white women of similar education and because they are viewed more favorably than either black men or white women by their white employers. Evidence about the motivational aspect of the argument is based on two sources: intensive interviews with thirty-one black women whose positions in law, medicine, dentistry, university teaching, journalism, and public relations set them apart as atypical occupational successes, and quantitative data on black women who were studied in 1964 by the National Opinion Research Center (NORC) when seniors at historically black colleges. The NORC data on senior women imply that college-educated black women in general, not simply the atypical group that has achieved top professional jobs, bring unusual motivational assets to the world of work. They are more self-confident about their abilities; they look at education more often as an investment in their futures; they are more motivated by economic rewards; even if married, they more often view careers as growing out of their own life aims instead of being supplementary to their husbands' work; and they show firmer commitments to work as indicated by having made their occupational choices earlier. Other researchers[60] add that black college women are less motivated by fear of success, the motive that has become popular in accounting for achievement inhibition among women.[61]

A careful look at available evidence on the aspirations and achievement motivations of black women and white women does not confirm such differences, at least at the college level. Black and white college women show very similar aspiration and motivation patterns.[62] The only reliable difference in the work motivations of college-educated black and white women is that black women more often expect to combine careers and family responsibilities. The National Opinion Research Center study of black and white graduating seniors in 1964 reported that 50 percent of the black women but only 25 percent of the white senior women expected to work after having children.[63] The work intentions of a sample of women whom Epps and Gurin have studied in ten historically black colleges, compared with white women attending a major university in the Midwest, differed less than these NORC results indicate. When asked, "Do you expect to work after you get married and before you have children?," 90 percent of the white women and 93 percent of the black senior women said yes. Working after the arrival of children distinguished them somewhat more. Half of the black women and 42 percent of the white women said they did intend to work after having children; 29 percent of the black and 28 percent of the white women were uncertain; 21 percent of the black but 30 percent of the white women definitely planned not to work after having children.[64]

Apart from these slight race differences in expectance of continuity of work experience, the educational and occupational goals of college women show marked racial similarities, not dissimilarities. Further, the sex differences that my colleagues and I have consistently found in the educational and occupational aspirations of black men and black women in college closely resemble data from national studies of college students. Three times as many men as women, both in the college population at large and in the black colleges studied, plan to pursue doctoral or professional degrees.[65] Figures on graduate degrees awarded also confirm similar sex disparities among blacks and whites. The male rate in earning the Ph.D. in the United States was nine to one; among blacks it was eight to two.[66] The male edge for masculine occupations was also approximately the same in the aspirations of black and white college seniors studied by the National Opinion Research Center.[67] For example:

Eight times as many men, both black and white, as women planned to enter the law.

Six times as many men, both black and white, as women planned to enter medicine.

Three times as many men, both black and white, as women planned to enter the physical sciences.

Eight times as many black men as women and thirteen times as many white men as women planned to enter engineering.

Twice as many black men as women and five times as many white men as women planned to enter business.

The sex-role conventionality reflected in the occupational choices of both black and white women is further shown by applying criteria used to define occupational role innovation in a study of white college women[68] to the women attending the black colleges studied. Women were classified as role innovators if they aspired to occupations in which less than 30 percent were women—that is, to occupations where women were underrepresented relative to their proportion in the experienced college-educated, civilian labor force. Women were classified as moderates if they aspired to occupations with 30 percent to 50 percent women, and as traditionalists if they planned to enter occupations with more than 50 percent women. Using these definitions, 19 percent of the white female seniors at major four-year universities were role innovators, another 19 percent were moderates, and 60 percent were traditionalists.[69] Applying the same criteria to the occupational choices listed by senior women in the sample of students attending black colleges, black women were every bit as conventional. Seventeen percent were role innovators, another 14 percent were moderates, and 68 percent were traditionalists.[70]

Black and white women, or black and white men, even among the college population, do not experience life the same way or hold the same attitudes about themselves and their worlds. Black women's reactions to the women's liberation movement attest to their own unique perspectives. The insightful analyses of black women by Toni Cade,[71] Joyce Ladner,[72] Gerda Lerner,[73] and Inez Reid[74] highlight unique themes in growing up black and female. Yet, sex-role demands and patterns of sex discrimination in society encourage women, black or white, to choose role-appropriate educational and occupational goals. This is perhaps particularly true of women who have been socialized through our educational institutions all the way to the college level. That this cannot be seen as cultural bias blinds us from facing the facts as they are. Sex discrimination has affected the aspirations of black women at the same time that they have had to cope with race discrimination as well. Again, these sex-role restrictions on the aspirations of black women in college are changeable. Because most colleges reinforce previous sex-role socialization does not mean they must. Some colleges we have studied did challenge and encourage their women students to disregard these sex-role influences on their future goals. More colleges can do that, although educators will hardly commit themselves to the goal of encouraging black women to go on to graduate and professional school and to enter demanding occupations if they accept the common misconceptions about black women in higher education and the labor market.

The Labor Market and Worker Expectations

The emphasis on expectancies in psychological research on the motivation of women and minorities fits particularly well with the supply issues suggested by a view of the market, or at least certain markets, as monopsonistic rather than competitive. An employer can profit when excluding groups of workers if the employer has market power and if such workers form a separate labor pool, particularly one that is less elastic. This means that we need to know if women and men, or blacks and whites, supply themselves differently even when equally trained and productive. We need information on worker perceptions of the market and their effects on expectancies of success. Do the perceptions of alternatives and beliefs about opportunities held by women and minorities reinforce sex and race segregation in the labor pool and/or make for different supply elasticities that can then be exaggerated by biased employers? This might happen if women and minorities:

Believe their opportunities are fewer.

Are more willing to take lower paying jobs at the bottom of a work category because they feel their alternatives are limited.

Are geographically less mobile (something more probable for married women than for single women or male minority workers).

Have less access to job information by knowing fewer people already occupying better jobs through which they could know about job openings.

Are aware that unions as worker monopolies control access to jobs they may prefer.

Realize that tests that are less valid for them will nonetheless form the basis of decisions about their hiring or promotion.

Such beliefs, judgments, and expectancies may not produce different supply elasticities in separate labor pools, particularly at the aggregate level; they would, however, with respect to supply for particular markets. Research on questions such as these is critically needed. It is psychological research that does not presume personality deficits that becomes productivity proxies for labor market experience. Instead, it focuses on the experiences and perceptions that women and minorities have of the market and how these affect their success in it. How does the discouragement of the woman applicant come about? How do workers conceive of the processes by which personnel offices manage to keep certain workers out of sales?

Psychologists from the situational tradition in motivation offer a theoretical framework that is particularly congenial to these supply questions. This framework distinguishes between expectancies as reflectors of the current situation and motives (or needs) as the more stable aspects of personality derived from earlier socialization. It helps us to understand that aspirations, like behavior, reflect expectations as well as needs, motives, and values. We particularly need this perspective in studying women since women do express aspirations different from those of men. One might be tempted to conclude, therefore, that women get what they want after all. But we can hardly know this if we do not first find out how much their stated preferences and aspirations reflect their expectations of what is possible.

Expectancies of success probably influence most women in the world of work, although they may operate somewhat differently for different groups of women. For example, highly educated women may shift their expectancies more rapidly than women with lower educational attainments when agreements, such as that established with American Telephone and Telegraph, open opportunities to women. Similarly, expectancies may figure more prominently for and require stronger interventions for change among women who are considering returning to the market in the middle years. Many people who counsel such women argue that lack of confidence and restricted expectancies severely affect whether these women actually try to continue their education, get training for new careers, and settle for low-paying jobs below their training and competencies.

The expectancies of women with much more continuous experience in the market would probably shift more readily if opportunities and alternatives were to expand for them. Yet, expectancies may operate very differently for older minority workers who have experienced many years of intermittent unemployment and constant underemployment than for younger workers, even those currently unemployed.

The research we need simply must disaggregate the analyses of expectancies by looking at their impact on behavior and their sensitivity to change in market opportunities among minority and women workers who have already had different experiences in the market and who are currently located in different types of local markets. Psychologists cannot carry out the needed research without the collaboration of economists and demographers who understand the critical ways in which markets vary and may thus condition the role of expectancies as supply characteristics.

Notes

1. See Irwin Katz and Patricia Gurin, eds., *Race and the Social Sciences* (New York: Basic Books, 1969).

2. Current Population Report Series P-60, 85 (December 1972), Table 49, pp. 115 and 119, "Median Earnings of Persons 25 Years Plus."

3. Richard B. Freeman, "Changes in the Labor Market for Black Americans, 1948-72," *Brookings Papers on Economic Activity*, 1 (1973), Table 2.

4. Orley Ashenfelter and James Heckman, "Changes in Minority Employment Patterns, 1966 to 1970," report prepared for the U.S. Equal Employment Opportunity Commission (February 1973), Table 1-1.

5. The index of occupational position is the average salary for a given group if its members had the same earnings in each occupation as the total population. Ibid.

6. Orley Ashenfelter, "Minority Employment Patterns, 1966," report prepared for the U.S. Equal Employment Opportunity Commission and the Office of Manpower Policy Evaluation and Research of the United States Department of Labor (April 1968).

7. Freeman, "Changes in Labor Market"; Ashenfelter and Heckman, "Changes in Employment"; Ronald L. Oaxaca, "The Persistence of Male-Female Earnings Differentials," paper prepared for the National Bureau of Economic Research Conference on Research on Income and Wealth (University of Michigan, 1974).

8. Henry Sanborn, "Pay Differences Between Men and Women," *Industrial and Labor Relations Review* 17, No. 4 (1964): 534-50.

9. Victor R. Fuchs, "Differences in Hourly Earnings Between Men and Women," *Monthly Labor Review* 94 (1971): 9-15.

10. Teresa Levitan, Robert P. Quinn, and Graham L. Staines, "Sex Discrimination Against the American Working Woman," *American Behavioral Scientist* 15 (1971).

11. Current Population Report Series P-60 (December 1972), Tables 49 and 52.

12. Ronald Oaxaca, "Male-Female Wage Differentials in Urban Labor Markets," *International Economic Review* 14, No. 3 (1973): 704.

13. Larry E. Suter and Herman P. Miller, "Income Differences Between Men and Career Women," *American Journal of Sociology* 78, No. 4 (1973): 962-975.

14. John E. Buckley, "Pay Differences Between Men and Women in the Same Job," *Monthly Labor Review* 94 (1971): 36-40.

15. Mary Hamilton, "A Study of Wage Discriminatory Sex: A Sample Survey in the Chicago Area" (Ph.D. dissertation, University of Pennsylvania, 1969).

16. Suter and Miller, "Income Differences," pp. 962-975.

17. Levitan, Quinn, and Staines, "Sex Discrimination."

18. Burton G. Malkiel and Judith A. Malkiel, "Male-Female Pay Differentials in Professional Employment," Working Paper No. 35 (Industrial Relations Section, Princeton University, 1972).

19. Janice Fanning Madden, "The Economics of Sex Discrimination" (Ph.D. dissertation, Duke University, 1972).

20. Orley Ashenfelter, "Minority Employment"; J.N. Morgan and Tecla Schrader, "Two Notes on Earnings Differentials by Sex and Race" (Survey Research Center, University of Michigan, 1971).

21. Orley Ashenfelter, "Minority Employment."

22. Walter Fogel, "The Effect of Low Educational Attainment and Discrimination on the Occupational Status of Minorities," Proceedings, Conference on Education and Training of Racial Minorities (Madison, Wisconsin, 1967).

23. Otis Dudley Duncan, "Inheritance of Poverty or Inheritance of Race?" in Daniel P. Moynihan, ed., *On Understanding Poverty* (New York: Basic Books, 1968).

24. Current Population Report Series P-60, 85 (December 1972), Table 58.

25. Freeman, "Changes in Labor Market"; U.S. 1970 Census of the Population, PC 27A Subject Reports, *Occupational Characteristics*, Tables 20 and 21.

26. Phyllis A. Wallace, "Employment Status of Black Women" (speech presented at the Southern Economic Association, Houston, Texas, 1973).

27. Ibid.

28. Otis Dudley Duncan, "Discrimination Against Negroes," *Annals of the American Academy of Political and Social Science* 371 (May 1967): 85-103; Duncan, "Inequality and Opportunity," *Population Index* 35 (1969): 361-366; Duncan, "Inheritance of Poverty"; Paul M. Siegel, "On the Cost of Being a Negro," *Sociological Inquiry* 35 (April 1965): 41-57; Orley Ashenfelter, *Minority Employment Patterns, 1966* (Industrial Relations Section, Princeton University, 1968); Fogel, "Low Educational Attainment."

29. Otis Dudley Duncan, "Inheritance of Poverty."

30. H. Proshansky and P. Newton, "The Nature and Meaning of Negro Self-Identity," in M. Deutsch, I. Katz, and A. Jensen, eds., *Social Class, Race, and Psychological Development* (New York: Holt, Rinehart & Winston, 1968).

31. Joseph H. Fichter, *Neglected Talents: Background and Prospects of Negro College Graduates*, Report No. 112 (Chicago: National Opinion Research Center, 1966); Patricia Gurin and Edgar Epps, *Black Consciousness, Identity and Achievement* (New York: John Wiley & Sons, forthcoming).

32. Ibid.

33. Fichter, *Neglected Talents*.

34. J.S. Coleman et al., *Equality of Educational Opportunity* (Washington, D.C.: U.S. Government Printing Office, 1966); Melvin Seeman, "Alienation and Engagement," in Angus Campbell and Philip E. Converse, eds., *The Human Meaning of Social Change* (New York: Russell Sage Foundation, 1972), pp. 467-527.

35. J. Veroff, L. McClelland, and D. Ruhland, "Varieties of Achievement Motivation," in M. Mednick, L. Hoffman, and S. Tangri, eds., *Women and Achievement* (New York: Holt, Rinehart & Winston, forthcoming).

36. R. Bloom and J. Barry, "The Determinants of Work Attitudes Among Negroes," *Journal of Applied Psychology* 51, (1967): 291-294.

37. J. Slocum, Jr., and R.H. Strauser, "Racial Differences in Job Attitudes," *Journal of Applied Psychology* 56, No. 1 (1972): 28-32.

38. William Cobb, "The Relationship Between Quality of Employment and Job Satisfaction Among Black and White Workers," in R. Quinn and T. Mangione, *The 1960-70 Survey of Working Conditions: Chronicles of an Unfinished Enterprise* (Ann Arbor: Institute for Social Research, 1973).

39. Seeman, "Alienation"; Coleman et al., *Equality of Opportunity*; Gerald Gurin, *A National Attitudes Study of Trainees in MDTA Institutional Programs* (Ann Arbor: Institute for Social Research, University of Michigan, 1970); Patricia Gurin, Gerald Gurin, Rosina C. Lao, and Muriel Beattie, "Internal-External Control in the Motivational Dynamics of Negro Youth," *Journal of Social Issues* 26, No. 3 (1969): 29-53.

40. Julian B. Rotter, "Generalized Expectancies for Internal Versus External Control of Reinforcement," *Psychological Monographs* 80, No. 1, whole no. 609, 1966.

41. Gurin and Epps, *Black Consciousness*.

42. Ibid.

43. Fichter, *Neglected Talents*.

44. William H. Sewell, "Inequality of Opportunity for Higher Education," *American Sociological Review* 36 (October 1971): 793-809.

45. Ibid.

46. Ibid.

47. Diane Delsa Hatch, "Differential Personal Change of Males and Females in Two College Environments" (Ph.D. dissertation, University of Michigan, 1971); S.S. Tangri, "Role Innovation in Occupational Choice Among College Women" (Ph.D. dissertation, University of Michigan, 1969).

48. Alexander W. Astin and Robert J. Panos, *The Educational and Vocational Development of College Students* (Washington: American Council on Education, 1969).

49. Jerry Lee Lamasnez Miller, "Occupational Choice: The Construction and Testing of a Paradigm of Occupational Choice for the College Graduate" (Ph.D. dissertation, Florida State University, 1959); Hatch, "Differential Personal Change."

50. A.W. Astin, *Progress of the Merit Scholars: An Eight-Year Followup*, NMSC Research Reports 1 (Evanston, Illinois: National Merit Scholarship Corporation, 1965); S.S. Angrist, "The Study of Sex Roles," *Journal of Social Issues* 25, No. 1 (1969): 215-232; J.L. Holland, "Exploration of a Theory of Vocational Choice and Achievement: A Four-Year Prediction Study," *Psychological Reports* 12 (1962): 547-594; W.L. Wallace, *Student Culture: Social Structure and Continuity in a Liberal Arts College* (Chicago: Aldine Publishing Company, 1966).

51. J. Crowley, T. Levitan, and R. Quinn, "The Seven Deadly Half-Truths About Women," *Psychology Today* (March 1973): 94.

52. Patricia Gurin and Daniel Katz, *Motivation and Aspiration in the Negro College* (Ann Arbor, Michigan: Institute for Social Research, 1966).

53. Gurin and Epps, *Black Consciousness.*

54. Crowley, Levitan, and Quinn, "Seven Deadly Half-Truths."

55. Conversations with Teresa Levitan and Robert Quinn relative to work in progress on working conditions of a national sample of American workers, Survey Research Center, University of Michigan, 1972.

56. Crowley, Levitan, and Quinn, "Seven Deadly Half-Truths."

57. Sewell, "Inequality of Opportunity."

58. Typically, race differentials are displayed as the income ratio of blacks to whites and separate ratios are presented for men and women. Likewise sex differentials are displayed as the income ratio of women to men and again separated for blacks and whites. When the absolute income figures (or occupational indices) themselves are also presented, the reader can see that black women typically fall at the bottom of the rank order of the four groups. Some papers (see Freeman, "Changes in the Labor Market") include *only* the ratio statistics. This especially encourages the misconception that black women are doing better than black men when the race differential ratios merely show that race discrimination is less for them than for black men. Black women can be

relatively less disadvantaged than black men (when each is compared to their own sex among whites) *and* less disadvantaged than white women (where each is compared to men of their own racial group) but still earn the least (or show the lowest occupational position) of the four groups. Many papers also fail to keep the *relative* comparison in focus and slip into language that implies absolute status when discussing black women.

59. Cynthia Fuchs Epstein, "Positive Effects of the Multiple Negative: Explaining the Success of Black Professional Women," *American Journal of Sociology* 78, No. 4 (1973): 912-935. While Epstein explicitly rejects the view of black women as "dominant" or as having fared unusually well in the market, the motivational discussion in the *American Journal of Sociology* consistently develops a picture of unusual motivational strengths. Had evidence been restricted just to the thirty-one women whom she interviewed intensively, the burden of the argument would have been very different. Atypical groups probably possess unusual motivational strengths either because of having brought greater potential to the job world or because of having developed stronger motivation through the job experience. A later discussion by Epstein ("Black and Female: The Double Whammy," *Psychology Today*, 7, 3, 1973, 57-61) indeed is restricted to considering just the atypical group she interviewed. Unfortunately, the discussion of motivation in the original article depended greatly on information gathered from senior women before entering the job world and thus applied not merely to a highly atypical group but to college-educated black women in general. It is that more general picture that is at issue since data reviewed here indicate that black women while still in college do not appear to have escaped sex-role inhibitions on work motivation.

60. Peter J. Weston and Martha T. Mednick, "Race, Social Class and the Motive to Avoid Success in Women," *Journal of Cross-Cultural Psychology* 1, No. 3 (September 1970): 284-291; Gwendolyn R. Puryear and Martha T. Mednick, "Black Militancy, Affective Attachment, and the Fear of Success in Black College Women," *Journal of Consulting and Clinical Psychology* 42, No. 2 (1974): 263-266.

61. Matina Horner, "Toward an Understanding of Achievement-Related Conflicts in Women," *Journal of Social Issues* 28, No. 2 (1972): 157-175.

62. Fichter, *Neglected Talents.*

63. Ibid.

64. Gurin and Epps, *Black Consciousness.*

65. Astin and Panos, *Educational and Vocational Development*; Fichter, *Neglected Talents.*

66. Helen Astin, *The Woman Doctorate* (Hartford, Connecticut: The Russell Sage Foundation, 1969); James A. Bryant, *A Survey of Black American Doctorates* (New York: The Ford Foundation, no date).

67. Fichter, *Neglected Talents.*

68. Sandra Schwartz Tangri, "Determinants of Occupational Role Innovation Among College Women," *Journal of Social Issues* 28, No. 2 (1972).

69. Ibid.

70. Gurin and Epps, *Black Consciousness.*

71. Toni Cade, ed., *The Black Woman* (New York: Signet, 1970).

72. Joyce Ladner, *Tomorrow's Tomorrow: The Black Woman* (Garden City, New York: Doubleday and Company, Anchor Books, 1972).

73. Gerda Lerner, *Black Women in White America: A Documentary History* (New York: Pantheon Books, 1972).

74. Inez Reid, *Together Black Women* (New York: Emerson-Hall, 1972).

Bibliography

Angrist, S.S. "The Study of Sex Roles." *Journal of Social Issues* 25 (1969).

Ashenfelter, Orley. "Minority Employment Patterns, 1966." Report prepared for the U.S. Equal Employment Opportunity Commission and the Office of Manpower Policy Evaluation and Research of the United States Department of Labor (April 1968).

Ashenfelter, Orley, and James Heckman. "Changes in Minority Employment Patterns, 1966 to 1970." Report prepared for the U.S. Equal Employment Opportunity Commission (February 1973).

Astin, A.W. *Progress of the Merit Scholars: An Eight-Year Followup.* NMSC Research Reports 1. Evanston, Illinois: National Merit Scholarship Corporation, 1965.

Astin, Alexander W., and Robert J. Panos. *The Educational and Vocational Development of College Students.* Washington: American Council on Education, 1969.

Astin, Helen. *The Woman Doctorate.* Hartford, Connecticut: The Russell Sage Foundation, 1969.

Bloom, R., and J. Barry. "The Determinants of Work Attitudes Among Negroes." *Journal of Applied Psychology* 51 (1967).

Bryant, James A. *A Survey of Black American Doctorates.* New York: The Ford Foundation, no date.

Buckley, John E. "Pay Differences Between Men and Women in the Same Job." *Monthly Labor Review* 94 (1971).

Cade, Toni. *The Black Woman.* New York: Signet, 1970.

Cobb, William. "The Relationship Between Quality of Employment and Job Satisfaction Among Black and White Workers." In *The 1969-70 Survey of Working Conditions: Chronicles of an Unfinished Enterprise*, R. Quinn and T. Mangine, eds. Ann Arbor: Institute for Social Research, 1973.

Coleman, J.S. et al. *Equality of Educational Opportunity.* Washington: U.S. Government Printing Office, 1966.

Crowley, J., T. Levitan and R. Quinn. "The Seven Deadly Half-Truths about Women." *Psychology Today* (March 1973).

Current Population Report Series P-60, 85 (December 1972).

Duncan, Otis Dudley. "Discrimination Against Negroes." *Annals of the American Academy of Political and Social Science* 371, (May 1967).

Duncan, Otis Dudley. "Inheritance of Poverty or Inheritance of Race?" In *On Understanding Poverty*, Daniel P. Moynihan, ed. New York: Basic Books, 1968.

Duncan, Otis Dudley. "Inequality and Opportunity." *Population Index* 35 (1969).

Epstein, Cynthia Fuchs. "Positive Effects of the Multiple Negative: Explaining the Success of Black Professional Women." *American Journal of Sociology* 78 (1973).

Fichter, Joseph H. *Neglected Talents: Background and Prospects of Negro College Graduates*, Report No. 112. Chicago: National Opinion Research Center, 1966.

Fogel, Walter. "The Effect of Low Educational Attainment and Discrimination on the Occupational Status of Minorities." Proceedings, Conference on Education and Training of Racial Minorities, Madison, Wisconsin, 1967.

Freeman, Richard B. "Changes in the Labor Market for Black Americans, 1948-72." *Brookings Papers on Economic Activity* 1 (1973).

Fuchs, Victor R. "Differences in Hourly Earnings Between Men and Women." *Monthly Labor Review* 94 (1970).

Gurin, Gerald. *A National Attitudes Study of Trainees in MDTA Institutional Programs.* Ann Arbor: Institute for Social Research, University of Michigan, 1970.

Gurin, Patricia, and Daniel Katz. *Motivation and Aspiration in the Negro College.* Ann Arbor, Michigan: Institute for Social Research, 1966.

Gurin, Patricia, Gerald Gurin, Rosina C. Lao, and Muriel Beattie. "Internal-External Control in the Motivational Dynamics of Negro Youth." *Journal of Social Issues* 26 (1969).

Gurin, Patricia, and Irwin Katz, eds. *Race and the Social Sciences.* New York: Basic Books, 1969.

Gurin, Patricia, and Edgar Epps. *Black Consciousness, Identity and Achievement.* New York: John Wiley and Sons, 1975.

Hamilton, Mary. "A Study of Wage Discriminatory Sex: A Sample Survey in the Chicago Area." Ph.D. dissertation, University of Pennsylvania, 1969.

Hatch, Diane Delsa. *Differential Personal Change of Males and Females in Two College Environments.* Ph.D. dissertation, University of Michigan, 1971.

Holland, J.L. "Exploration of a Theory of Vocational Choices and Achievement: A Four-Year Prediction Study." *Psychological Reports* 12 (1962).

Horner, Matina. "Toward an Understanding of Achievement-Related Conflicts in Women." *Journal of Social Issues* 28 (1972).

Ladner, Joyce. *Tomorrow's Tomorrow: The Black Woman.* Garden City, New York: Doubleday and Company, Anchor Books, 1972.

Lerner, Gerda. *Black Women in White America: A Documentary History.* New York: Pantheon Books, 1972.

Levitan, Teresa, Robert P. Quinn, and Graham L. Staines. "Sex Discrimination Against the American Working Woman." *American Behavior Scientist* 15 (1971).

Madden, Janice Fanning. "The Economics of Sex Discrimination." Ph.D. dissertation, Duke University, 1972.

Malkiel, Burton G., and Judith A. Malkiel. "Male-Female Pay Differentials in Professional Employment." Working Paper No. 35, Industrial Relations Section, Princeton University, 1972.

Miller, Jerry Lee Lamasnez. "Occupational Choice: The Construction and Testing of a Paradigm of Occupational Choice for the College Graduate." Ph.D. dissertation, Florida State University, 1959.

Morgan, J.N. and Tecla Schrader. "Two Notes on Earnings Differentials by Sex and Race." Survey Research Center, University of Michigan, 1971.

Oaxaca, Ronald. "Male-Female Wage Differentials in Urban Labor Markets." *International Economic Review* 14 (1973).

Oaxaca, Ronald. "The Persistence of Male-Female Earnings Differentials." Paper prepared for the National Bureau of Economic Research Conference on Research on Income and Wealth, University of Michigan, 1974.

Proshansky, H., and P. Newton. "The Nature and Meaning of Negro Self-Identity." In *Social Class, Race, and Psychological Development*, M. Deutsch, I. Katz, and A. Jensen, eds. New York: Holt, Rinehart and Winston, 1968.

Puryear, Gwendolyn R., and Martha S. Mednick. "Black Militancy, Affective Attachment, and the Fear of Success in Black College Women." *Journal of Consulting and Clinical Psychology* 42 (1974).

Reid, Inez. *Together Black Women.* New York: Emerson-Hall, 1972.

Rotter, Julian B. "Generalized Expectancies for Internal Versus External Control of Reinforcement." *Psychological Monographs* 8 (1) whole No. 609, 1966.

Sanborn, Henry. "Pay Differences Between Men and Women." *Industrial and Labor Relations Review* 17 (1964).

Seeman, Melvin. "Alienation and Engagement." In *The Human Meaning of Social Change*, Angus Campbell and Philip E. Converse, eds. New York: Russell Sage Foundation, 1972.

Sewell, William H. "Inequality of Opportunity for Higher Education." *American Sociological Review* 36 (October 1971).

Siegel, Paul M. "On the Cost of Being a Negro." *Sociological Inquiry* 35 (April 1965).

Slocum, J., Jr., and R.H. Strauser. "Racial Differences in Job Attitudes." *Journal of Applied Psychology* 56 (1972).

Suter, Larry E., and Herman P. Miller. "Income Differences Between Men and Career Women." *American Journal of Sociology* (1973).

Tangri, S.S. *Role Innovation in Occupational Choice Among College Women.* Ph.D. dissertation, University of Michigan, 1969.

Tangri, Sandra Schwartz. "Determinants of Occupational Role Innovation Among College Women." *Journal of Social Issues* (1972).

U.S. 1970 Census of the Population, PC 27A Subject Reports, *Occupational Characteristics*, Tables 20 and 21.

Veroff, J., L. McClelland, and D. Ruhland. "Varieties of Achievement Motivation." In *Women and Achievement*, M. Mednick, L. Hoffman, and S. Tangri, eds. New York: Holt, Rinehart and Winston, in press.

Wallace, Phyllis A. "Employment Status of Black Women." Speech presented at the Southern Economic Association, Houston, Texas, 1973.

Wallace, W.L. *Student Culture: Social Structure and Continuity in a Liberal Arts College.* Chicago: Aldine Publishing Co., 1966.

Weston, Peter J., and Martha T. Mednick. "Race, Social Class and Motive to Avoid Success in Women." *Journal of Cross-Cultural Psychology* 1 (September 1970).

Comments

Carolyn Shaw Bell

Gurin's paper argues that we need more information on labor supply functions, and that the particular kind of information needed requires psychological research regarding the beliefs and perceptions of women and minorities about markets, opportunities, and likelihood of success. As one example of useful findings, Gurin reviews research suggesting that women and minorities resemble white males in their work-related goals and values but differ sharply in their sense of personal control.

These are the kind of issues that economists usually file under the ceteris paribus assumption, or take as parameters of a given supply situation. Gurin points out that in economic terms her prescription would lead to a sharper delineation of the shape and slope of the supply schedule, and therefore its elasticity. Elasticity, of course, determines the extent of employer power that can be exercised in a monopsonistic labor market. Two further responses to Gurin's paper may be taken by those who believe that social and psychological questions can also present viable economic issues.

First, the theory of choice (and perhaps the construction of utility functions) may be reviewed from the perspective of the individual's decision to supply labor. One piece of economic theory, the permanent income hypothesis, presently incorporates the notion of expectancies; what implications does this hold for the labor supply function? Second, it may be recognized that while the marketplace serves a primary function of providing information to participants, the feedback mechanism consists of more than changing relative prices.

The economist's supply function focuses on the individual's decision to supply a particular quantity and type of labor to a particular market, given the price prevailing in that market and the opportunity cost to the individual of the time and effort involved. The simplest kind of function finds the quantity of labor offered at a low price to be less than that at a high price. Presumably this relation reflects the individual's alternatives for using time, given the opportunities for consumption or investment in human capital through education and training. The shape of the function differs between individuals, depending on the manner in which inherited and acquired tastes and skills influence their perception of labor market opportunities and alternative uses of time.

The individual, however, is not only a supplier of labor. He or she is also a complete human being for whom a particular job or employment opportunity represents much more than the specific situation of work assignment and wage payment. A job may represent the port of entry into the labor market or progress in a career; it may be a temporary mainstay between two periods of education or a part-time supplement to retirement income; or it may be a step upward or a downgrading, a tentative exploration of a new field or the beginning of a long-term commitment. To the individual involved, the job is part of a life experience. Thus, the same job can provide different life experiences to different people.

While economists certainly know this to be true of their own career patterns and probably those of their personal friends, the concept of expectancies has not been built into the decision-making models that generate supply functions. Gurin's article should lead us to insist on a long time frame, a kind of "permanent employment" theory in which the worker perceives a current job in relation to past accomplishments and future prospects. Using the language of the permanent income theorists, employment may contain a transitory element and a permanent element. The former refers to the job as a stage in an expected path of progress; the latter, to the job as arrival at or attainment of a given level of success. The economist may then question whether men and women differ in ratios of transitory to permanent elements. If, for example, the position of bank teller means, for a man, a six-month's assignment in an executive training program, his work effort and productivity may be quite different than that of a woman for whom the same position means a dead-end job, with no possibility of promotion or transfer.

Gurin points out that a job does carry significance to the particular person in terms of that person's aspirations. Women generally hold lower aspirations than men, and any shift tends to be toward lower rather than higher levels of aspiration. These and other sex differences in attitudes toward work, of course, reflect women's expectancies. And, like the expectations of blacks for less success and a smaller measure of control over their personal lives, these attitudes appear to be wholly realistic.

Approaching labor supply in terms of human beings may, in fact, call for a reconsideration of the permanent income hypothesis itself. Crudely put, this theory (and its variations) state that a consumer unit at any point in time works out expected lifetime income and then plans consumption and savings out of current income accordingly. Yet, calculation of expected income also requires plotting the size and composition of the income unit. Although there is little discussion of the income unit among permanent income theorists, it is probably safe to assume that most economists are thinking in terms of family. This means, however, that calculating expected income must also predict the employment and income generated by each working member, for the majority of husband-wife families today contain two working partners. Perhaps more important, the calculation must include some prediction about the "permanence" of the income unit itself. Realistically, adults today should expect to belong to more than one family during a lifetime. Gurin's article urges us to pay more attention to individuals as people than as abstract economic units, and it may be useful to recognize that there is no a priori reason for individuals to share the same expectancies, or even consonant expectancies, about lifetime employment or lifetime income just because they are married to each other.

The second theme for economists to consider in Gurin's article is the notion of information generated in the marketplace. Her review of studies on sex and race concludes that expectations of success influence job motivation for women and blacks differently than for white males, and she urges future research on how these expectations are formed. Some tentative evidence suggests that experiences in the labor market (what happens in the first job) has a marked influence. Aside from the examples cited by Gurin, the continuing controversy over coeducation may be noted: whether women's colleges help women to achieve self-confidence and experience in leadership or hinder women by shielding them from the "real world" of male dominance and male discrimination. Both parties to the controversy argue in terms of how best to prepare women for employment; both cite reports from working women about their experiences on the job. Evidently, what happens in a work situation tells a woman something about the job and its costs and benefits, but it also conveys a message about herself as a person. And this latter information obviously affects the woman's subsequent decisions, through its impact on her perceptions of job opportunities and her own expected lifetime employment pattern.

The market has long been admired by economists (and others) for its automatic adjustment process which incorporates an elaborate and sensitive feedback mechanism. Economists have tended to focus on changes in relative prices as the primary element in this feedback process and to pay little attention to the other types of information provided by the market. In fact, business adjusts to many indicators other than price: the rate of new orders, the age of accounts receivable, suppliers' quoted delivery times, reports from sales people about "soft" markets, reactions by bankers to financial statements, and so on. Most of this information, however, refers to events that happen (or fail to occur) in impersonal, market transactions.

The market influence Gurin discerns has an impact on people, not just economic events, and provides information that affects personal goals and efforts. Labor market economists have come to recognize the "discouraged worker" as a particular type of unemployment, and Gurin suggests that similar psychological descriptions may be useful in identifying other types of economic behavior. There is, of course, a further implication that changes in economic events can follow from changes in attitudes, feelings, expectations, or motivations. The possibility that we can expect economic policy to include programs for psychological intervention may seem remote. The implications of Gurin's article for social policy program, however, clearly call for such intervening action, to change the feelings that blacks and women have about themselves.

Gurin's article is an appeal to economists to remember that they are social scientists, dealing with people. If that stance proves unpalatable, economists will become increasingly helpless in dealing with functions, like that of labor supply, that represent people's choice decisions. The psychology used by economists represents, for the most part, inventions by economists, from Adam Smith's citing a "natural" inclination on the part of mankind to higgle and bargain to Lord Keynes' citing a "well-known propensity" on the part of men to spend more as their incomes increase, but not in the same proportion. Economists may do better if they turn to psychologists and their research for information about human behavior.

Comments

Lotte Bailyn

In "The Role of Worker Expectancies in the Study of Employment Discrimination," Patricia Gurin approaches the problem of employment discrimination by analyzing job behavior in terms of a psychological theory of motivation. In doing so she contributes to our understanding of the process of career development.

The traditional explanation of employment differentials between men and women, or blacks and whites, has been based on an implicit assumption that careers evolve by means of the following chain of events:

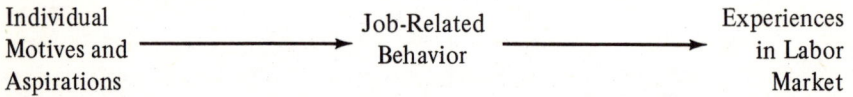

Individual   Job-Related   Experiences
Motives and ⟶   Behavior   ⟶   in Labor
Aspirations   Market

Women, for instance, have lower aspirations than men and thus are less productive on the job. The fact, therefore, that their experiences in the labor market (in the form of wages or promotions) are less good is a direct reflection of their initial unequal input.

What Gurin has done by analyzing motives in terms of the expectancy-value model is to rearrange the elements in this chain. The expectancy-value theory views motivation as a function of two elements; the strength of a motivational tendency is seen as the product of an individual's *expectancy* or belief that a particular activity will have a particular consequence, and the *value* or attractiveness of this consequence to the individual. Gurin, through her incisive review of the literature, establishes that the primary difference between blacks and whites, and, though more complex, between men and women, does *not* lie in the value or attractiveness to them of careers but in their realistic evaluation of the probability of being successful in these careers. Thus, the process of career development is seen in a very different way:

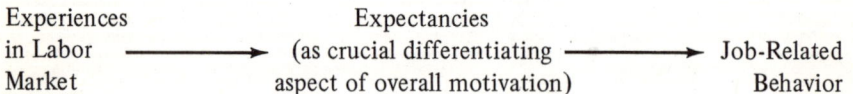

Experiences   Expectancies
in Labor   ⟶   (as crucial differentiating   ⟶   Job-Related
Market   aspect of overall motivation)   Behavior

Different experiences in the labor market, which in the traditional view are seen as the rational *consequence* of different motivations and behavior, are now seen to be at the *root* of these presumed psychological differences.

The divergent implications of these two views for research into employment differentials by race and sex and for policies dealing with these differences are

42

obvious. By highlighting the role played by actual work experiences in the development of people's careers, Gurin—and others in this volume who have come to a similar conclusion (Bergmann and Polachek)—underline the importance of studying and changing the objective conditions of employment in order to equalize people's work opportunities.

Gurin has made a significant contribution to our understanding of the work experiences of "disadvantaged" groups, and the type of research she recommends is badly needed. But we can also benefit by research in another tradition: by a more qualitative analysis of the way careers actually develop in specific people. Such studies can often provide special insight into the processes by which experiences are translated into expectations and the ways these personal responses, in turn, help determine an individual's subsequent career.

3

Research Needs I: What Psychological Research on the Labor Force Participation of Women Is Needed?

Judith Long Laws

Introduction

The labor force participation of women raises numerous psychological questions that deserve empirical investigation. These questions may be grouped into three programmatic research concerns.

1. The development and change of women's work orientations and labor force attachments within a life-cycle context.

2. The sex composition of the labor force, subsuming experimental and quasi-experimental variations on the sex of leaders and coworkers, with performance-based dependent variables.

3. Employer attitudes and behavior, including studies of change attempts and their effectiveness, as well as cases of "backlash" and mechanisms of circumvention.

Research questions in each of these areas are outlined below.

Development and Change in Women's Work Orientations

Two related research programs, one experimental and one naturalistic, are needed in this area. The first might take off from existing research findings that identify conflicts inhibiting goal-related striving in women and suggest mechanisms for neutralizing such conflicts.[1] Such studies will need replication. The next stage would be the development of programs that incorporate the techniques found to be effective in producing change.

A second application of experimental techniques would be to sample individuals confronted with the major "decision" or inflection points that are relevant for occupational behavior, and to ask, for example, "Does exposure to peers or adults who encourage or discourage various occupational aspirations affect the occupational attainment of young people?"

In order to study women's labor force behavior in a coherent manner, a framework of the female life cycle must be adopted. Within this framework certain major stages or statuses in a sex-role "program" can be identified. These have implications for the kind of labor force behavior (and even attitudes, orientations, and aspirations) that are "appropriate" for a woman at particular stages of development.

The need for longitudinal studies of individual careers is urgent. Individual cross-sectional studies that are currently available compare pseudo-cohorts constituted *after* major points of divergence in the lifelong process of choice. Similarly, a comparison of the percentage of college women electing professional careers with the percentage of women students in professional schools or practicing in the professions overlooks the "dropouts." Without longitudinal data on individual careers, questions regarding the critical factors influencing such choices cannot be answered.

Existing research affords several promising starting points in the life cycle where changes seem to occur in the work-relevant orientations of females. Studying the forces that play on the individual at these points may reveal the determinants affecting the choice of one path rather than another.

Currently available research indicates that the following are such inflection points:[2]

The onset of the *social* status of adolescence (fifth grade).

The end of adolescence, whether high school graduation for the terminal student or college graduation (coming to terms with the adult sex role).

Marriage, and the child-intensive phase of the family life cycle.

The "empty nest" stage when child care demands are greatly diminished.

This list is not exhaustive and longitudinal research may indicate other important inflection points. Divorce, for example, is a common event that occasions major changes in the balance of family and work responsibilities. This phenomenon, however, has not been studied in the context of labor force behavior; indeed, single women tend to be ignored in many analyses of women in the labor force.

During each of the critical periods cited, the factors highlighted by previous research come into play. Of particular importance are reference figures and role models. Therefore, research on the work orientation of women should study (1) available models for particular occupations (for many occupations these will be exclusively male, and for others, exclusively female); (2) "life-style" role models that demonstrate the range of patterns for combining work and family commitments (these will be exclusively female); (3) boyfriends and potential mates; and (4) other peers.

In the past, research on reference figures and role modeling has emphasized positive effects; role models are assumed to provide a positive pattern, inspiration, and encouragement. However, data on the lowering of aspiration levels by young women indicate that "significant others" may be a potent source of *discouragement*, rather than encouragement, for occupational aspiration.[3] Research on reference figures implies that the young girl who perseveres in her high occupational aspirations is exceptional not in her motivation or her ability, but in the support she receives from significant others.[4]

The emphasis placed on role modeling is not new in the study of occupational choice. Traditionally, the idea of role modeling has been limited to figures in face-to-face interaction with the focal person. This narrow focus ignores the effects of vicarious learning, which may be extremely important. Vicarious learning involves the observation by the perceiver of a model engaging in some activity. The learning of the activity by the perceiver is mediated, however, by a number of factors that militate toward "identification" with the model; gender has been shown to be one such factor. Furthermore, the *motivation* of the perceiver is engaged by her perception of the outcomes rewarding the model as a consequence of the behavior. Limitation or reproduction of the modeled behavior tends to occur only when the model has been rewarded (or successful) in the behavior. Conversely, the perceiver will inhibit, or perhaps even "forget," the observed behavior if she perceives that the model is punished for it.

The issue of providing role models for occupational attainment in women appears to be extremely complex. The individual may be affected, even at some distance, by the perception that women are occupying jobs that are responsible, prestigious, challenging, or "masculine." This perception alone can broaden her perceived set of options. However, if the model is not rewarded with success, the perceiver is unlikely to strive to follow the example. One consequence of this is that the practice of tokenism in organizations is not likely to be effective in starting a chain of role modeling.

Individual difference factors such as personality variables may have their effect within rather than across the "tracks" created by options made available to an individual at different stages of the life cycle. Certainly, the need for achievement, the motive to avoid success, and Julian Rotter's internality/externality variables should have predictive power at this level of analysis.

The research resulting from this approach, though extremely broad in scope, promises to yield information that is available through no other means. Moreover, it has the potential of revealing a set of "tracks" or careers representing different combinations of options at different stages of the life cycle and at different levels of the social and occupational structures.

At each stage of the life cycle it is important to ascertain feelings about work, occupations, and the actual and intended behaviors involved in labor force participation. Given the previous research, it would not be surprising to find extraordinary achievement motivation coupled with a very ordinary occupational "choice" in young women whose perceived options and social support are restricted. A comparison with cohorts of males would be strategic for this research. Differences in the experience of encouragement/discouragement may be critical predictors of the differential occupational attainment of females and males. From a practical point of view, such data would aid in the design of programs and policies that are appropriate to the target population. Another contribution of such a research program would be an expansion of the current incomplete understanding of the psychological factors affecting the formation and development of work orientations in women.

Sex Composition of the Work Force

Descriptive studies of the sex composition of the labor force have proven useful, and will continue to be so. However, there is a significant lack of experimentally oriented research at the level of the establishment or individual company. Companies with a large enough number of workers and sufficient organizational flexibility give the researcher the opportunity to vary important conditions in a quasi-experimental design. Two important sets of studies concern (1) *women in positions of leadership* and (2) *women as coworkers.* There is a tradition of research on leadership and on group cohesion and productivity in industry, originating within the discipline of social psychology. However, this research has tended to neglect women.

F.E. Fiedler's extensive series of studies suggests that a number of factors add up to task situations that affect the difficulty of the job of the leader.[5] Factors included here are (1) the degree to which the task is structured; (2) the legitimacy or power of the leadership position (independent of its present incumbent); and (3) the group climate. Each of these (in the experimental situation) can be manipulated through instructions and definitions of the situation. Given the number of assumptions made about women as leaders, it is probably crucial to approximate a degree of experimental control rather than to allow these factors to vary accidentally.

A program of research could begin with comparisons of the effectiveness of female and male leaders when Fiedler's parameters are varied. If sex differences are found, they may point to different leadership styles that pay off for females and males. However, it seems likely that controlling (or matching on) task structure, group climate, and legitimacy will reveal similar leadership effectiveness in both sexes.

A second major focus of research should be the sex composition of the work group. Competing hypotheses in this area are (1) that sex composition, or sex ratio, makes a qualitative difference in the performance or climate of the work group; and (2) that variables known to affect these outcomes override any sex effect. The relevant research literature here directs attention to the following variables: task interdependence/independence; group versus individual rewards; and presence or absence of a common goal.[6] Within these pairs, the first variable predicts group cooperation; the second, competition and disruption.

A number of hypotheses that predict differential effects of mixed-sex versus same-sex work groups are available. Valerie K. Oppenheimer[7] predicts that as the sex ratio approaches equality, there will be a tendency for subgrouping along gender lines. Other research indicates that the practice of tokenism may militate against the entry of significant numbers of women into management and nontraditional professions.[8] Moreover, following the work on racial succession in residential areas, it might be predicted that there is a "tipping point" that, if exceeded by the proportion of the minority group, indicates that a particular job will be abandoned by the majority group. Another hypothesis implies that men will find the presence of women so disruptive that their work will suffer. All of these hypotheses can be tested by systematiclly varying the sex ratio of work groups while controlling other variables. Finally, when the effects of sex of leader and sex composition of work group have been investigated, the interaction effects associated with combinations of these two factors may be explored.

Employer Attitudes and Behavior

If attention is directed to the *situation* that the female worker confronts rather than focusing on the individual, the effects of the structural features of the labor market are so overwhelming that the behavior of the individual is proportionately reduced in scope. Therefore, it is particularly critical to look at the behavior and attitudes of those who direct the implementation of organizational policy.

A first step in this research program would be to collect data on employer attitudes and policies in order to ascertain the degree of change needed. A second step would be to attempt to ascertain what incentives are effective for changing employer policies toward women. A third step would be to focus on attitudinal change—the techniques and the outcomes of change attempts. It would be interesting to examine the temporal relationship between changes in policy and changes in attitude.

Additional research is needed to identify the specific mechanisms used by employers to deny equal opportunity to women. Particularly critical is the identification of new procedures introduced to circumvent pressure for affirmative action and compliance with recent legislation. To date, some of these procedures have taken the form of "budget squeezes," retaliation against activists, tokenism, and lobbying activities, as well as adherence to the seniority (LIFO) principle in lay off from nontraditional jobs.

Conclusion

This paper has attempted to outline a broad programmatic approach to the numerous psychological questions raised by the labor force participation of women. The first important area of program research would involve both experimental and naturalistic studies of the development and change in the work orientation of women over the female life cycle. The adoption of a life-cycle framework would permit identification of the major stages and critical inflection points where changes occur in the career aspirations of females. Such an approach would also highlight the influence of role models in encouraging or discouraging occupational choices. A second research area would focus on experimentally oriented studies of the sex composition of the labor force at the individual company level. Critical questions to be explored here would include the effectiveness of women in positions of leadership and of work groups with varying proportions of women. The final programmatic research area would focus on the behavior and attitudes of employers. Such employer studies may be expected to have important implications for the implementation of equal opportunity policy.

Notes

1. The experimental findings of H.S. Farmer and M.J. Bohn, "Home-Career Conflict Reduction and the Level of Career Interest in Women," *Journal of Consulting Psychology* 17 (1970): 228-232; and M.L. Katz, "Female Motive to Avoid Success: A Psychological Barrier or a Response to Deviancy?," Educational Testing Service, 1973, demonstrate that when occupational aspiration or striving can be seen as less deviant, women are less motivated to inhibit career concerns.

2. A number of studies show a "flight into femininity" at about fifth grade (D.G. Brown, "Masculinity-Femininity Development in Children," *Journal of Consulting Psychology* 21, 1957: 197-202). Late in adolescence a curtailment of aspirations has repeatedly been observed (E. Matthews and D.V. Tiedman, "Attitudes Toward Career and Marriage and the Development of Life Style in Young Women," *Journal of Consulting Psychology* 11 (1964): 375-383; and M. Schwenn, "Arousal of the Motive to Avoid Success" (Junior Honors Paper, Harvard University, 1970)). The influence of motherhood upon labor force participation has often been studied (Valerie K. Oppenheimer, *The Female Labor Force in the United States: Demographic and Economic Factors Governing its Growth and Changing Composition* (University of California, Berkeley: Population Monograph Series #5, 1970), but not that of divorce or bereavement).

3. Boyfriends or potential mates may be particularly influential (S. Tangri, "Determinants of Occupational Role Innovation Among College Women," *The Journal of Social Issues* 28, 1972: 177-199; P. Hawley, "What Women Think Men Think: Does it Affect Their Career Choice?," *Journal of Consulting Psychology* 18, 1971: 193-199; A. Peplau, "The Impact of Fear of Success, Sex Role Attitudes and Opposite Sex Relationships on Women's Intellectual Performance: An Experimental Study of Competition in Dating Couples," Ph.D. dissertation, Harvard University, 1973). Negative attitudes of men-in-general are

also perceived by women (J.L.A. Birnbaum, "Life Patterns, Personality Style, and Self Esteem in Gifted Family Oriented and Career Committed Women," Ph.D. dissertation, University of Michigan, 1971; Matthews and Tiedman, "Attitudes Toward Career and Marriage") and documented for men (Oppenheimer, *The Female Labor Force*, pp. 44-46; B.M. Bass, J. Krusell, and R.A. Alexander, "Male Managers' Attitudes Toward Working Women," *American Behavioral Scientist* 15, November/December 1971: 221-236).

4. Cf. Tangri, "Determinants of Occupational Role"; E. Almquist and S. Angrist, "Role Model Influences on College Women's Career Aspirations," *Merrill-Palmer Quarterly* 17 (1971): 273-279; Birnbaum, "Life Patterns."

5. F.E. Fiedler, "Leadership and Leadership Effectiveness Traits: A Reconceptualization of the Leadership Trait Problem," in *Interpersonal Behavior*, L. Petrullo and B.M. Bass, eds. (New York: Holt, Rinehart and Winston, 1961).

6. M. Deutsch, "An Experimental Study of the Effects of Cooperation and Competition upon Group Processes," *Human Relations* 2 (1949): 199-231; L.K. Miller and R.L. Hamblin, "Interdependence, Differential Rewarding, and Productivity," *American Sociological Review* 28 (1963): 768-778; B.H. Raven and H.T. Eachus, "Cooperation and Competition in Means-Interdependent Triads," *Journal of Abnormal and Social Psychology* 67 (1963): 307-316.

7. Valerie K. Oppenheimer, Testimony before the Federal Communications Commission (Docket No. 19143), August 1972.

8. J.L. Laws, "The Psychology of Tokenism," mimeographed, 1972.

Bibliography

Almquist, E., and S. Angrist. "Role Model Influences on College Women's Career Aspirations." *Merrill-Palmer Quarterly* 17 (1971): 273-279.

Bass, B.M., J. Krusell, and R.A. Alexander. "Male Managers' Attitudes Toward Working Women." *American Behavioral Scientist* 15 (November/December 1971): 221-236.

Birnbaum, J.L.A. "Life Patterns, Personality Style, and Self Esteem in Gifted Family Oriented and Career Committed Women." Ph.D. dissertation, University of Michigan, 1971.

Brown, D.G. "Masculinity-Femininity Development in Children." *Journal of Consulting Psychology* 21 (1957): 197-202.

Deutsch, M. "An Experimental Study of the Effects of Cooperation and Competition Upon Group Processes." *Human Relations* 2 (1949): 199-231.

Farmer, H.S., and M.J. Bohn. "Home-Career Conflict Reduction and the Level of Career Interest in Women." *Journal of Consulting Psychology* 17 (1970): 228-232.

Fiedler, F.E. "Leadership and Leadership Effectiveness Traits: A Reconceptualization of the Leadership Trait Problem." In *Interpersonal Behavior*, L. Petrullo and B.M. Bass, eds. New York: Holt, Rinehart, and Winston, 1961.

Hager, R.L., and A. Kaher. "Discrimination Against Competent Women." 1974.

Hawley, P. "What Women Think Men Think: Does it Affect Their Career Choice?" *Journal of Consulting Psychology* 18 (1971): 193-199.

Katz, M.L. "Female Motive to Avoid Success: A Psychological Barrier or a Response to Deviancy?" Educational Testing Service, 1973.

Laws, J.L. "The Psychology of Tokenism." Mimeographed. 1972.

Matthews, E., and D.V. Tiedman. "Attitudes Toward Career and Marriage and the Development of Life Style in Young Women." *Journal of Consulting Psychology* 11 (1964): 375-383.

Miller, L.K., and R.L. Hamblin. "Interdependence, Differential Rewarding, and Productivity." *American Sociological Review* 28 (1963): 768-778.

Oppenheimer, Valerie K. *The Female Labor Force in the United States: Demographic and Economic Factors Governing its Growth and Changing Composition.* U.C. Berkeley, Population Monograph Series #5, 1970.

Oppenheimer, V.K. Testimony before the Federal Communications Commission (Docket 19143), August 1972.

Peplau, A. "The Impact of Fear of Success, Sex-Role Attitudes and Opposite Sex Relationships on Women's Intellectual Performance: An Experimental Study of Competition in Dating Couples." Ph.D. dissertation, Harvard University, 1973.

Raven, B.H., and H.T. Eachus. "Cooperation and Competition in Means-Interdependent Triads." *Journal of Abnormal and Social Psychology* 67 (1963): 307-316.

Schwenn, M. "Arousal of the Motive to Avoid Success." Junior Honors Paper, Harvard University, 1970.

Tangri, S. "Determinants of Occupational Role Innovation Among College Women." *The Journal of Social Issues* 28 (1972): 177-199.

4

Research Needs II: Towards More Useful Modes of Research on Discrimination in Employment and Pay

Barbara R. Bergmann

Can economists do research which will prompt action toward ending discrimination? Most research work by economists has been concerned with trying to determine how discrimination works and the general direction of its effects on wages and employment of particular groups. It has also been attempting to discover empirically how or whether discrimination has in fact affected the wages and employment of blacks and women.[1] While some of this work has been interesting, an impartial observer would have to conclude that its impact on the process of ending discrimination has not been large.

I believe the reason for this lack of impact is a simple one. National policy on ending discrimination is set. Although the speed with which we go forward is at issue, the direction is not. Much research effort has been devoted to estimating that the national average of pay differentials between men and women or between blacks and whites, after correction for differences in education and years of experience, is "only" x percent. However, such findings will not change the direction of national policy, whether the x is 10 percent or 40 percent. Some researchers have "results" which argue that blacks should attribute their lowly jobs and pay to bad genes, bad education, and/or bad luck and women should attribute their lowly jobs and pay to "their (sic) home responsibilities." Still, some women and blacks have been able to uncover obviously discriminatory practices in the firms they work for and they have the law on their side.

Action towards ending discrimination must come at the level of the establishment, the firm, and the department. If research is to have an important impact on that action, it will have to address the issues that arise at those levels. I believe that in order for researchers to truly contribute to the action, they will have to devote themselves to finding, describing, and bringing to public notice important and/or egregious cases of discrimination. They also must devise ways to help business firms in effectively changing their behavior toward their black and female employees and in placing these workers in jobs previously reserved for white males.

I recently have seen an excellent project, done by a group with little formal research training, on discrimination by private employment agencies in the Washington metropolitan area.[2] The group gathered their data by sending male and female students claiming identical qualifications to the agencies to apply for

This paper is based on the work of the Project on the Economics of Discrimination which is supported by a grant administered by the U.S. Department of Labor.

jobs. They found that most employment agencies relegated women to clerical jobs, while numbers of comparable men were referred to management training positions. The report gives the results by agency name and also points out the obvious sexism in the agencies' telephone directory advertisements. Undoubtedly, putting the finger on particular firms will strike many economists as unscholarly, as not what they were trained to do, as, in a word, naderesque. Yet, the report may have more effect on actual employment practices than the ten best "scholarly" articles on discrimination ever written.

Perhaps a more "respectable" version of this mode of research is work that can be done in conjunction with regulatory agencies. Banks, insurance companies, airlines, trucking firms, and utilities seem to be obvious loci of occupational segregation by race and sex. The state and federal agencies which regulate them, if properly approached, should be interested in ending illegal practices by the firms they regulate and should be able to obtain and supply to researchers data on pay and employment practices of individual firms. Surely, the Bell Telephone System case, presented at the Federal Communications Commission hearings, should be the model for many similar proceedings.[3]

Economists have had few opportunities to help individual business firms in changing their practices. Economists traditionally have refrained from the survey work, experimentation with small groups, and participant observation methods of data gathering which tend to improve the data gatherer's insight into the way discrimination operates within an actual firm.[4] Yet even in their current state of detachment from experience with the operations of a firm, economists have a considerable potential for contributing to a firm's planning. They can help to formulate goals, pointing out among other things that women and black males together constitute 45 percent of the labor force and should in time have 45 percent of many if not all of the jobs currently reserved for white males. They can demonstrate the importance of hiring white males for jobs previously relegated to women or black males. They can help to formulate timetables, by showing how the firm's natural labor turnover provides the "room" for integration.[5] They can help to design incentive schemes which will ease the pain of transition to a color-blind and sex-blind system. They can help to devise new wage scales which will take account of the fact that for certain jobs the supply pool of applicants will be considerably larger than before and for other jobs the pool will be smaller.[6] They can examine the promotion process, which may be the heart of the problem.[7] They can do backup work in developing information which helps in recruiting blacks and women for management training programs.[8] They can find successful cases of affirmative action and describe them as models for others.[9]

The work is there and the hands are there to do it. However, the hands must be reallocated from theoretical work and from running regressions on aggregative data. In short, in research on discrimination we need less basic science and more applications to particular situations.

Notes

1. For a list of the work produced by one group of economists interested in discrimination see "Research Reports by Members of the Project on the Economics of Discrimination," College Park, University of Maryland.

2. See Maryland Public Interest Research Group, "An Analysis of Employment Agency Practices in Montgomery and Prince George's County, Maryland," College Park, in press.

3. See Phyllis A. Wallace, ed., *Equal Employment Opportunity and the AT&T Case*, Cambridge, MIT Press, 1976.

4. When I suggested at a recent economists' meeting that money and banking experts seldom talk to bankers and might learn something from doing so, I was reproved by a well-known economist. He said, "I talk to them every day, and I never find out a thing."

5. See Barbara R. Bergmann and W. Krause, "Evaluating and Forecasting Progress in Racial Integration of Employment," *Industrial and Labor Relations Review*, April 1972, 399-409.

6. See Barbara R. Bergmann, "The Effect on White Incomes of Discrimination in Employment," *Journal of Political Economy*, March/April 1971, 294-313.

7. For a start on this work see Peter B. Doeringer and Michael S. Piore, *Internal Labor Markets and Manpower Analysis*, Lexington, Mass., D.C. Heath, 1971.

8. This type of work is being done at the University of Texas under the direction of Ray Marshall.

9. A project for doing this has been started at a major not-for-profit research organization.

5

Black Employment in the South

Ray Marshall

Introduction

This paper summarizes the major findings of the Negro Employment in the South (NES) project.[1] The main objective of the NES project was to analyze black employment patterns in thirteen southern states with a view to making policy recommendations to improve black employment opportunities. The specific questions raised were: (1) What are the black employment patterns and trends?, (2) What are the main explanations for the patterns and trends?, (3) What kinds of public policies are most effective in improving black employment opportunities?

The major areas studied in the NES project were rural and nonmetropolitan places, with special emphasis on agriculture; metropolitan areas, with detailed field work and analyses in Atlanta, Birmingham, Houston, Louisville, Memphis, Miami, and New Orleans; federal employment; state and local government employment; minority contractors in the construction industry; and comparative studies of the South and the rest of the country.

The research procedures included a detailed literature review and statistical and econometric analyses using data from the Equal Employment Opportunity Commission (EEOC), the Bureau of the Census, the Department of Labor, the one percent social security sample, the Survey of Economic Opportunity, and field surveys in all of the major standard metropolitan statistical areas (SMSAs).

The principal statistical measures of black employment patterns were *penetration rates*, expressing the extent to which blacks had entered various industries and occupations, and *indexes of occupational position*, measuring the extent to which blacks had moved up in those industries and occupations. In some cases, other measures, such as an index of tokenism and measures of segregation within a firm or industry, were used.

This paper is divided into three sections. The first describes the conceptual framework used in the NES project. The behavioral model used is contrasted with the neoclassical model of traditional economic theory, and, to a lesser extent, with multiple labor market theories. The second section summarizes the major empirical findings of the NES project. The final section outlines the recommendations made by the NES study group.

Theory of Discrimination

A theoretical or conceptual framework for empirical studies was developed at the outset of the NES project. Although the project was policy oriented, it was recognized that effective public policies must be based on sound theories that isolate the basic causal relationships affecting discrimination. Conceptually, emphasis was placed on a theoretical framework for *employment* rather than *income* discrimination. In other words, the focus of the project was on explaining differences in employment patterns rather than income differentials.

Perhaps the most widely accepted theoretical work on the economics of discrimination is the neoclassical model developed by Gary Becker,[2] who was primarily concerned with direct or overt discrimination which manifests itself as unequal treatment in the labor market. Writers in the neoclassical tradition, however, do not agree on details; they merely use the same basic theoretical approaches. In Becker's analysis, employers with a "taste for discrimination" require black workers to accept lower wages than whites for equally productive labor. Becker termed the black-white wage differential as a proportion of the white wage the "discrimination coefficient," which he considered in practice to be quite large. However, Becker felt that discriminating employers would be at a disadvantage in competitive markets in the long run, so to him the persistence of discrimination is evidence of monopoly power in product markets. The neoclassical model thus implies that discrimination could be effectively combatted by making product markets more competitive.

Other economists—notably Finis Welch, Barbara Bergmann, and Kenneth Arrow—have made significant improvements in the neoclassical model. Welch[3] uses a model similar to Becker's to demonstrate that discrimination is caused more by the preferences of employees to work with members of their own race than by employer "tastes for discrimination." If a worker's wage is a decreasing function of the proportion of his race in a firm's work force, it is possible to show that cost minimization in a competitive equilibrium requires total segregation within a labor force rather than combinations of black and white workers who receive different wages, as implied by Becker's model. Welch notes, however, that because blacks and whites have different levels of education they are complementary and not substitutes.

Bergmann[4] uses a Becker-type theoretical model to explain the stability and breakdown of occupational segregation. She assumes two occupations—one prestigious and one menial—that require equally skilled labor as well as a crucial black-white wage differential for each occupation that makes employers indifferent to the hiring of black versus white workers. On the basis of these assumptions, occupational segregation will be stable if the difference between marginal productivities in the two occupations lies between the crucial occupational wage rate differences. If the marginal productivity of blacks in the prestigious occupation rises to the point where it exceeds that in the menial occupation by more than the crucial differential between black and white wages, blacks will be hired into the prestigious occupations. Bergmann also argues that employers can gain from discrimination if they pay blacks wages that are below marginal productivity and if they are able either to exercise monopolistic power in the labor market or to reach easily policed "gentlemen's" agreements to restrict blacks and women to certain jobs.

Some of the most significant improvements in the neoclassical model have been made by Kenneth Arrow, whose objective was to analyze discrimination without lumping social factors "into an uninformative category of imperfection or jumping to a precipitate rejection of neoclassical theory with all its analytical power."[5] Arrow's model, like Becker's, assumes full employment, competition, and profit and utility maximization. If all employers have equal tastes for discrimination, whites will be paid more than their marginal products and blacks will be paid less, the differences between wages and marginal products reflecting the "discrimination coefficient" or "the price the employer is willing to pay, in terms of profits, for reducing his (black) labor force (or increasing his white labor force) by one." However, if employers have different tastes for discrimination, the tendency will be toward segregated work forces, because only the least discriminatory firms will survive in a competitive market over the long run.

Arrow also incorporates "tastes for discrimination" by foremen and white workers into his model and relaxes the usual assumptions of convex indifference surfaces and costless adjustments. Presumably, both white workers and foremen will be willing to work for less in situations where the ratio of white to total labor is greater if they have "tastes for discrimination." The assumption of convex indifference curves must be relaxed because it assumes integration of black and white workers, at least in the short run, whereas discrimination coefficients by white workers, employers, and foremen will result in segregation over the long run. Similarly, the assumption of costless employment adjustments is relaxed to allow for personnel investments associated with hiring, so that the wage rate in equilibrium for a nondiscriminating employer will equal the marginal product of labor less the personnel investment. Personnel investments therefore permit racial wage differentials to continue and changes in employment to occur only where changes in wages are large.

Finally, Arrow considers an alternative model of employer discrimination based on perceptions of reality rather than the "taste for discrimination." If a personnel investment is required to determine the true productivities of workers, and the probability of hiring a qualified white worker is greater than the probability of hiring a black worker, white wages will be higher than black wages by at least the amount of the net personnel investment required to determine whether or not blacks are qualified.

A large number of attempts have been made to measure discrimination by using models containing "objective" labor market or "productivity" factors like education, age, and industrial structure to predict black income or occupational position and to attribute the residual to discrimination. While these models are useful, particularly in assigning weights to different factors associated with black income and occupational differentials, they add little to our *theoretical* understanding of the causes of discrimination because they do not explain the residual. Moreover, it clearly is hazardous to ascribe all of a residual to discrimination. Nevertheless, these empirical models provide valuable clues to the nature of the underlying causal relationships in the theory of employment discrimination.

A theory of discrimination has clear implications for policy. In the neoclassical model, discrimination can be reduced only by decreasing monopoly power in product and labor markets or by "educating" white workers and employees to the view that discrimination is bad. This kind of educational campaign is not likely to be very effective if whites accept the neoclassical model which shows them gaining at the expense of blacks.

This is not to argue, however, that the neoclassical model offers no other suggestions for measures to improve black employment patterns, because these patterns could be improved without reducing discrimination if (1) black workers accepted lower wages for equally productive labor; (2) black workers increased their productivity relative to whites; (3) measures were taken in Arrow's alternate model to equalize the employer's probability of hiring qualified black workers relative to whites. However, the "taste for discrimination" in the neoclassical model is determined outside the system and is ordinarily assumed to be a desire by whites to employ or work with other whites. The model therefore offers little explanation for how these tastes are formed by, or interact with, market forces.

Just as neoclassical economic theory offers little insight into the dynamics of discrimination, it has little explanation, apart from discrimination and human capital differentials, for why black workers are more concentrated in certain labor markets or occupations than whites. The neoclassical model solves this difficult problem by assuming homogeneous labor supplies and thus provides little insight into labor market segmentation. Labor economists have traditionally devoted considerable attention to the heterogeneous nature of labor markets, and they make a distinction between internal and external labor markets. Internal labor markets are caused by personnel costs and increasing specificity of jobs within firms; they are isolated from external market forces except at so-called "ports of entry" where workers are hired from the open market.

Because blacks have been barred from many of the "ports of entry" through which workers are hired from the external labor markets, they have been denied access to on-the-job training and seniority that would permit them to train for higher paying jobs. Blacks are also among those who are relegated to the largely structureless external labor markets that are unprotected by the "web of rules" shielding those in the internal labor markets from outside competitive pressures. Employers screen out blacks and others by using devices designed to select workers who are most likely to meet their criteria for success in the internal labor markets. Dual labor markets are perpetuated because workers in the unstable external sector adapt to employment instability, making this condition self-perpetuating. In other words, institutionalized behavior patterns perpetuate segmentation without the necessity of overt discrimination.

A "radical" variant of multiple labor market hypothesis provides for segmentation by race, among other things. Some radical economists argue that segmentation occurs not only because of technological and labor market forces operating within the economy, which usually manifest themselves in uneven development of various sectors under capitalism, but also because of conscious capitalist efforts to divide the proletariat and thereby prevent class identification and organization.[6]

While multiple labor market analyses provide useful insights into the operation of labor markets, they provide little help with the basic quest for an explanation of the causes of racial discrimination. The radical assertion that segmentation results in part from a conscious effort by capitalists to prevent proletarianization has some historical merit, but it is incomplete and of limited value in understanding contemporary racial employment patterns. There is little evidence that employers, or capitalists, rather than white workers or the white community, are mainly responsible for racial employment patterns of blue-collar workers. There is no doubt that capitalists have *used* racism and occupational divisions for their purposes, but they did not *create* the racism that segments black workers for their purposes. It is also difficult to see how hiring black strikebreakers caused segmentation because their hiring actually integrated many jobs for the first time.

The neoclassical model was also found to be of very limited value as a theoretical framework for understanding racial discrimination in employment. The NES project required that the concept of discrimination be differentiated into direct or overt discrimination where various actors make conscious decisions based on race and institutionalized behavior patterns that perpetuate black exclusion from certain jobs. Moreover, although various forms of discrimination have some common characteristics and are based on the same racial motives, each form requires different explanatory processes—discrimination in housing or public accommodations is not the same as discrimination in upgrading in the internal labor markets.

The NES project findings indicate that discrimination is much more of a status than a physical phenomenon. Whites do not object primarily to working with blacks but many have refused to work with them on equal terms on the same jobs. Because blacks have been branded as "inferior" people, many white workers have considered their status to be threatened when required to work with blacks on equal terms.

The neoclassical model also defines discrimination in a narrow and unrealistic way—a taste for which maximizing agents are willing to pay—in order to force this phenomenon into the price theory mold. Price theory is only partially applicable to discrimination, however, because it is only partially a market or monetary phenomenon. *Job control* appears to be a broader and more realistic concept than wages as the primary concern of white workers. Wages are only one aspect of a job and are not the dynamic equilibrating force determining employment structures that the neoclassical model assumes them to be. It seems very unrealistic, for example, to assume that white workers would demand that blacks with equal productivity be paid lower wages for doing identical work.

Wage differentials for perfect substitutes are relatively unimportant for workers in the same firms and occupations. White workers, especially if unionized, recognize that they would be replaced by blacks, and wage scales and other working conditions would be undetermined if they permitted wage differentials. The main manifestation of wage differentials for even near substitutes is where qualified black journeymen are hired as laborers or helpers regardless of their qualifications. This is more a manifestation of status then an unwillingness to work with blacks unless the latter accept lower wages. Moreover, it is more common for white workers to want to exclude blacks from particular occupations than to insist on or permit wage differentials. What is required, therefore, is a model that will explain the diverse patterns observable rather than one that will merely be able to handle either segregation or integration.

An Alternative Formulation

The conceptual framework found to be most useful for the NES project is a behavioral model that incorporates features of the neoclassical and multiple labor market models, but specifies the motives of the various actors and the contexts within which they operate on the basis of empirical evidence rather than a priori deductive reasoning. This model, which is similar to that developed by John Dunlop in his *Industrial Relations Systems,*[7] assumes discrimination by whites (or blacks if they have the power) to be motivated by a combination of status and job control—that is, whites are concerned about their occupational status and will attempt to monopolize job opportunities for themselves. They also develop mechanisms to improve their power relative to employers and competitors who would weaken their job control. In this formulation, wages merely constitute one aspect of the job. Other considerations include security, safety, prestige, general working conditions, participation in rule making, and mechanisms to control entry to jobs and occupations.

The model also assumes racial employment patterns in any given situation to be products of the power relationships among the actors and the specific environmental contexts in which they operate. These relationships and contexts can be empirically determined to some extent and, while relatively stable in the short run, change through time and involve dynamic mutual causation rather than the simple causal relationships contemplated by the neoclassical model.

The Actors

The main actors involved in the determination of racial employment patterns are managers, white workers, black workers, unions, and government agencies responsible for the implementation of antidiscrimination and industrial relations policies. The key environmental features influencing racial employment patterns include economic and labor market conditions, community race relations, the distribution of power in the larger community, industry structure and growth potential, labor market skills, and educational requirements of various companies and industries.

Employers

The neoclassical model is most useful in helping to understand management attitudes and motives. The profit-maximizing assumption seems to be an accurate predictor of top management behavior. This is not to argue that management is not motivated by status considerations. But in large companies, management suffers little loss of status from deciding that blacks should be hired in blue-collar occupations. However, status is a factor that causes management to resist hiring blacks in those managerial occupations (or occupational career paths) leading to managerial positions. In other words, management has limited status motives for excluding blacks from blue-collar occupations, but stronger status motives for barring "inferior people" from white-collar jobs.

The neoclassical profit-maximizing model was enlarged to include factors other than productivity that impinge on profits. Employers, for example, have to consider profit implications from the reactions of other actors in the employment process. For example, a firm might lose profits if it is denied government contracts, if white workers strike or boycott, if black workers strike or boycott, or if its racial actions cause it to lose sales. Similarly, management will use personnel screening and selection procedures to minimize personnel costs and maximize the probability of selecting qualified applicants. In short, the employer's profit-maximizing calculations must be broadened to include forces ordinarily assumed away in the neoclassical model; if not, prediction is possible in only a very abstract and theoretical sense.

Management hiring decisions are influenced by firm size, industry structure, and the nature of labor supplies. The strongest factor influencing the ability of black workers to combat discrimination is not marginal productivity of each worker but total labor supplies to meet management requirements if whites strike or boycott. In this case, the conclusions of the neoclassical and bargaining models are contradictory. Other things equal, the larger the supplies of labor, the lower the marginal products and the less likely blacks are to be hired at given wage rates. In the bargaining model, larger supplies of labor increase bargaining power. Whites will rarely be able to exclude large supplies of blacks qualified to take their place. Moreover, where total labor supplies are adequate, employers frequently prefer minority workers for certain kinds of jobs. This is because the limited job options available to blacks and their traditional employment in those occupations make them dependable sources of labor. Blacks have been preferred for menial and disagreeable occupations, but also for some higher paying jobs such as musicians, athletes, in the trowel trades in the construction industry, as waiters, longshoremen.

Company size and structure affect management's hiring practices. Consumer-oriented industries are more likely to be influenced by racial pressures in product markets than firms producing intermediate or producers' goods. Traditionally, consumer-oriented firms have been reluctant to hire blacks to serve white customers, but black boycotts and government pressures have caused these companies to do so.

Laws and other public policies influence management relationships with white customers and white workers by making it possible to shift the blame for a management decision to hire blacks to the government. Moreover, government policies influence prevailing racial sentiments by providing the moral weight of what appears to be the attitude of the majority as well as the force of law. The most important initial impact of the law probably is to cause managers who wish to do so to hire blacks for this reason; subsequently, tougher measures must be adopted to deal with discrimination by those who are disposed to discriminate.

The neoclassical model assumes that competitive pressures will produce equalitarian employment patterns because employers with no "taste for discrimination" will be able to bid productive resources away from those who discriminate. However, many forces isolate the labor market from competition and weaken competitive pressures. The neoclassical hypothesis is difficult to test empirically, because employment is influenced by a complex constellation of these forces, some of which are reinforcing and some countervailing. For example, studies that find negative correlations between product market concentration ratios and black employment could be measuring industry skill requirements, rather than discrimination, because skill requirements are highly correlated with concentration ratios, especially in manufacturing.

Competitive firms are likely to be labor intensive and to pay low wages, so it is not surprising to find black employment concentrated in this sector, but it is doubtful that competitive market forces had a great deal to do with forcing such firms to hire blacks. Industries with the highest product market concentration ratios are also the most capital intensive, have relatively high skill requirements, and are more likely to be growth industries in terms of employment. However, because blacks have lower levels of education and fewer technical skills per capita than whites, it would be surprising to find blacks equally represented in these industries, even in the absence of discrimination.

Size might also be an important determinant of black employment patterns, though size alone rarely seems to be a decisive factor. Large employers have larger internal labor markets and, therefore, might provide attractive employment opportunities, particularly where there are growth and upgrading potentials; whites have therefore sought to monopolize the better jobs in these firms. If white workers are powerful relative to employers, they will be able to restrict blacks to menial occupations. The black community or government agencies might exert counterpressures to get blacks hired; their success, of course, will depend on the amount of pressure they can exert on employers and white workers. Blacks can get the better jobs in larger firms if they have sufficient supplies of labor to meet an employer's requirements. Smaller employers are more likely to be able to hire blacks exclusively for certain jobs because their labor demand is relatively small.

By ignoring group strategy, the neoclassical model assumes that monopolists are more likely than competitive firms to discriminate. However, organized pressure from black workers and the black community could cause employers with monopoly power to hire more blacks, particularly where the black community combines measures to increase the supplies of black labor and exerts pressure to reduce racial barriers. To the extent that employers avoid blacks because the probability of finding qualified black workers is less than the probability of finding qualified whites, a strategy to increase the probability of recruiting a qualified black worker would increase black employment.

Neoclassical assumptions about the racial practices of competitive firms not only ignore the fact that monopolistic firms might provide more conspicuous targets for group strategy, but also assume full employment, which would make it difficult for employers to meet their labor requirements from one race alone. The presence of unemployment and other labor market "imperfections" explains why such competitive industries as agriculture and textiles have provided very limited employment opportunities for blacks. The textile industry hired very few blacks because it could satisfy its demand from the white labor pool alone, until whites moved into higher wage industries. Textile employers were already having trouble recruiting and retaining white workers when the federal government brought pressure on them to hire more blacks. This combination of events produced relatively rapid increases in black employment in the textile industry during the 1960s and early 1970s. However, these changes were not brought about as much by product market considerations as by a combination of government pressure and labor market conditions that made employers receptive to those pressures.

The bargaining model gives less weight than the neoclassical model to the influence of attitudes on racial employment patterns. Attitudes are assumed to influence race relations in the larger community, but have less direct impact on employment decisions. Further, in the bargaining framework the power relations between the actors and the environment within which they operate are the immediate forces influencing employment patterns. In other words, because of these power relations, the actor's behavior will not necessarily be determined by his racial attitudes. Moreover, racial attitudes are more likely to be influenced by the position imposed on the actors by these power and environmental relationships than the reverse. This is not to argue that attitudes are of no importance, but merely that they are marginal and not a basic determinant of racial employment patterns.

White Workers

As noted earlier, the bargaining model assumes that white workers are motivated primarily by status and job control considerations in excluding blacks from "their jobs." However, whether or not whites succeed in excluding blacks depends on their ability to bring pressures to bear on an employer. If whites are in sufficient supply to fill particular occupations, in the absence of countervailing powers employers will find it profitable to hire only whites. However, if blacks are in sufficient supply to meet labor requirements, an employer might turn to them to weaken white unions. He will not necessarily pay black workers a different wage, but their presence will tend to moderate wage pressures unless blacks and whites form a united bargaining front.

Similarly, the bargaining power of white workers would be weakened even if blacks were in helper or other mislabeled occupational categories while actually performing the same jobs as whites. Bigoted whites are not likely to quit good jobs because of their racist attitudes, but neither are they likely to demand wage differentials to compensate for their prejudices. Even assuming that they have adequate knowledge of alternatives, prejudiced whites are likely to stay on their jobs if moving is costly in terms of loss of seniority, good wages, and the advantages of specialized nontransferable job skills in places where they have worked.

Unions

White workers will use the unions they control to preserve and ration job opportunities.[8] Consequently, the union does not ordinarily create job discrimination but might be used to perpetuate the exclusion of blacks from certain jobs or to strengthen job segregation within plants.

Race enters union operating procedures in a variety of ways. Different kinds of unions have different motives, procedures, and control mechanisms, and therefore will react differently to the presence of black workers or potential workers. If there are no black workers in an industry or trade, unions are motivated by job control and status considerations to keep them out. Whether unions are able to bar blacks depends largely on their control of entry into certain occupations. Craft unions, for example, ordinarily have considerable control of the supply of labor. The main job control instruments of craft unions are control of training, entry into the trade and union, and job referrals. In order for blacks to penetrate these crafts and unions, they must ordinarily either threaten the unions' control instruments or inflict monetary losses on them. Because of their entrenched powers, the racial practices of craft unions are likely to be changed less by direct threats than by appeals that offer to help preserve basic union control processes in exchange for the admission of blacks.

In cases where there are supplies of black workers who can replace striking or boycotting whites, unions ordinarily have not been successful in excluding blacks. Union conditions would clearly be undermined by exclusion unless black competitors could be relegated to nonunion positions or otherwise restricted so they could not compete directly with union members. In the case of unions like the carpenters and bricklayers, for instance, blacks could not be excluded in the South, but they could be segregated, and generally were, before World War II.

Industrial unions have generally adopted different procedures, mainly because they confront different situations, not because their members have had any more or less racial prejudice than craftsmen, although job status considerations seem to have been weaker in the case of industrial unions. But the major difference between craft and industrial unions is that the latter have little direct influence over hiring. In order to organize their jurisdictions, industrial unions must therefore appeal to the workers hired by an employer. Thus, if blacks have been hired in competition with white workers, both the union's ability to organize and its bargaining strength will depend on its ability to attract blacks.

The growth of industrial union membership, and black participation in those unions, was augmented by events during the 1930s. The power of black workers to change union racial practices was strengthened when the Railway Labor Act of 1926 and the National Labor Relations Act of 1935 established government-supervised elections to determine whether unions would be given representation rights. These legal developments gave industrial unions motives for catering to black workers in order to gain their support in representation elections and in order to avoid prosecution by courts, the National Labor Relations Board, and other government antidiscrimination agencies. But there were other motives as well, because the industrial unions formed during and after the New Deal had broad political and social objectives that required them to form political alliances with black leaders. The political objectives have carried over to the AFL-CIO.

Union racial practices are also influenced by union structure. Because federations and national unions have broader political objectives than locals, the motive for racial equality increases when moving one from the local to the national level. Moreover, national craft unions have also stronger motives than their locals to take in blacks because the national's power depends to some extent upon the size of its membership, whereas the local often conceives its power as depending more narrowly on control of labor supplies in local labor markets.

Although the racial practices of unions will depend on the union's structure (local, national, federation, craft, or industrial), and the impact of blacks on the union's ability to carry out its primary objectives through its usual control mechanism, all kinds of counteracting forces impinge on the racial practices of a local union. Local leaders interested in keeping their jobs must consider their relations with the white membership, the black membership, and employers. If blacks are organized into effective political forces within unions, or if there are many blacks in jurisdictions the union is trying to organize, the union's leaders will be more responsive to black interests. If there are few or no blacks and the local's white members are either racists or have strong interests in restricting job opportunities to white members and their relatives, they will resist the admission of blacks. However, there are forces tending to overcome white control of job opportunities. They include more pro-black attitudes in the larger community; government measures to increase black employment opportunities; pressures on locals from their nationals (making the power relationship between national local unions and between the national and the AFL-CIO or other unions important linkages in the power transmissions channels influencing local union racial practices); and the power and organization of black workers outside the unions.

Black Workers

Black workers outside craft unions derive their power mainly from the extent to which they can reduce costs or provide dependable labor supplies for employers, or threaten the wage rates and job control procedures of discriminating white union members and their leaders. These factors, in turn, depend primarily on the number of blacks in a labor market who possess the necessary skills to compete with white union members, and secondarily on the extent to which the black community and antidiscrimination forces are organized to overcome white resistance to the admission of blacks. Even if civil rights forces are well organized to achieve this objective, they will have limited impact unless they produce black applicants for employment, upgrading, apprenticeship, and/or journeymen status who meet the qualifications imposed by unions and employers, or unless they successfully challenge the standards and specifications themselves. These considerations make it obvious that an effective strategy to overcome local union resistance will ordinarily require giving considerable attention to local labor market conditions and the control mechanisms used by locals to regulate labor supplies and control jobs.

Environmental Factors

The specific and immediate forces affecting black employment patterns are influenced by such environmental factors as the relative amount and quality of education available to blacks, race relations in the larger community, the age and sex composition of the black work force, alternative income sources available to black workers and their families, housing patterns and transportation costs relative to the location of jobs, the physical and emotional health of blacks relative to whites, whether an industry is growing or declining in terms of employment, black and white migration patterns, the structure of industry in terms of its customers (blacks, whites, other employees, or government), general business conditions, skill requirements and job structures within industry, the black community's relative accessibility to job information, and the processes through which employers and unions recruit and train workers for jobs.

While all of these factors are important determinants of black employment patterns, some are more important and measurable than others. General business conditions are very important because tight labor markets facilitate the employment and upgrading of blacks. However, this view must be qualified because experience clearly shows that tight labor markets are not sufficient because of change. Most of the cities studied had low official employment rates but stable racial employment patterns between 1920 and the 1960s. Moreover, there is a difference between a labor market where unemployment is declining and one where unemployment is low and stable. In addition, the overall unemployment rate obscures particular labor market conditions where blacks are able to get jobs. Finally, concerted efforts to change institutional arrangements can make it possible for black employment to increase in a particular category even when white employment is falling, as was the case between 1966 and 1969 in many of the cities studied.

The extent to which *education* is a significant variable in black employment has become controversial. Some observers argue that education is not important because blacks seem to gain very little with increasing education and, indeed, blacks with higher levels of education are discriminated against relatively more than those with lower levels of education.[9] However, education is a much more complicated variable than this simple analysis would imply. For one thing, the importance of education was in a state of dynamic flux during the 1960s as employers and unions formalized their entry requirements in response to civil rights forces. At the same time, broadening job opportunities increased blacks' motives to acquire education and rising incomes increased their ability to do so. Moreover, the relative quality of black education undoubtedly rose as a result of continued urbanization of the black population and the racial ferment following World War II.

Another measurement problem with respect to education involves establishing the relationship between education and productivity (which is highly correlated with income).[10] Education and other factors influencing black job opportunities strongly affect the kinds of jobs blacks are likely to get. Lifetime income-earning abilities are influenced by the kinds of job ladders people get on because experience and on-the-job training opportunities vary with different kinds of jobs. Education tends to be used as a screening device for jobs with higher levels of return per year of experience. In the past blacks, regardless of their level of education, have been barred from jobs with upward occupational mobility. If these jobs are opened up to them, and there is some evidence that they have been, returns to education for younger blacks would be greater than returns to their parents, a trend reinforced by the declining gap in the quality of education. As a consequence, estimates based on returns to average levels of education for blacks would understate the future significance to them of increasing their levels of education.

Summary

In order to put the bargaining model framework in perspective, a number of empirical and theoretical studies of employment discrimination were examined in the NES project. Because of its wide acceptability among economists, the neoclassical model was examined in considerable detail. Although it provided some useful analytical insights, it forces the problem of racial discrimination into the price theory mold. As such, the neoclassical model does not adequately define discrimination or provide sufficient understanding of the basic factors influencing black employment patterns to form the basis for policy prescriptions to promote equal employment opportunities. A broader bargaining model that specifies different variables for various kinds of discrimination (overt and institutional) and for different aspects of employment opportunity (employment or penetration rates and upgrading or occupational position) was thus favored. Moreover, because the employment patterns of black women are determined by different factors from those of black men, different models were specified for each sex.

Specifically, the conceptual model found to be most useful was one that considered the motives and power relationships between various actors—employers, white workers, black workers, government agencies—and the environment in which these actors operate. These environmental influences include such factors as race relations in the community, business conditions, and product and labor market conditions.

Employment patterns are products of profit-maximizing decisions made by employers, influenced to varying degrees by actual and anticipated reactions from unions, white employees, black employees, the black community, customers, government officials, and public opinion. The reactions of white workers, who are influenced by job status and control of job opportunities, are particularly important in understanding racial employment patterns. Sometimes whites use unions to accomplish their objectives, but labor organizations vary in their racial practices according to their product market orientations and the nature of their customers. Public opinion influences employment decisions mainly through laws and regulations concerning discrimination, but these laws and regulations affect a given type of actor in different ways. It is therefore important for public policy to be based on an appropriate conceptual model. Because it is too narrow, the neoclassical model was found to provide inadequate policy prescriptions.

Summary of Major NES Empirical Findings

Because it covered so many different subjects, it is not possible to discuss the findings of the NES project in detail here. However, a summary of the NES empirical findings, arranged according to the subject studied, together with policy recommendations, is presented below.

Rural and Nonmetropolitan Areas

1. Despite rapid outmigration, agriculture is a more important source of employment for blacks in the South than any four manufacturing industries. Blacks were 30 percent of southern farmers in 1950 and 14 percent in 1969; there were 40 percent as many white farmers in 1969 as in 1950 but only 13 percent as many blacks. Only 24,144 black-operated farms in 1969 were in Class I-5 (that is, with gross sales of $2,500 and over).

2. There were about 250,000 nonwhite paid farm workers in the South in 1969, who constituted about half of the total hired farm labor force.

3. Fewer white farm operators were farming much more land in 1969 than in 1964; for blacks, land and farms declined. In 1969 the average black farm in the I-5 class was 139 acres, as compared with 400 acres for all farms.

4. There has been a shift to off-farm work and income for farm families. Farmers with sales below $5,000 earned about three fourths of their income off the farm. A slightly smaller percentage of blacks reported off-farm work in 1969 as compared with whites, 58 percent and 54 percent, respectively.

5. Blacks and many rural whites have not been prepared by education and experience for nonfarm jobs. Of these black males who left southern agriculture between 1950 and 1969, 80 percent had less than seven years of education, and

52 percent had less than four years. Nevertheless, the best educated blacks tend to migrate, and their income and employment compare favorably with that of urban-born blacks with similar characteristics.

6. Manufacturing employment has grown faster in rural than in urban areas, but blacks have not shared proportionately in the gains.

The fastest nonagricultural growth has been outside black population centers.

Even in the population centers, blacks have not shared equitably in employment gains. Blacks are most underrepresented in white-collar jobs. The greatest black employment gains have been where manufacturing employment growth is greatest; industry skill requirements are lowest; black work experience is greatest; and black education levels are highest, although this is a weaker factor than work experience in determining black employment gains.

Inadequate black employment opportunities in the 244 counties with 5,000 or more blacks in their populations are caused by discrimination on the demand side and the lack of competitive labor market attributes by blacks on the supply side. However, available data and techniques were not sufficient to resolve the issue of which of these factors is more important.

7. Small farmers have been displaced in part because of the regressive nature of U.S. agricultural policy.

With respect to black farmers, there has also been discrimination in the administration of agricultural programs.

There are no across-the-board economies of size in agriculture in terms of costs per unit of output. However, technological requirements for optimal-sized farms have increased capital requirements to the point where they are beyond the reach of most black farmers in the South.

It is conceivable that public policy could significantly reduce the shift of black farmers and farm workers out of agriculture, improve the nonfarm opportunities of rural blacks, and facilitate the movement of blacks from rural to urban areas.

8. Rural manpower programs could play an important role in improving the economic opportunities of blacks, but the potential of these programs is largely unrealized. There is a special program for extending manpower facilities to rural areas because of the scattered nature of their populations and the paucity of organizations to administer programs. Nevertheless, a number of programs have considerable promise for rural areas, especially programs that relate manpower and economic development, like the "start-up" training concept and Concerted

Services in Training and Education (CSTE). Other approaches that seem to have considerable promise include Operation Hitchhike, to extend employment service functions into rural areas, and public employment programs like Operation Mainstream, to provide jobs for persons not likely to be absorbed into the private sector. Relocation projects also have a limited role to play in a rural manpower strategy.

Metropolitan Employment Patterns

In 1970, for the first time, a majority of southern blacks lived in metropolitan areas. EEOC data for 1966 and 1969 show the following:

1. Black females increased their share of metropolitan employment while the share held by black males changed very little.

2. Black males increased their share of nonmetropolitan employment, but not as much as black females.

3. Overall, the greatest gains were made in nonmetropolitan areas, although blacks still had a greater share of metropolitan jobs. Moreover, relative to whites, black occupational positions were higher in nonmetropolitan areas than in metropolitan areas.

4. Blacks increased their share of white-collar jobs in metropolitan areas but remained much more heavily concentrated than whites in the operative, laborer, and service categories.

5. Black women are more evenly represented across occupations, but not across industries, than black men. Black women were virtually absent from white-collar jobs in major industries in some southern SMSAs where larger numbers of white women were employed.

6. These metropolitan-nonmetropolitan employment differences reflect the growth of white-collar jobs in metropolitan areas and blue-collar jobs in nonmetropolitan areas.

7. The main findings of the city studies (Atlanta, Birmingham, Houston, Louisville, Memphis, Miami, and New Orleans) follow:

First, there were general improvements in black political power and more black participation in previously segregated schools and community facilities during the 1960s.

Second, black employment patterns, relative to those of whites, apparently did not change very much between the 1920s and the 1960s, but there were noticeable improvements in black income and employment during the last half of the 1960s. Nevertheless, blacks remain two or three times as likely as whites to be concentrated in the operative, laborer, and service categories; in 1969, 73 percent of black women and 82 percent of black men were concentrated in these categories.

Government Employment

1. Opportunities for blacks in government employment were generally superior to those in the private sector.

2. The highest black penetration rates were ordinarily in local units of government; the lowest were in state governments. The best relative occupational positions were in federal employment.

3. Black employment in state and local government was mainly at the token level, although there were exceptions in every substantial unit of government. The main exceptions to tokenism were in "traditional" jobs historically held by blacks (menial jobs and jobs in segregated institutions) and "new traditional" jobs; the latter are professional, technical, or nonmenial jobs traditionally closed to blacks, but where, as a result of pressure from blacks, a black skin is becoming a requirement.

4. Relative to their proportion of the population, blacks are underrepresented in federal employment in the South and overrepresented in the rest of the country. However, in the South blacks are overrepresented in Wage Board and underrepresented in General Schedule jobs.

5. In the federal service there was considerable variation in black employment by agency. Agencies with relatively low black employment were the Departments of Agriculture, Transportation, and Justice; the National Aeronautics and Space Administration; the Internal Revenue Service; the Soil Conservation Service; the Federal Housing Administration; and the Air Force.

6. Departments and agencies with black participation above their proportion of the population (19 percent) were the EEOC (48 percent), OEO (27 percent), GSA (40 percent), Veterans Administration (27 percent), and the Department of Commerce (19 percent).

7. As with private employment, black employment varies inversely with the ratio of white-collar to total employment. As in state and local government, blacks are overrepresented mainly in those agencies with large black client groups.

Determinants of Black Employment

A regression study of black employment in southern SMSAs, a study that attempted to quantify factors reflecting institutional discrimination, used the relative black-to-white index of occupational position as the dependent variable and the independent variables of education, age, employment growth rates, geographic area of the SMSA, industry skill levels, and the proportion of nonagricultural employment in manufacturing.

The model explained 70 percent of the variance in men's occupational position but only 50 percent for women, indicating, as expected, that the range for possible overt discrimination was much greater for women than for men. All variables except geographic market size were significant for men, but education and the percentage of manufacturing employment were the most powerful positive variables while industry skill requirements was the most important negative variable.

Different variables were associated with the female index of occupational position. The labor market size variable was not important for men, but was highly significant for women. The most important explanatory variables for women were concentration relative to whites in ages twenty to thirty, market size, economic growth, and relative education above twelve years. As contrasted with their significance in the equation for men, the elementary education and occupational skill requirements variables were not significant for women.

The following were some of the major conclusions concerning additional causal relationships.

1. Although there is some controversy regarding the influence of *education* on black employment opportunities, education is a significant factor determining black employment patterns, especially for younger blacks who receive more and better education than their elders. Nevertheless, on-the-job training is a more important determinant of black employment opportunity than education.

2. Industry structure is important for males, particularly skill requirements of the industry. This probably explains inadequate black representation in growth industries and in those with product market concentration ratios.

3. Transportation was an important factor explaining black participation in low-wage but not in high-wage jobs. Because black women are more likely than black men to be in low-wage service jobs, the size of labor markets was a significant determinant of their employment opportunities.

4. Black workers and employers use different labor market information systems for white-collar jobs. The employment service was rarely used by either black workers or employers for white-collar jobs. Moreover, the employment service, with few exceptions, had a very poor image in black communities.

5. Unions were not basic causes of racial employment patterns, but they formalized those patterns through collective bargaining procedures. Craft unions have perpetuated the exclusion of blacks from certain trades while industrial unions have perpetuated job segregation within plants. The racial practices of unions were determined mainly by their structure and the number of blacks in the union or trade. In general, racial discrimination is a membership rather than a leadership problem, so the degree of racial discrimination varies directly with the extent to which unions are controlled by white members.

6. Antidiscrimination laws are necessary, but not sufficient, means of improving black employment opportunities. Outreach programs, when used with antidiscrimination measures, can be effective means to improve black employment patterns.

Recommendations

The main recommendations concerning black employment opportunities are outlined below.

Rural Employment

1. Programs to help small farmers should be established. The Department of Labor could help train small farmers in some marketable nonfarm skill (like welding and equipment operation) to permit them to supplement their income.
2. The programs of the Rural Manpower Service (RMS) could be strengthened to improve the availability of manpower services to rural blacks; particularly, rural areas could receive larger shares of manpower funds and the RMS should continue its experiments to adapt manpower programs to the unique characteristics of rural areas. Programs like CSTE, start-up training, and public employment programs targeted at disadvantaged groups should be encouraged. The CSTE concept of establishing development coordinators in rural counties seems promising because there are very limited numbers of program administrators in these areas.
3. Because of the leadership and organizational problems of small farmers and agricultural workers in rural areas, National Labor Relations Act coverage should be extended to agricultural workers. As farm sizes increase and agricultural work becomes more regularized, the distinctions between farm and nonfarm workers are eroded. There is no reason why agriculture should not be covered by the National Labor Relations Act on the same basis as other industries.
4. Similarly, other protective legislation should be extended to agricultural workers. For example, farm workers should be covered by unemployment insurance, workmen's compensation, and other legislation.
5. The Department of Agriculture should give greater attention to programs to improve the incomes of small farmers. These include conducting research on labor-intensive crops, developing technology for small farms, providing technical services to small farmers and their organizations through the land-grant college system, and encouraging low-income cooperatives and other organizations of small farmers.

Government Employment

1. Outreach programs should be established to recruit, prepare, and place black workers in government jobs where they are absent or have only token representation. Outreach programs should also be established wherever there are

large-scale government projects like the Tennessee-Tombigbee Waterway project in Mississippi and Alabama.

2. The antidiscrimination machinery within the federal government could be strengthened by a number of measures:

The creation of an independent enforcement machinery at every level of government, responsive to the chief executive, with responsibility for receiving and adjudicating discrimination complaints, reviewing minority employment patterns, and making periodic reports.

The transfer of ultimate antidiscrimination responsibility within the federal government from the Civil Service Commission, which has other functions to perform, to the EEOC, which should have no higher objective than eliminating discrimination.

The appointment of a special investigating team by the President to examine those federal agencies and geographic areas where minorities have very low penetration rates and occupational positions. Special attention should also be devoted to key agencies and quasi-public committees—like those of the economic development districts, the Army Corps of Engineers, and the Department of Agriculture—which make important decisions affecting human research development. This investigating team should have full power to require agencies to furnish whatever information it needs to perform its duties.

In addition, federal statistical agencies should take measures to coordinate and improve their statistics on racial employment patterns because there is a special need to make these statistics comparable enough to facilitate comparative analysis. Sufficient data on the characteristics of federal employees are also needed to facilitate analysis of employment patterns.

Private Employment

1. Adequate personnel should be provided to the Office of Federal Contract Compliance and the EEOC to enable these agencies to carry out their enforcement and review functions. Both of these organizations are currently grossly understaffed.

2. Particular attention should be directed to outreach programs to place blacks in white-collar jobs in nonmetropolitan areas.

3. The NES project shows that industry skill requirements have a strong negative correlation with black male employment patterns. Whether this finding is due to discrimination by employers in upper level jobs or to inadequate training and education of blacks is not known. However, both factors are present. Training and education for the more highly skilled jobs thus appears to

be an important precondition for improvement in minority representation in higher paying jobs. However, because it would be tragic to encourage minorities to train for jobs closed to them because of discrimination, education and training efforts should be carefully coordinated with outreach and antidiscriminatory machinery.

4. In order to facilitate upgrading, job training and eduation should be more readily available to accommodate those who wish to upgrade themselves. Key institutions that are centrally located in rural areas might be designated as federal job upgrading centers and given special funds to achieve this objective. Particular attention should be given to the education and training facilities of the 244 predominantly black counties in the deep South where economic development is lagging, at least in part because of inadequate human resource development.

Notes

1. The project was directed by the writer and sponsored by the Office of Research and Development of the Manpower Administration, U.S. Department of Labor, with some financial and data help from the Office of Economic Opportunity. However, neither agency necessarily endorses the views expressed in this paper. I am grateful to all of the participants in the NES project, but especially to Virgil Christian and Arvil Van Adams, for their help with the project upon which this paper is based. The project was initiated by Phyllis Wallace when she was at the Research Department of the Equal Employment Opportunity Commission. Howard Rosen, Ellen Sehgal, and Mary Bedell of the Office of Research and Development, Manpower Administration, not only supported the project financially, but with their advice and encouragement as well. A book based on the project, *The Employment of Blacks in the South*, edited by Ray Marshall and Virgil Christian, is forthcoming from The University of Texas Press. For a fuller critique of the economic theory of discrimination see Ray Marshall, "The Economic Theory of Racial Discrimination," *Journal of Economic Literature* (September 1974).

2. Gary S. Becker, *The Economics of Discrimination* 2nd ed. (Chicago: The University of Chicago Press, 1971).

3. F. Welch, "Labor-Market Discrimination: An Interpretation of Income Differences in the Rural South," *Journal of Political Economy* (1967). Welch's argument is reviewed and the part of it that shows total segregation in work forces and equal wages under competition is put in mathematical terms in Kenneth Arrow's *Some Models of Racial Discrimination in the Labor Market* (Santa Monica, Calif.: Rand Corporation, February 1971).

4. Barbara Bergmann, "Occupational Segregation, Wages and Profits When

Employers Discriminate by Race and Sex," mimeographed (College Park, Maryland: University of Maryland, Project on the Economics of Discrimination, 1970).

5. Kenneth Arrow, "The Theory of Discrimination," in *Discrimination in Labor Markets*, Orley Ashenfelter and Albert Rees, eds. (Princeton, N.J.: Princeton University Press, 1973).

6. Michael Reich, David Gordon, and Richard Edwards, "A Theory of Labor Market Segmentation," *American Economic Review/Papers and Proceedings* (May 1973): 359-365.

7. John Dunlop, *Industrial Relations Systems* (New York: Henry Holt and Company, 1958).

8. Similarly, there are few examples where blacks have used unions they control to bar whites from some jobs, though black power in the larger community has not been strong enough to give blacks control of very many "good" jobs.

9. See, for example, Lester Thurow, *Poverty and Discrimination* (Washington, D.C.: Brookings Institution, 1969).

10. For a more detailed discussion of this point see Sar Levitan, Garth Mangum, and Ray Marshall, *Human Resources and Labor Markets* (New York: Harper & Row, 1972).

Bibliography

Adams, A.V. *Toward Fair Employment and the EEOC: A Study of Compliance Procedures Under Title VII of the Civil Rights Act of 1964.* Columbus, Ohio: Center for Human Resource Research, Ohio State University, 1972.

Adams, A.V. "A Theory of Labor Market Discrimination with Independent Utilities." *American Economic Review* 63, 2 (May 1973): 296-302.

Alexis, M. "The Political Economy of Labor Market Discrimination: Synthesis and Exploration." In *Patterns of Discrimination*, A. Horowitz, and G. von Furstenberg, eds. Lexington, Mass.: D.C. Heath-Lexington Books, 1974.

Arrow, K.J. "Models of Job Discrimination" and "Some Models of Race in the Labor Market." Chapters 2 and 6 in *Racial Discrimination in Economic Life*, A.H. Pascal, ed. Lexington, Mass.: D.C. Heath-Lexington Books, 1972.

Arrow, K.J. "The Theory of Discrimination." In *Discrimination in Labor Markets*, O. Ashenfelter, and A. Rees, eds. Princeton, N.J.: Princeton University Press, 1974.

Ashenfelter, O. "Discrimination and Trade Unions." In *Discrimination in Labor Markets*, O. Ashenfelter, and A. Rees, eds.

Becker, G.S. *The Economics of Discrimination.* 2nd ed. Chicago: The University of Chicago Press, 1971.

Bergmann, B.R. *Occupational Segregation, Wages, and Profits when Employers Discriminate by Race and Sex*. Mimeographed. Project on the Economics of Discrimination. College Park, Maryland, 1970.

Bergmann, B.R. "The Effect on White Incomes of Discrimination in Employment." *Journal of Political Economy* 79, 2 (March/April 1971): 294-313.

Doeringer, P., and M.J. Piore. *Internal Labor Markets and Manpower Analysis*. Lexington, Mass.: D.C. Heath-Lexington Books, 1971.

Dunlop, J. *Industrial Relations Systems*. New York: Henry Holt and Company, 1958.

Edgeworth, F.Y. "Equal Pay to Men and Women for Equal Work." *Economic Journal* 32 (1922): 431-457.

Fisher, L. *The Harvest Labor Market in California*. Cambridge, Mass.: Harvard University Press, 1953.

Franklin, R.J., and S. Resnik. *The Political Economy of Racism*. New York: Holt, Rinehart, Winston, 1974.

Freeman, R.B. "Changes in the Labor Market for Black Americans, 1948-72." *Brookings Papers* 1 (1973): 67-120.

Gordon, D.M. *Theories of Poverty and Underemployment: Orthodox, Radical, and Dual Labor Market Perspectives*. Lexington, Mass.: D.C. Heath-Lexington Books, 1972.

Heistand, D.L. *Discrimination in Employment: An Appraisal of the Research*. Ann Arbor, Mich.: Institute of Labor and Industrial Relations, University of Michigan; Detroit: Wayne State University with the National Manpower Policy Task Force, 1970.

Kerr, C. "The Balkanization of Labor Markets." In *Labor Mobility and Economic Opportunity*, E.W. Bakke, et al., eds. Cambridge, Mass.: Massachusetts Institute of Technology Press; New York: John Wiley, 1954.

Kerr, C., J.T. Dunlop, F. Harbison, and C.A. Myers. *Industrialism and Industrial Man*. Cambridge, Mass.: Harvard University Press, 1960.

Killingsworth, C.C. *Jobs and Incomes for Negroes*. Policy Papers in Human Resources & Industrial Relations No. 6. Ann Arbor, Mich.: Institute of Labor and Industrial Relations, University of Michigan; Detroit: Wayne State University with National Manpower Policy Task Force, 1968.

Krueger, A.O. "The Economics of Discrimination." *Journal of Political Economy* 71, 5 (October 1963): 481-486.

Marshall, R. *The Negro and Organized Labor*. New York: John Wiley, 1965.

Marshall, R. *The Negro Worker*. New York: Random House, 1967.

Marshall, R., and V. Christian, eds. *The Employment of Blacks in the South*. The University of Texas Press, forthcoming.

McCall, J.J. *Racial Discrimination in the Job Market: The Role of Information and Search*. Santa Monica, Calif.: Rand Corporation, 1971.

Phelps, E.S. "The Statistical Theory of Racism and Sexism." *American Economic Review* 62, 4 (September 1972): 659-661.

Piore, M.J. "Jobs & Training." In *The State and the Poor*, S. Beer and R. Barringer, eds. Cambridge, Mass.: Winthrop, 1970.

Piore, M.J. "Notes for a Theory of Labor Market Stratification." Working Paper No. 95. Cambridge, Mass.: Massachusetts Institute of Technology, 1972.

Thurow, L. *The Economics of Poverty and Discrimination.* Washington: Brookings Institution, 1969.

Walker, J.L. *Economic Development, Black Employment, and Black Migration in the Nonmetropolitan Deep South.* Mimeographed. Center for the Study of Human Resources, University of Texas at Austin, 1973.

Welch, F. "Labor Market Discrimination: An Interpretation of Income Differences in the Rural South." *Journal of Political Economy* 75, 3 (June 1967): 225-240.

Comments

Michael Piore

Ray Marshall's paper is a first-rate job of bringing together an understanding of the specific practices of particular industries, combining that understanding with theory and with data, and then bringing the whole to bear on policy problems. It is the kind of thing we ought to be teaching our students to do. Instead, we seem to have taught them a much more rigid approach to economic analysis, one which is not only confined by a fairly limited body of economic theory but which leads them to view anything done outside the confines of that theory as "sloppy" and second rate. Operating with what Marshall calls an eclectic theory is perhaps "sloppy," but as his paper demonstrates, there is nothing second rate about it. To do it well takes tremendous finesse. It also takes courage because answers do not automatically appear. However, Marshall's paper demonstrates that courage has its rewards in the form of real insights into policy.

One perspective, however, is somewhat obscured by operating at the particular level at which Marshall's paper is written. The Marshall paper and the NES study are directed at the identification of specific policy instruments that can be brought to bear upon particular problem areas. However, the possibility that there is a single pattern that underlies discrimination is obscured. This is a theme of long standing in the literature on employment discrimination. In that literature, it has two basic variations. The first is that there is a single basic pattern of discrimination throughout the South. That is, one does not find isolated examples of discrimination, say, in construction, textiles, agriculture, or industry, but some underlying set of forces work for discrimination in all these places at once. This view suggests that policy instruments must be aimed at cracking the whole system. At some point, the attack upon specific industries and individual practices will do more than break down discrimination in each of the separate compartments—it will change the whole system, moving us to a nondiscriminatory social order.

The other basic variant of this theme in the literature is that the pattern of discrimination in the South is fundamentally different from racial patterns in the North and that one needs to examine these two patterns separately and to develop different strategic approaches in attacking them. This theme feeds into a third theme in discussions of racial policy in this country—that is, in some sense the South is going to change and become the "new" society long before the North because the southern pattern of race is easier to change than the northern pattern. In concentrating on the relationship between specific policy instruments and specific industries, the larger questions tend to be obscured. It is, thus, important to go back and think about the possibility that these relationships are part of a larger, more holistic, process.

82

6

Modeling a Segmented Labor Market

Charles C. Holt

Introduction

The job search of the labor market attempts to go beyond static neoclassical microeconomic theory in coming to grips with dynamic labor market adjustment processes, associated frictions, and structural problems. It visualizes a complex set of dynamically interacting labor markets characterized by great heterogeneity of jobs and workers, massive turnover flows in and out of the labor force and between jobs, and limited information that leads to substantial investments in search. Workers' aspirations for income and satisfaction interact with those of employers for high output and low labor costs. Human capital is accumulated by a worker through his sequence of job experiences, both within and between firms. Wages and working conditions are bargained for by workers individually and collectively through unions. The movements of workers between jobs are often impeded by barriers related to race, sex, age, and class, as well as by geography and occupation. The analytic study of the equilibrium and dynamic characteristics of such a complex nonlinear stochastic process is so unwieldy that computer simulation is indicated for any model incorporating realistic complexity.

Knowledge of labor market structure and processes is urgently needed by policy makers. Labor market processes have important effects on inflation and unemployment, and there is growing evidence that our inflation and unemployment objectives cannot be achieved without structural improvements in the labor market.[1] Yet the design of programs and policies to achieve structural change requires better knowledge of both structure and process. At present, in evaluating manpower programs to determine whether they are meeting their designed objectives, it is quite difficult to measure the direct impacts on participants and virtually impossible to detect diffuse indirect effects. Better prediction and evaluation of program effects, especially indirect ones, thus

This research was supported by funds from the Office of Manpower Research, Manpower Administration, U.S. Department of Labor, under Grant No. 92-11-72-36 to The Urban Institute, and by the National Science Foundation and the Ford Foundation. Opinions expressed are those of the author and do not necessarily represent the views of the Urban Institute or its sponsors.

The author is deeply indebted to his colleagues Ralph E. Smith, Richard S. Troikka, William J. Scanlon, and Jean E. Vanski.

An earlier draft of this paper was presented at the December 1973 meeting of the Economic Society where helpful comments were received from David Cass, Robert E. Hall, Robert Lucas, and Christopher Sims.

requires a greater understanding of basic labor market relationships. Moreover, because the success of any efforts to change labor market structure will be strongly affected by the level of aggregate demand, policies impinging on output, inflation, growth, efficiency, income distribution, and equity across racial and sexual groups need to be designed jointly. Consequently, structural models that accurately capture important characteristics of the labor market will have significant policy uses at both the macro and micro levels.

This paper briefly examines the processes and structural relations important in the labor market and the kinds of policy issues that could be clarified by an econometric model of the system. It then compares and contrasts alternative model types and chooses a model formulation. Using a group transition framework, it also presents a plan for estimating and testing a sequence of successively more realistic models. The data issues and econometric problems raised by this effort are also considered. Finally, the first Urban Institute model of a demographically segmented labor market is discussed briefly.

The Structure of the Labor Market

Economists have traditionally described the actors and institutions in the labor market and their patterns of behavior from the perspective of profits, income, productivity, work satisfaction, and collective organization by workers and employers. Although these concerns must be taken into account in any labor market model, the dynamics and uncertainties of the market processes also need to be included. This paper focuses on these considerations.

The major states and processes through which workers and job vacancies flow are illustrated in Figure 6-1. The boxes represent stocks of workers and jobs, and processes that occur between the stocks. Most flow lines are identified by pairs of letters that indicate the source and destination for each flow. For example, the vertical line ET in the center of the diagram is the flow of workers from the status of employment into that of training.

The relationships embodied in Figure 6-1 may be illustrated by an example. Consider the repercussions of an increase in the number of job vacancies. An increase in demand for industry output stimulates a flow of new vacancies, PV, at the lower left of the diagram. (This flow can be negative if demand contracts.) The upward flow of vacancies subsequently increases turnover. As vacancies are matched with unemployed workers by placement transactions, an addition is made to the new-hire flow, H, which goes into employment.

These employment pairings eventually terminate either by employer-initiated layoffs or by employee-initiated quits, with the result that the vacancy flow, $EV + JV$, goes back from employment to the external labor market if it is not canceled by a negative PV, which decreases the total number of jobs in the system. A corresponding flow of workers, $EU + ET$, enters unemployment and

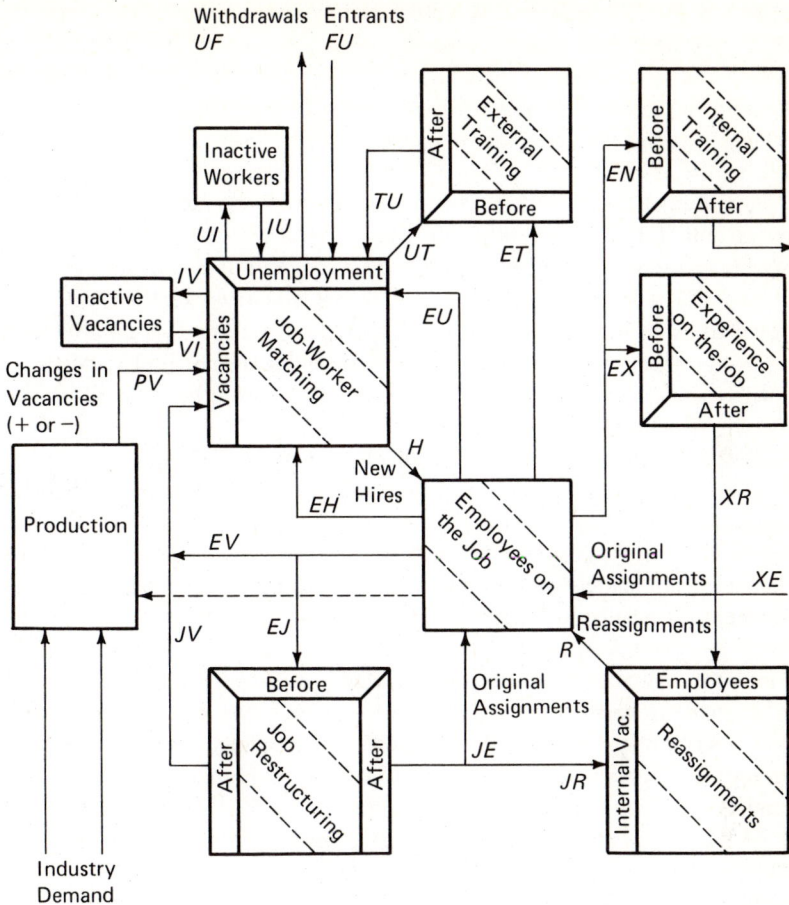

Figure 6-1. Structure of the Labor Market

external training. On the termination of external training, the flow into unemployment, *TU*, occurs. "Training" here is broadly interpreted to include any program that "transports" the worker occupationally, geographically or otherwise between market segments.

The stock of unemployment is also influenced by the *net* flow from inactive workers who are not searching, *UI – IU*, and by the net flow of entrants and withdrawals from family "employment," *FU – UF*. The stocks of inactive workers and employers are those who have ceased to search for employment or recruits, respectively, and are not effectively in the market. Estimates have been made of such net changes in worker "participation" in job search and, hence, of inclusion in the "labor force." A similar phenomenon occurs when employers, after a long period of search, despair of finding workers to fill certain job vacancies and stop searching. Some employed workers search for new jobs while still employed and do not quit their old jobs until they can start new ones. This job-change flow of workers is shown as EH, which becomes a component of the new-hire flow, H.

The internal labor market within the firm (on the right of the diagram) operates both formal and on-the-job training. The increased capability of the worker may result in an upgraded reassignment, R, but this is not always the case. Despite increased experience or training, some workers are left on (or returned to) their original job assignments, XE, especially when employment is not growing. When increased experience and training do not lead to better jobs internally, workers may use their skills to acquire jobs in other firms. This is one reason why employers tend to underinvest in training.

As the labor force develops through the accumulation of experience, employers may engage in job restructuring in order to keep up with the increasing skills, JE, or their workers, or to adapt the jobs for reassignment to other employees, JR. Also, when the structure of vacancies in the external labor market does not match well with the capabilities of the unemployed workers, employers may adapt the vacancies to the available supply by restructuring jobs, JV.

Flows in the labor market are emphasized here because they are surprisingly large relative to sizes of the stocks. For example, the total *annual* flow of separations from firms is almost half the size of employment. Moreover, the flow relationships, coupled with the population and the demand for production, determine levels of employment, unemployment, labor force, and vacancies. Each of the flows in Figure 6-1 represents decisions by workers or employers to change states or statuses.

Neoclassical economic theory provides an analysis of an elaborate system equilibrium in which all firms and workers optimize their welfare by responding to market-generated prices. However, the traditional theory needs to be extended and supplemented before it will be adequate to explain the complex microdynamic decisions important in the labor market. Heterogeneity of jobs and workers, and imperfect knowledge, introduce a second allocating variable that can be as important as price. "Availability" has utility for both workers and employers and can motivate decisions to act as surely as prices or wages. Lack of availability triggers the costs of "delay," "search," or both, and hence has the dimensions of time, information, and uncertainty. In the static classical world of perfect information both time and information are omitted, so price constitutes a sufficient statistic for decision making.[2] A full understanding of the functioning and structure of the labor market requires new areas of analysis as well as recognition that decision making is not done by an "economic man" who only maximizes functions, but by a complex person with socially influenced attitudes, emotions, and bounded rationality.

The income and cost motivations and the resulting market clearing wages and prices must be incorporated into the behavioral relations of a simulation model. For example, hire flows should be regulated not only by the sizes of stocks of workers and vacancies but also by the offering and acceptance of wages that represent the aspirations of employers and workers. Aspirations, as represented by acceptance wages, guide market search, including duration and wage outcomes. Such market wages constitute the opportunity cost to workers for not quitting their present employment. The quits that do occur constitute the cost to the employer of not raising the wages of his present employees.

Segmentation of Labor Markets

Workers are highly differentiated by skill, ability, experience, location, preferences, race, sex, and family responsibilities. Similarly, jobs are highly differentiated by skill requirements, inducements, location, and often extraneous restrictions. Important behavioral consequences follow from these differences; thus, it is necessary in modeling labor markets to distinguish among *many* groups of workers (symbolically $i = 1, 2, \ldots, I$) and *many* groups of jobs ($j = 1, 2, \ldots, J$) in the various activities of the labor market system.

The behavioral interactions in the labor market influenced by these variables can have the effect of segmenting the market. Hiring, reassignment, employment, and separation inherently involve worker-job pairing, either creating pairs or dissolving them. The behavior of such a pair needs to be analyzed in terms of its composition (that is, a worker of type i and a job of type j). It is useful to analyze the interactions in terms of a rectangular array identified by types of workers and types of jobs. For example, Figure 6-2 shows a segmented array of workers paired with jobs in the employment relation through the process of hiring.

Training, experience, and restructuring involve "transformations" of workers or jobs from one type to another. For example, Figure 6-3 shows the transition of workers from one category before training (row) to another category after training (column). Such transitions need to be analyzed in terms of probability. Each type of training program would have a transition type. Health service, rehabilitation, work experience, and other types of employment-related "transformation" programs can be described in this way. Educational programs will affect the attributes workers possess when entering the labor force and should be formally included in a model.

There are important two-way causal relationships between work and schooling through the accumulation of human capital and the opportunity costs of doing so. Moreover, because workers and employers have income and profit motivations, their participation in training, relocation, and other programs to transform people and jobs will be influenced by the opportunity costs of real wages and lost output, as well as the benefits. For example, employer losses of

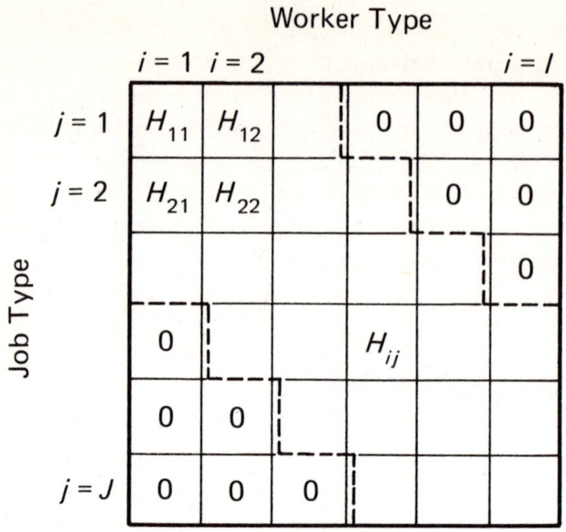

Worker Type

H_{ij} is the number of workers of type i hired to work on jobs of type j.

Figure 6-2. The Segmentation of Hiring

general and specific human capital through turnover further complicate decisions with respect to workers with different characteristics.

Additional discussion of the market search and hiring process underscores the significance of segmentation. If workers and vacancies are ordered in terms of their geographic (or occupational) "closeness" to each other, with "high" skill on one end and "low" skill on the other end of the i and j groups, respectively, most of the placements resulting from market search would be expected to pair workers and jobs of "similar" skill levels (or locations). For example, it is unlikely that a worker of low skill will find a job requiring high skill. This is indicated in the box representing the job-worker match process in Figure 6-2 by the zeros in the off-diagonal hiring cells. It is also indicated, though more crudely, in Figure 6-1 by large zeros in the off-diagonal corners of the various boxes.

Because of the heterogeneity and complexity of jobs and workers, and the costs of obtaining and analyzing relevant information, the search and match processes involve large elements of chance; hence, relationships are likely to hold only in probability terms. The match probabilities are highest in the diagonal band where jobs and workers are "similar" in the relevant sense. Patterns of zeros *within* the diagonal band of Figure 6-2 would indicate discrimination or exclusion in hiring on racial, sexual, union, or other grounds.

There is likely to be an asymmetric relationship between skill levels—that is,

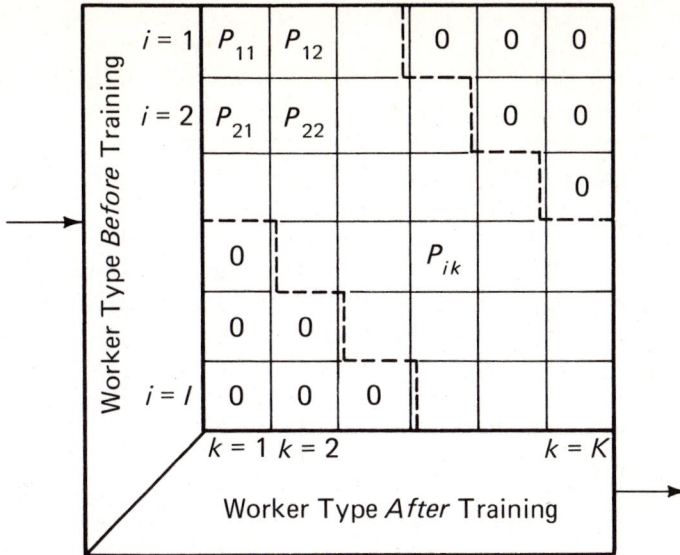

P_{ik} is the probability that a worker of type i will be transformed to type k as a result of a particular training program.

Figure 6-3. Transformation of Workers Between Segments of Training

a high skill level worker being able to fill a low skill job, but not vice versa. This dominance would eliminate the zero probabilities in one corner and further ensure them in the opposite corner. Moreover, the off-diagonal zeros in Figure 6-3 reflect the fact that *great* changes in worker type, as the result of training, are extremely unlikely, although not impossible.

The duration of employment relationships depends on the productivity, satisfaction, earnings, and labor costs of employment matches. These, in turn, depend on interactions among the hiring, internal training, work organization, job restructuring, and reassignment processes of a firm. The speed of placement depends on the interaction of search efficiency, external training, job restructuring, and aspirations for earnings and labor costs.

The foregoing discussion is intended only to suggest the ranges and kinds of behavior and processes that interact to determine the dynamic and equilibrium properties of the labor market. For policy analyses it is necessary to be able to predict changes in aggregate wages and unemployment and in various groups of workers that result from various programs and policies.

Knowledge Base

Although more needs to be learned before adequate system models can be constructed, a foundation of theoretical and empirical work does exist on which modelers may build. An immense amount of factual quantitative information about the labor market has been collected by the government. In spite of its complexity, enough work has now been done to know that this information can be analyzed successfully, even at the micro level, provided that adequate care is taken in formulating behavioral hypotheses and in applying econometric techniques appropriate for the microdynamic processes involved. Research done at the Urban Institute provides several examples of such work.

A simple theory of a compartmentalized labor market is obtained by assuming that the barriers that segment labor markets are impenetrable. One result is a theoretically relevant measure of unemployment dispersion across compartments which, because of the nonlinearity of the wage response relation, is related to an increase in the rate of wage inflation. Empirical tests indicate that this measure of the demographic dispersion of unemployment[3] has a statistically significant effect on the wage inflation rate.

The simple hypothesis that the more job vacancies that exist, the smaller the level of unemployment, can be reduced to rigorous form by analyzing the probability relations that determine hire and turnover flows, including those in and out of the labor force.[4] This theory, in its simplest form, yields a linear logarithmic relation with a negative slope between vacancy and unemployment rates. This relation suggests that market responses to changes in unemployment correspond to percentage changes in vacancies. That is, a reduction in unemployment rates from 8 percent to 4 percent will cause vacancies to rise by a certain factor, and a further reduction of unemployment from 5 percent to 2 percent will increase vacancies again by the same factor. This is a vivid example of how the "full employment ceiling" operates. The relationships tend to be highly nonlinear.

The analysis of behavioral probabilities relates directly to allocation by availability, which has already been discussed briefly. Availability is affected, of course, by both demand and supply conditions in the external labor market (by job vacancies and by workers competing for them). Thus, on theoretical grounds, the ratio of vacancies to unemployment is a relevant measure of availibility. The stocks that affect availability are, in turn, influenced by the behavioral probabilities regulating flows between those stocks. Differences in employment turnover probabilities have been found to account for most of the differences in unemployment rates of various groups—blacks and whites, teenagers and adults, and so forth.[5] These probabilities are inversely related to the durations in various labor market states, durations which, in turn, can affect the probabilities. Also, random sorting processes can affect the compositions of workers and jobs in a particular stock.

Possible economies of scale in the labor markets of large cities have been offered as an explanation for growing urbanization. Such economies could operate through the waiting, information, and risk aspects of availability. Labor market availability may be better for both workers and employers in large cities because of increased efficiency of information search, decreased waiting time between opportunities to be hired or to hire, and consequent reductions of risk. Success in recruiting by employers and in job search by workers depends, respectively, on wage offers and aspiration wages, so price and availability effects can interact strongly.[6]

Classical theory finds that a firm's survival depends on positive profits, but manpower theory adds a second condition for survival: the hire rate of a firm must make good its separations, or it will lose its work force. A firm that is already losing money may find that raising wages is preferable to losing its previous human capital investments through turnover.[7] This may explain, at least partially, why when vacancies increase, wage inflation can become intense, even though the unemployed still far outnumber the vacancies. The quit threat may have more clout in influencing wages than the strike threat by a union.[8] The lowering of hiring standards can aid in recruitment but will not stem an increased quit flow in a tight market. There are, of course, limits to the lowering of hiring standards. These limits are set by possible morale problems that might occur with present employees, if new employees receive inequitable treatment— for example, are paid higher wages or are hired through the setting of lower quality standards. Hiring decisions affect not only the labor costs of the new workers but the productivity of the whole organization as well. Further, there are theoretical grounds for expecting relations to exist between training, wage, turnover, unemployment, and education; and for these, in turn, to affect the expectations and behavior of employers and particular groups of workers.[9]

Modeling Alternatives

One important phenomenon in the labor market that requires study is unemployment. Insight into the requirements for a model formulation may be gained by examining the types of causal relationships involved in determining the stock of unemployed workers. This stock is determined by *how long* it takes a person to find a job or to drop out of the labor force, and by *how many* people flow into unemployment from jobs or by entering the labor force. Each of these actions by workers, or by workers and employers jointly, is influenced by a constellation of personal and firm attributes, and of general market factors such as the level of aggregate demand. However, only probability statements about the occurrence of such events can be made. There is little hope of finding deterministic relations to describe the behavior that occurs in labor markets. This conclusion, of course, does not rule out the aggregation of events occurring at the worker level for purposes of modeling, but it does mean that the inherent stochastic character of such events must be recognized and dealt with explicitly.

Although time in labor market operations is actually continuous and can be simulated using such programs as SIMSCRIPT,[10] a discrete time approximation is sufficient, especially if the time period is short. A recursive model may then be utilized, avoiding the need to solve simultaneous equations in the simulation computations.

In addition, because data collection is usually periodic and because discrete changes of state are important in the labor market, discrete time approximations are made in the modeling effort discussed here, although the possible consequences of that approximation are noted.

The probability that a person will leave unemployment in a month is about 50 percent. To capture this behavior, the model must utilize a very short time period. A month, however, is the shortest time period feasible in terms of the data available. The shortness of this period provides another reason to frame an analysis in probabilistic terms—there is little time aggregation.

Statistical analysis indicates that the labor market, in some respects, acts as an integrated system. For example, unemployment rates for different regions, occupations, and demographic groups tend to rise and fall along with changes in the level of aggregate demand. Yet, these unemployment rates have quite different averages and sensitivities to changes in national production and its industrial composition. Accordingly, while a unified model of the whole labor market system is needed, that model should be segmented in order to reflect important systematic differences in behavior. The segmented structure of labor market processes is perhaps best described by a model that is loosely coupled through probability relationships. (This loose coupling is another reason for expecting that an adequate model can be made recursive.)

The mathematical structures of various types of models and their suitability for modeling labor market processes are discussed below. The first type of model is composed of linear difference equations. Although this is the most commonly used formulation for econometric models, it is better adapted to approximating aggregated relationships than it is to the complex, nonlinear stochastic dynamics of the labor market. Moreover, with a sufficiently short time period to utilize a recursive model, there is no need to assume linearity in order to estimate simultaneous relationships.

The second type of model is a Markov process with a constant matrix of transition probabilities. This formulation, in terms of the probabilities of changing states, is well adapted to deal with the stochastic segmented character of the labor market. It is a simple linear system with a well-developed body of mathematical theory. Unfortunately, the rigidity of the Markov process prevents it from dealing with the variable probabilities of the labor market that are functions of changing personal and environmental factors. Moreover, the labor market involves compound events, like the matching of a worker with a job in the employment relation. Events depending on the availability of both "components" cannot be expressed economically in terms of a Markov process.

With respect to issues of stochastic equilibrium (as contrasted to dynamics), an iterative analysis in terms of Markov matrices might be useful, even where the probabilites are not constant. However, this is not an adequate reason for adopting this formulation of the model.

A third type of model has been developed by Guy Orcutt and others.[11] A microanalytic model would be a natural formulation for labor market modeling because it could be used to model the behavior of individual workers and employers. Such a model could be composed of a sample of thousands of workers behaving very much like the actual economy of millions of workers because the sample of random events in the model would be large in statistical terms. An additional advantage is that nonlinear operating characteristics that determine the probabilities of various events in such models can often be estimated directly from large and representative random samples of microdata on individuals and firms. This type of model is especially powerful if a large number of attributes of individual workers or employers are important in predicting behavioral probabilities.

Orcutt's microanalytic models bear a strong family resemblance to discrete-event job shop simulation models and similar business models and games, but his work is distinguished by the serious attention it gives to statistical estimates of behavioral parameters in contrast to judgmental estimates. However, it is rare for consistent data to be available for all relevant aspects of any system, so Orcutt's model strategy serves as a device for pooling empirical estimates and theoretical knowledge from diverse sources.

A fourth type of model groups similar workers and firms and carries out the system simulation in terms of the sizes of groups in various states, taking into account various group attributes.[12] The probabilities of transfers of individuals between the groups are then estimated. Such group-transition models attempt to capture as much of the heterogeneity in behavior between groups as possible while attaining the simplicity of modeling that comes from having groups as internally homogeneous as feasible. Within this modeling framework a great deal of flexibility can be used in assigning individuals to groups with particular characteristics, in moving the members of these groups through different states, in transferring individuals between groups, and in changing the attributes of whole groups.

Estimation Alternatives

Several broad approaches to the estimation of model parameters can be distinguished. With a computer simulation model this problem cannot be bypassed as it might be with a purely mathematical formulation using symbolic parameters. In order to run a simulation model, the computer requires the researcher to supply specific numerical values of the model parameters. These may be supplied by: (1) statistical estimates from consistent integrated sets of empirical measurements; (2) statistical estimates from fragmented and incomplete sets of empirical measurements; (3) interviews with actors in the labor market (or other socioeconomic system being modeled); and (4) judgmental estimates by the researcher.

Sufficient data to use approach (1) are lacking, so approach (2) is the "best" possible approach on hard empirical grounds. Approaches (3) and (4) are less expensive than (1) and (2), and can often serve as the basis for learning a great deal about the characteristics of the simulation model.[13] Unfortunately, it is easy to confuse knowledge about a simulation model with "guesstimated" parameters and knowledge about the actual system the model attempts to capture.

Sensitivity testing is often advanced as a method for determining whether a system's performance is sensitive to the values of the parameters. Sometimes an assertion is made that large systems are inherently insensitive to their parameter values. Unfortunately, the conclusions from sensitivity tests are conclusions about the characteristics of the particular model and, again, do not necessarily apply to the real system the model is supposed to represent. Sensitivity analysis can serve as a useful guide for determining which parameters are critical and, hence, merit special attention, but even in a given model structure some parameters will be sensitive in some regions of parameter space while others will be sensitive in others. Hence, any conclusions about the value of additional data are necessarily conditional on the knowledge already available.

Simulation models can be used to obtain implications from a stated set of quantitative premises. Such a computer model is a tool of deductive logic that will yield valid conclusions but leave open the truth of the premises, and, hence, the truth of the conclusions. Used in this way, judgmental estimates are certainly appropriate. Tobin, Nichols, Bergmann, and Chinitz and Kadanoff have formulated and tested labor markets in this spirit—which has thrown interesting and relevant light on the micro search and turnover dynamics of the labor market.[14]

Although the simulation modeler aspires to use his model to predict how the real world will behave, he is under much greater pressure to carefully develop the theoretical specification, find relevant data bases, and use appropriate statistical methods. These requirements are difficult enough to meet where the objective is to predict the system's response to exogenous variables within their range of usual variation. However, the requirements are even more critical for predicting the effects of changes in economic structure that have not previously occurred. Yet that is precisely what is needed if simulation models are to help answer such questions as how manpower programs can influence the Phillips curve or how equal opportunity legislation can affect the employment of blacks and women.

Selection of Group-Transition Models

For reasons discussed above, the choice of model type for The Urban Institute effort was quickly narrowed to microanalytic models and group-transition models. One important consideration in making the final choice was the basic data to be used.

The Current Population Survey (CPS), which samples 55,000 households monthly, is one of the richest sources of labor market observations. The samples in successive months are matched and the changes in labor market status are determined. Unfortunately, the monthly data are not available in matched micro form and would be extremely costly to process if they were, but the matched data tabulated by groups in various dimensions can be obtained in machine-readable form.

The National Longitudinal Surveys of Labor Market Experience consist of microdata available from the Department of Labor. The Survey of Economic Opportunity led to the Income Dynamics Annual Surveys. Unfortunately, these sets of longitudinal microdata have incomplete labor market histories within the year. The decision was made to put prime reliance on the "CPS Gross Change" data that are still largely unexploited.

The number of groups in a group-transition model tends to rise as the product of the number of dimensions used to define groups. As a result, the models can quickly become large. In spite of this, the design of the model can remain quite simple, with lower estimation and operating costs for a microanalytic model.

In selecting a model formulation, the area of its application needs to be taken into account because even models that purport to be "structural" are but crude caricatures of a complex world. The policy concern of this study is primarily the *broad* structural and demand issues rather than income distribution and poverty, where personal attributes and motivations are likely to be more important.[15] Thus, a microanalytic model would clearly be more suitable.

The "individual" in a microanalytic model actually serves as a proxy for a group. This becomes clear when sample results are scaled up to make predictions about the whole population. In this respect, the two approaches are similar, but there are still significant differences. In the group-transition model the number of groups depends on the number of different types of behavior that are distinguished. The size of each group and state, which is determined by the model, indicates the "weight" of that group in the population. In a microanalytic model, behavioral patterns that occur frequently are reflected by modeling a large number of such nearly identical individuals. In a group-transition model, a transition probability is multiplied by the size of the group to determine the transition flow. This yields an expected value estimate of the flow, free of random variability. The microanalytic model actually draws random numbers, compounds probabilities, and yields the full richness of stochastic dynamics. For large systems the results should be equivalent, but researchers need to be sensitive to the possibility that divergences can occur. The complexities of large nonlinear stochastic systems defy both analytic treatment and full understanding by the researcher.

Although other researchers are developing microanalytic models for labor market applications, group-transition models were judged to be more suitable for using the CPS gross flow data and somewhat simpler for the policy applications studied here, which stress interactions between aggregate demand and structural programs. Actually, a great deal needs to be learned about the potentialities of both kinds of simulation models.

Data, Econometric Methods, and Computing

In assessing the needs of a modeling effort and planning its successive stages, it is useful to take stock of the availability of data, econometric techniques, and computing capabilities required.

Evaluation of Available Data

Presently available data are, of course, incomplete, but are used rather than collecting new data. In general, vacancy and wage aspiration data are weak, data on job restructuring are entirely absent, and there is very little direct evidence on internal training, on-the-job learning, or job changes that do not involve unemployment. Most of the other data are available, though fragmented, and are somewhat weak in geographic terms. Fragmented data can be integrated through a model and a comprehensive theoretical framework.

The most serious general data weakness is the lack of adequate data on vacancies, with respect to both quality and disaggregation. This reflects a general neglect on the demand side of most labor market research. The second important weakness is the very limited data available detailing the work experience, which accounts for the concerns and characteristics of *both* workers and employers. Although fairly rich data on employment and the supply of labor permit inferences about what the demand for labor must have been, this weakness becomes critical in relation to the design of manpower programs and the study of their effects on the observed system parameters.

The Current Population Survey offers tabulations on employment, unemployment, and out-of-the-labor-force, including flows between those states disaggregated demographically, occupationally, and industrially. There are also CPS data on unemployment by reason of entry and duration. Earnings are collected in the March CPS, but only in May 1973 were wage rates added to the regular monthly surveys.

The National Longitudinal Surveys of Labor Market Experience consist of microdata that are available from the Department of Labor. The Survey of Economic Opportunity led into the Income Dynamics Annual Surveys. Unfortunately, these sets of longitudinal microdata have incomplete labor market histories within the year.

There are monthly data on vacancies from Help Wanted Advertising, and Job Openings Pending at the Employment Service.[16] The help-wanted proxy for vacancies comes from a sample of cities, with no occupational detail. The Employment Service data are biased toward low skills; however, the computerized Job Bank files have yet to be exploited for research and could be increasingly important.

The Bureau of Labor Statistics (BLS) survey of manufacturing employers yields data by state on labor turnover that distinguish between quits and lay offs, but not on whether turnover flows from firms are through unemployment, out-of-the-labor-force, or to another job. Employment, earnings, labor productivity, hours, and insured unemployment data are also available monthly from the BLS by industry.

Extensive new annual longitudinal surveys of microdata have been collected by the Bureau of the Census for the Department of Labor and the Office of Economic Opportunity. Although they are rich in data on worker attributes and motivations, their monthly histories of work, unemployment, and labor force withdrawal are incomplete.

The Department of Labor has commissioned a survey of job search methods by workers and recruitment methods by employers. Administrative data from manpower, unemployment compensation, and social security programs are available. Sociological surveys have been made which concentrate on occupational mobility, and educational surveys have been made which include employment follow-ups.

The data sources mentioned above are illustrative of those available. Although massive data collection efforts have been made, there are still no coherent and comprehensive data bodies spanning the employment function, including both worker-employer behavior and the work experience. Nevertheless, there are more than enough data to work with, and with more work, still other data sets will be ready for computer analysis.

Econometrics Related to the Data

Certain problems relate to particular characteristics of the data. Many CPS tabulations are incomplete in that certain combinations of variables are cross-tabulated, but each variable is not tabulated against all the others. This means that there are certain marginal totals without all the inner cell counts.[17] For example, tabulations on labor market stocks are more detailed than those on gross flows. These deficiencies in the tabulations undoubtedly arise from the traditional analyses by BLS and the Bureau of the Census, which try to attach meanings to the frequency counts of individual cells. For this reason the bureau is quite reluctant to show "small" cells. This is of less concern for regression analyses in which an individual cell count constitutes only one observation among many in grouped data. In the gross flow data some of the weighting factors are random, depending on how many individuals can be matched in successive months. The statistical analysis ideally should be carried out at the sample level, but unadjusted data on stocks are not available, nor are the weighting factors that would be needed to deflate population estimates to get back to the original samples.

Additional CPS data issues relate to sampling variability, respondent response errors, representativeness of the sample (both migrant and population growth are excluded from the gross change data), inconsistent sequential responses leading to rotation biases among the different CPS panels, and misclassification of the labor market status of the interview respondent and household members on which he or she reports. The CPS gross flow data indicate changes in labor market stocks of workers, and so forth, which are inconsistent with the changes in stocks reported. Although this fact has inhibited use of these data in the past, cyclically changing adjustment factors to correct the data have been estimated with encouraging results. When annual microdata are used for their greater richness of worker attributes, inferential estimates of monthly labor market histories will be needed, though based on incomplete questions and recall. The fragmentation of the data sources clearly poses problems of combining incomplete estimates and reconciling duplicative ones.

Econometrics Related to the Models

Other econometric issues derive from the group-transition model itself. What kinds of individuals can be grouped without adversely affecting simulation accuracy must be determined, and estimates of probability functions need to be bounded by zero and one. Hence, these functions are inherently nonlinear. Because transition probabilities from a state must sum to unity, residual errors are inherently correlated across equations, and the probability functions are constrained. Thus, statistical efficiency would indicate simultaneous estimation models.

Real time is continuous, but The Urban Institute model uses discrete monthly time. Behavioral theory applies to probabilities in continuous time, but the probabilities observed in discrete time are complex mixes of the continuous time probabilities. Although the Urban Institute model predicts the discrete time observations, some of the microdata treat time continuously.

The estimation problems associated with probability functions have received increasing attention in econometrics literature. McFadden and Nerlove and Press have presented maximum likelihood estimates based on individual observations.[18] Earlier, Theil developed linear regression techniques for dealing with grouped data, and Scanlon has generalized their application for The Urban Institute model.[19] In using the grouped data available from the CPS, the kinds of individuals who can be grouped without adversely affecting estimation or simulation accuracy must be considered. If individuals who have different probability functions are grouped, an errors-in-variable problem is introduced, which results in inconsistent and biased estimates.

The short monthly time period poses two econometric problems. The residual errors are likely to be autocorrelated, and estimating the seasonal patterns by dummy variables is a bit wasteful of parameters.

In the estimation of wage dynamics, both wage aspirations of workers and hiring standards of employers are important theoretical concepts which, unfortunately, are usually unobserved. Their treatment poses subtle econometric problems. Although we need a short time period to observe transition flows in the labor market, the time lags associated with wage-price dynamics and changes in expectations are thought to be quite long—perhaps one year or more. These two requirements must be reconciled.

Probability functions for transitions between particular states can be estimated jointly for all groups with a gain in sample size if the parameters are the same across groups.[20] If not, probability functions must be estimated individually. However, in either case the fact that the probability functions reflect similar behavior should improve the quality of the estimates.

Sequence of Labor Market Models Planned

Although the complexities of the labor market dictate that their modeling be tackled in stages, it will be useful to first lay out the ultimate system in broad outline and then to consider a tentative plan for the successive stages of a structural labor market model.

Design of the Group Transition Model

Figure 6-4 indicates the design of the simulation model of labor market processes. It incorporates in a more compact form the market structure, processes, and programs shown in Figure 6-1, except that inactive vacancies and workers have been dropped and wage variables have been made explicit.

The workers in the model are assigned to groups, each of which is identified by the index i ($i = 1, 2, \ldots, I$), where groups are defined in terms of such worker attributes as demographic characteristics (age, race, and sex), occupational experience, location, wage aspiration, education, and family responsibilities. These groups, in turn, are divided into subgroups, each of which is identified by its status: out-of-the-labor-force, N_i; unemployed, U_i; employed in jobs of type, j: $J_j E_i$; external training, T_i; and internal training, I_i. External training can be broadened to encompass relocation and other "transformation" programs.

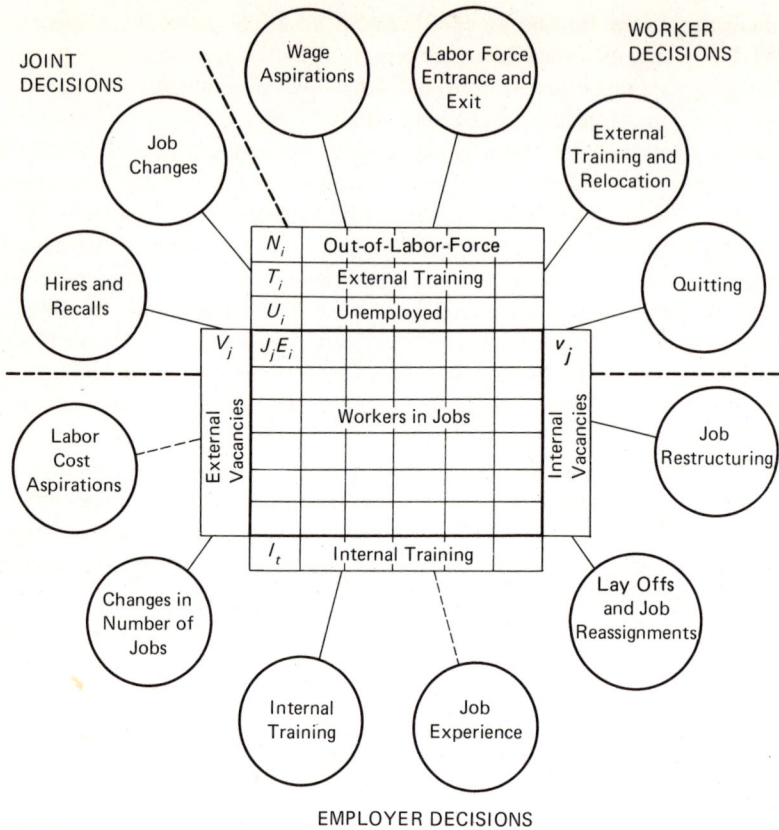

Figure 6-4. Simulation Model of the Labor Market and Programs

Jobs are assigned to groups identified by the index j where the groups are defined in terms of such job attributes as occupation, region, wage, and experience requirements. These job groups are further subdivided by their states as vacancies that are accessible from the external labor market, V_j; vacancies that are accessible only within the firm v_j; and jobs that are currently filled by workers of type $J_j E_i$.

At any time the simulation model would maintain counts of both the workers and the jobs in each group-state and have information on the attributes associated with each. The central cells of Figure 6-4 correspond to these group-states of paired groups of workers and jobs. For simplicity, all group-states are referred to as "groups."

The surrounding circles in Figure 6-4 designate decisions for workers or jobs to change their groups (including states and i or j designations) or to change certain attributes of the groups. (The latter circles are connected through dotted lines.) These decisions can be grouped roughly as worker decisions (4 upper right), employer decisions (6 bottom), and joint worker-employer decisions (2 upper left). Governmental intervention, in the form of programs, laws, and regulations, can impact many of these decisions and will not be explicitly indicated. The various decisions, processes, and transformations contained in the outer circles can be thought of as "operating" each period on the status of the labor market by changing its distribution of workers and jobs among the various states and attributes.

The attributes are updated monthly to indicate (1) the accumulation of on-the-job experience; (2) employer decisions on wage offers for new employees and changes in wage rates for present employees; and (3) changes in worker wage aspirations. Next, changes are made in the number and composition of jobs in response to exogenously given aggregate demand. Then, each of the following usually probabilistic transformation processes are brought to bear: matching unemployed workers and vacancies, changing employment from one job to another, entering or retiring from the labor force, moving from one geographic location to another, changing occupations through training, quitting work, restructuring vacancies to make them better fit the supply of unemployed labor, laying off workers and reassigning workers to different jobs, and training workers internally. Many of these processes will be influenced by unionization and other institutional factors.

Both wage and labor cost aspirations will be influenced by prices, so the model must incorporate supplementary relationships that indicate the effect of wage changes on prices, and prices on wages. This would be done initially in simple relations but might ultimately be done by interfacing the model with an econometric model of the balance of the economy.

A few examples of the mechanics of the model may be helpful. Assume that a group of workers in a particular type of job have certain wage aspirations and respond to the availability of vacancies offering better wages by quitting with a certain probability per month. Multiplying this probability by the count of workers in that group yields a prediction of the number of quits from the group that will occur that month. These quits transfer the workers to the corresponding group of unemployed workers with the same attributes; they also vacate an equal number of jobs and transfer them to the group of vacancies with the same attributes. The employer response in the model may be to try to fill those vacancies with new hires or to reassign (upgrade) other workers to those jobs, depending on the expected recruiting time, and so forth. These responses would be estimated by using the corresponding probability functions.

A Sequence of Models

The labor market is much too complex to attempt to cope with all aspects at once. Also, different policy issues require stress on different aspects of the labor market structure. Hence, a sequence of models, each with increasing detail and refinement, is planned by The Urban Institute. The differences in labor market experiences and behavior by different age, sex, and race groups will be stressed. Then, to see more clearly the effects of upgrading and the accumulation of human capital, occupational segmentation will be added. Finally, geographic segmentation will be introduced, data permitting. Microdata may permit the addition of more specific human capital, family, and motivational attributes.

The models will be driven by aggregate demand and its components. Linking the latter to the labor market may require disaggregation to the industry level. All of these models should try to relate unemployment and its composition to inflation. Union power will be analyzed as the need is indicated by the empirical work.

These models should be useful in making forecasts of the labor market impacts of changes in demand and its composition. In exploring the impacts of structural policies and programs, the models should yield predictions of indirect impacts. However, for such applications the models may need to be extended in order to introduce specific program parameters. These models should help to identify the differential behaviors and attributes that account for the high unemployment rates and low earnings of women, blacks, and other groups. The inclusion of vacancies and wage responses should also help to relate these problems to aggregate demand and the structural problems that contribute to skill shortages and inflation.

The Urban Institute's First Race-Age-Sex Model

The Urban Institute's initial demographic model provides an illustration of the strategic approach outlined above.[21]

The effect of exogenous aggregate demand on the labor market is reflected in the model by the total number of jobs, J (vacancies plus employment), without any disaggregation by type of job. Population is also exogenous, and is disaggregated into eight mutually exclusive demographic groups by age, sex, and race.

The model determines the labor participation, employment, and unemployment of each group by predicting the probabilities of transition between these states. The probability functions depend on the tightness of the labor market reflected in the ratio of aggregate vacancies to unemployment, seasonal factors, and time trends that indicate behavioral changes resulting from variables not explicitly included in the analysis. Average transition probabilities are shown in Table 6-1. The corresponding average monthly flows between various labor market states for the different demographic groups are presented in Table 6-2.[22] The model attempts to predict the seasonal and cyclical fluctuation of these probabilities and flows.

Table 6-1
Average of Monthly Transition Probabilities, July 1967-June 1972

	Employment to Unemployment $E \rightarrow U$	Employment to Out-of-Labor Force $E \rightarrow N$	Unemployment to Unemployment $U \rightarrow E$	Unemployment to Out-of-Labor-Force $U \rightarrow N$	Out-of-Labor-Force to Labor Force Entrant $N \rightarrow L$	Labor Force Entrant to Employment NE/NL
Teens (16-19)						
White Males	0.033	0.121	0.338	0.332	0.203	0.707
Black Males	0.065	0.151	0.242	0.365	0.199	0.533
White Females	0.026	0.142	0.302	0.406	0.146	0.683
Black Females	0.056	0.188	0.167	0.438	0.133	0.432
Adults (20+)						
White Males	0.009	0.013	0.385	0.124	0.072	0.754
Black Males	0.018	0.021	0.350	0.157	0.099	0.701
White Females	0.009	0.058	0.316	0.336	0.043	0.771
Black Females	0.014	0.064	0.241	0.377	0.075	0.661

Source: Unadjusted CPS gross flow data.
Note: All figures are probabilities per month, except the right column which is a probability.

Table 6-2
Average Monthly Gross Flows July 1967-June 1972 (in Thousands)

	Employment to Unemployment EU	Employment to Not-in-Labor-Force EN	Unemployment to Employment UE	Unemployment to Not-in-Labor-Force UN	Not-in-Labor-Force to Employment NE	Not-in-Labor-Force to Unemployment NU
White Male Adults	396	578	435	141	474	155
White Male Teens	102	383	144	139	358	148
Nonwhite Male Adults	78	93	79	37	75	32
Nonwhite Male Teens	22	55	28	39	49	43
White Female Adults	210	1,329	308	325	1,135	337
White Female Teens	66	358	110	145	342	159
Nonwhite Female Adults	50	216	60	99	168	86
Nonwhite Female Teens	11	46	18	46	38	50
Total	935	3,058	1,182	971	2,639	1,010

Figure 6-5 shows a schematic diagram of the demographic model, which is an application of the general scheme shown in Figure 6-4. The center cells indicate the group-state variables[23] incorporated into the model and the circles indicate the processes, typically probability, that operate on these variables. The state-group variables are workers: out-of-the-labor-force, N_i; unemployed U_i; and employed, E_i. Additional variables are the aggregates: labor force, L_i; population, P_i; total unemployment, U; and total employment, E. If X_i is assumed to stand for each of the above group-state variables, the demographic attributes of age, sex, and race are indicated as follows:

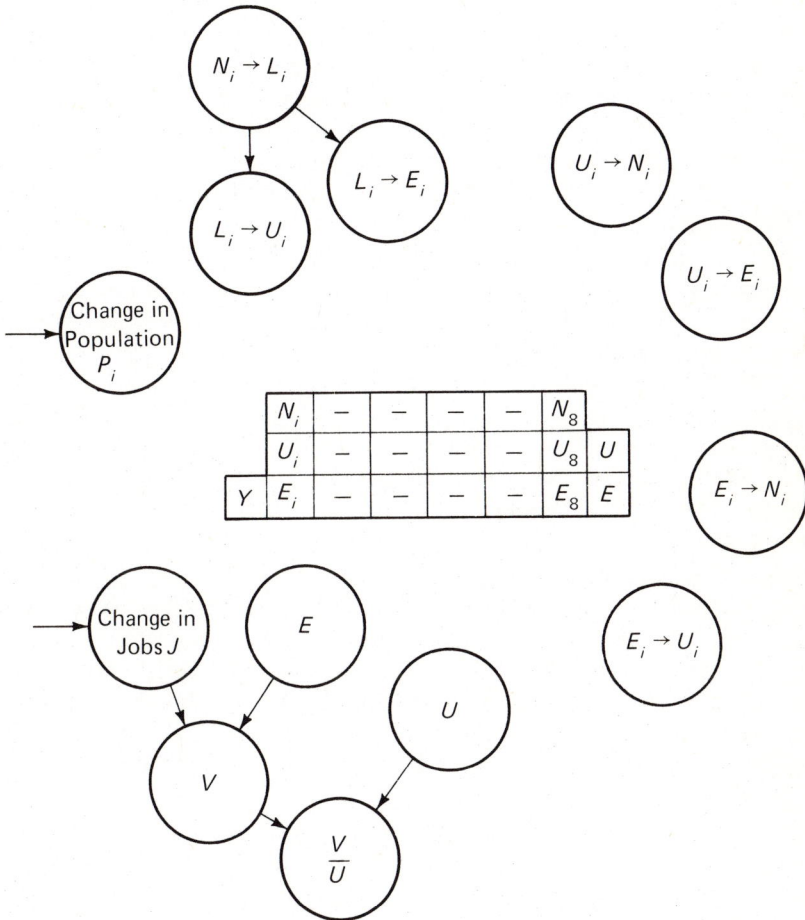

	N_i	—	—	—	—	N_8	
	U_i	—	—	—	—	U_8	U
Y	E_i	—	—	—	—	E_8	E

Figure 6-5. Demographic Model of the Labor Market

$$X_i \, (i = 1, 2, \ldots, 8) = N_{asr} \qquad \begin{matrix} (a = 16\text{-}19, 20+) \\ (s = M, F) \\ (r = W, B) \end{matrix}$$

The circles indicating the probability processes in Figure 6-5 are labeled to illustrate which flow they regulate. For example, $U_i - N_i$ indicates the probability that the unemployed workers in demographic group i will appear in out-of-the-labor-force (be in group-state N_i) in the following month.

The model does not distinguish between different kinds of jobs. At the end of the month the job stock, J, is compared to employment, E, and the unfilled vacancies V, is determined as a residual. The ratio of vacancies to unemployment influences the probabilities of all labor market transitions during the following month. The relative sizes of these two critical stocks is assumed to be an index of the opportunities for employment and recruitment and, therefore, to influence all of the decisions relating to the labor market. Although the effects of wages and price influences do not enter explicitly, they are reflected implicitly through their responses to market tightness.

The transition probabilities and the corresponding flow functions are shown in Equations (6.1)-(6.8) of Table 6-3 where, for example, EN_i is the expected flow from employment to out-of-the-labor force for group i, and the bracketed expressions represent the transition probabilities. There are eight flow equations of this type for each of the eight demographic groups, making a total of sixty-four behavioral equations.

The preliminary estimates of these probability functions were made using least-squares regressions in the log form. A representative sample of these regression estimates is shown in Tables 6-4 and 6-5. The UE transition of Table 6-4 is one of the best fits and the UN transition of Table 6-5 is one of the weakest, judging by the values of $\bar{R}^2$ and .85 and .43, respectively, for adult white males, the largest single group of workers. The corresponding $\bar{R}^2$'s for black teen-aged males are .55 and .21, respectively. The poor fits for black teen-aged males, one of the smallest groups, arise from high sampling variability.

In general, the results are encouraging. They have theoretically expected signs and show reasonable consistency across groups. Statistical significance is high in many cases, especially considering the fact that monthly flows are predicted. Serial correlation is present, but acceptable. However, the estimates indicate the necessity of obtaining additional vacancy data that better reflect the employment opportunities of blacks.

There is little developed theory about the behavior of labor market flows, as distinct from stocks. The signs of the cyclical sensitivity parameters of two of the flows were thus surprising. In a "good" labor market with a high ratio of vacancies to unemployment, relatively low probabilities of workers dropping out of employment or unemployment to leave the labor force would be expected. The results, however, show high probabilities. (See the significant positive signs

Table 6-3
Demographic Model Structure

For each of eight race, age, sex groups:[a]

Employment to Not-in-Labor-Force	$EN_i = [\alpha_{1,i} \dfrac{V^{\beta_{1,i}}}{U_{-1}} \, \gamma_{1,i}^T \, e^{K^{\Sigma\delta_{1,i,K}S_K}}] \cdot E_{i,-1}$	(6.1)
Unemployment to Not-in-Labor-Force	$UN_i = [\alpha_{2,i} \dfrac{V^{\beta_{2,i}}}{U_{-1}} \, \gamma_{2,i}^T \, e^{K^{\Sigma\delta_{2,i,K}S_K}}] \cdot U_{i,-1}$	(6.2)
Not-in-Labor-Force to Labor Force	$NL_i = [\alpha_{3,i} \dfrac{V^{\beta_{3,i}}}{U_{-1}} \, \gamma_{3,i}^T \, e^{K^{\Sigma\delta_{3,i,K}S_K}}] \cdot N_{i,-1}$	(6.3)
Employment to Unemployment	$EU_i = [\alpha_{4,i} \dfrac{V^{\beta_{4,i}}}{U_{-1}} \, \gamma_{4,i}^T \, e^{K^{\Sigma\delta_{4,i,K}S_K}}] \cdot E_{i,-1}$	(6.4)
Unemployment to Employment	$UE_i = [\alpha_{5,i} \dfrac{V^{\beta_{5,i}}}{U_{-1}} \, \gamma_{5,i}^T \, e^{K^{\Sigma\delta_{5,i,K}S_K}}] \cdot U_{i,-1}$	(6.5)
Probability of Successful Labor Force Entry	$\dfrac{NE}{NL_i} = [\alpha_{6,i} \dfrac{V^{\beta_{6,i}}}{U_{-1}} \, \gamma_{6,i}^T \, e^{K^{\Sigma\delta_{6,i,K}S_K}}]$	(6.6)
Not-in-Labor-Force to Employment	$NE_i = \dfrac{NE}{NL_i} \cdot NL_i$	(6.7)
Not-in-Labor-Force to Unemployment	$NU_i = NL_i - NE_i$	(6.8)
Employment	$E_i = [E_{i,-1} + (NE'_i + UE'_i - EN'_i - EU'_i)] \cdot \dfrac{\overline{P}_i}{\overline{P}_{i,-1}}$	(6.9)
Unemployment	$U_i = [U_{i,-1} + (NU'_i + EU'_i - UN'_i - UE'_i)] \cdot \dfrac{\overline{P}_i}{\overline{P}_{i,-1}}$	(6.10)

Table 6-3 (cont.)

Not-in-Labor-Force $\qquad\qquad N_i = [N_{i,-1} + (UN'_i + EN'_i - NU'_i - NE'_i)] \cdot \dfrac{\overline{P}_i}{\overline{P}_{i,-1}}$ $\qquad$ (6.11)

For aggregate economic conditions:[b]

Employment $\qquad\qquad E = \underset{i}{\Sigma}\, E_i$ $\qquad\qquad\qquad\qquad\qquad\qquad\qquad$ (6.89)

Unemployment $\qquad\quad U = \underset{i}{\Sigma}\, U_i$ $\qquad\qquad\qquad\qquad\qquad\qquad\qquad$ (6.90)

Vacancy Index $\qquad\quad V = k(\overline{J} - E)$ $\qquad\qquad\qquad\qquad\qquad\qquad\qquad$ (6.91)

Vacancy-Unemployment $\quad \dfrac{V}{U} = V/U$ $\qquad\qquad\qquad\qquad\qquad\qquad\qquad$ (6.92)
Ratio

---

[a]In Equations (6.1) - (6.6), α, β, γ, and the δ_K represent parameters from estimated behavioral relationships. The variables T and the S_K represent time trend and seasonal dummies, respectively. In Equations (6.9) to (6.11), the prime notation signifies that the estimated flows have been adjusted to correct for biases in the gross flow data. Correction factors were estimated outside the model. The P represents exogenous cohort population.

[b]In Equation (6.91), $\overline{J}$ represents exogenous job stock, $\overline{J} = 1/k\ \overline{V} + \overline{E}$, $\overline{V}$ and $\overline{E}$ are the nonseasonally adjusted Help Wanted Advertising Index and aggregate employment respectively, $1/k$ is a scaling factor used to generate a vacancy level from the index.

on β in Table 6-5.) The phenomena involved thus appear to be more complex. First, there may be cyclical shifts in the *kinds* of people who are both employed and unemployed. For example, in a tight labor market there may be more people who have a relatively low attachment to the money economy as well as relatively attractive alternatives for household activities. Second, in a tight labor market workers are upgraded into better jobs, opportunities for overtime are high, the risk of lay off is low, and the employment costs of reentering the labor market are low. These may combine to make work more attractive, but they also make the worker better off so that he can more readily afford to drop out of the labor force for a while.[24] These hypotheses may be tested with further disaggregation by attributes relating to labor market attachment.

The effect of changes in population size resulting from births, deaths, and movements between age groups on the size of age-sex-race groups is estimated by multiplying the three state-groups by the ratio between the corresponding populations in successive months. This adjustment for population change and updating stocks by accumulating the flows is shown in Equations (6.9)-(6.11) of Table 6-3. Thus, there are eleven equations for each of eight demographic groups, yielding eighty-eight equations.

The simulation model incorporated the estimated probability functions. The

Table 6-4

Parameters Determining Probability of Unemployment to Employment Transition

$$ln(UE_i/U_{i,-1}) = \text{Constant} + \beta_{uei}ln(V/U)_{-1}g_{uei}t + S1_{uei} \cdots S11_{uei} + \epsilon_{uei}$$

	White Males	Black Males	White Females	Black Females
Teens (16-19)				
Constant	−0.257	0.020	−0.508[a]	−1.038[a]
	(−1.990)	(0.057)	(−2.683)	(−2.527)
β_{uei}	0.284[a]	0.470[a]	0.184[a]	0.309
	(4.948)	(2.986)	(2.179)	(1.687)
g_{uei}	−0.0003[a]	−0.003	−0.004[b]	−0.002
	(−0.196)	(−0.802)	(−2.019)	(0.394)
F (11, 46) Seasonals	13.36[a]	4.19[a]	4.03[a]	4.46[a]
$\bar{R}^2$	0.809	0.554	0.615	0.421
D.W.	2.225	2.154	2.368	2.568
Adults (20+)				
Constant	−0.191[b]	0.088	−0.182	−0.764[a]
	(−2.023)	(0.342)	(−1.609)	(−3.444)
β_{uei}	0.220[a]	0.229[a]	0.298[a]	0.112
	(5.247)	(2.601)	(5.929)	(1.137)
g_{uei}	−0.003[a]	−0.007[a]	−0.002[b]	−0.008[a]
	(−3.009)	(−2.578)	(−2.053)	(−3.573)
F (11, 46) Seasonals	11.68[a]	5.73[a]	1.73	1.81
$\bar{R}^2$	0.849	0.594	0.812	0.556
D.W.	2.013	2.228	2.071	2.207

Note: *t*-statistics are shown in parentheses below the regression coefficients.

D.W. designates the Durbin-Watson statistic.

[a]Significance at the .98 level.

[b]Significance at the .95 level.

model was then run monthly through the five-year sample period as a self-contained system, with only jobs and population given exogenously. Table 6-6 shows the mean absolute percentage error for each of the groups and the aggregate during this run. Further adjustments for the biases in the gross change data subsequently improved the regression estimates and reduced these errors by about one third.

In order to explore the dynamics of the model, it was allowed to reach a static equilibrium undisturbed by seasonal or trend effects. Then the job stock was suddenly increased by an amount equal to about one third of the vacancies. The job stock was later restored to its original level. About two thirds of the adjustments occurred in three months.

When the model is further validated, it may be used to predict the impact of

Table 6-5
Parameters Determining Probability of Labor Force Exit from Unemployment

	White Males	Black Males	White Females	Black Females
Teens (16-19)				
Constant	−0.373	−0.552	−0.553	−0.326
	(−2.21)[a]	(−1.60)	(−4.15)[b]	(−1.31)
β_{ui}	0.242	0.228	0.0933	0.183
	(3.21)[b]	(1.48)	(1.57)	(1.65)
g_{ui}	−0.00084	0.00397	−0.00193	0.00047
	(−0.48)	(1.11)	(−1.39)	(0.18)
$F(11, 46)$ Seasonals	8.44[b]	2.44[a]	6.66[b]	2.59[a]
$\bar{R}^2$	0.65	0.21	0.57	0.24
S.E.	0.138	0.281	0.109	0.203
D.W.	1.60	1.50	1.86	1.72
Adults (20+)				
Constant	−1.237	−1.799	−0.455	−0.108
	(−6.78)[b]	(−5.57)[b]	(−4.83)[b]	(−0.53)
β_{ui}	0.309	−0.026	0.190	0.314
	(3.80)[b]	(−0.18)	(4.54)[b]	(3.48)[b]
g_{ui}	0.00112	−0.00374	−0.00206	0.00204
	(0.59)	(−1.11)	(−2.10)[a]	(0.97)
$F(11, 46)$ Seasonals	2.69[a]	0.90	6.30[b]	1.56
$\bar{R}^2$	0.43	0.03	0.72	0.26
S.E.	0.149	0.263	0.077	0.165
D.W.	1.73	1.83	1.83	2.43

Note: *t*-statistics are shown in parentheses below the regression coefficients.
D.W. designates the Durbin-Watson statistic.
[a]Significance at the .95 level.
[b]Significance at the .98 level.

various levels of aggregate demand on the unemployment and labor participation rates of various demographic groups. The effect of changes in the demographic composition of the population on labor market equilibria may also be explored. However, while each group can have unique responses to the aggregate vacancies and unemployment, in its present form the model does not allow differential responses to different kinds of vacancies. Nevertheless, it would be possible to conduct experiments to determine the effects of women experiencing the labor market probabilities of men, blacks experiencing those of whites, and so forth. The results of such experiments, however, must be interpreted very carefully.

Work currently under way on successive models links the vacancy variable to gross national product as the demand variable, introduces the inflation response to labor market tightness, makes turnover rates responsive to wage rates

Table 6-6
Errors in Historical Simulation July 1969-June 1972

	Vacancies Mean Absolute % Error	Employment Mean Absolute % Error	Unemployment Mean Absolute % Error	Not-in-Labor-Force Mean Absolute % Error
Aggregate	13.6	0.3	14.2	1.2
White Male Adults	–	0.4	16.7	3.0
White Male Teens	–	1.9	13.1	3.0
White Female Adults	–	0.7	14.7	0.7
White Female Teens	–	2.3	11.2	2.3
Nonwhite Male Adults	–	0.8	14.2	2.5
Nonwhite Male Teens	–	7.3	20.5	4.3
Nonwhite Female Adults	–	1.0	14.5	1.7
Nonwhite Female Teens	–	7.7	14.6	3.2

and earnings, and increases age groupings from two to four. This latter extension has raised the number of demographic groups to sixteen and the number of equations in the RASST (race-age-sex-search-turnover) model to 180.

Later work will attempt to relate wage offer and acceptance aspirations to transition probabilities. Some economists will be quite uncomfortable with the absence of price allocation in the initial model and the resulting dependence on allocation by availability to regulate the system. Although this was partially the result of data deficiencies, the short-term dynamics of the labor market appear to be more strongly influenced by changes in availability than by changes in wages and prices.

Conclusion

This paper has attempted to examine in broad terms a wide range of unresolved issues: labor market processes, structure, and behavior; alternatives for formalizing their quantitative and dynamic characteristics in a system model that can be estimated, validated, and manipulated; data, econometric, and computing difficulties; and a strategy for progressing from simple to successively more complex system models and applications. The effects of attitudes, institutions, and economic motivations that constitute barriers to equality of employment opportunity should be revealed quantitatively in a model of a segmented labor market by their impacts on its dynamic processes. For example, the differentials in unemployment between groups can be traced to their differences in hiring probabilities and turnover rates. Such a model can be used to study the direct and indirect effects of changing these behavioral relations, but much more work is needed to refine and validate the models and to relate changes in their parameters to various programs, policies, and attitudes. The strategy outlined in this paper will permit the simultaneous handling of many interconnected markets in validated quantitative terms. In this way it will be possible to better understand the operation of labor markets and to formulate more effective methods of governmental intervention through structural and aggregate demand measures.

Notes

1. L. Ulman, ed., *Manpower Programs in the Policy Mix* (Baltimore: The Johns Hopkins University Press, 1973). C.C. Holt, C.D. MacRae, S.O. Schweitzer, and R.E. Smith, "Manpower Programs to Reduce Inflation and Unemployment: Manpower Lyrics for Macro Music" (The Urban Institute Paper 350-28, December 1971).

2. Kenneth Arrow in his presidential address, "Limited Knowledge and

Economic Analysis," to the American Economic Association, analyzed the theoretical necessity in a dynamic economy for markets in future contracts for all goods (K.J. Arrow, "Limited Knowledge and Economic Analysis," *American Economic Review* (March 1974): 1-10). He observed the general absence of such markets in real operating economies except for a few basic commodities. Allocation by availability reflected in lead time for delivery and the resulting backlogs and unfilled orders undoubtedly plays a similar role to that of future prices. When a good that usually is kept in stock for immediate delivery is exhausted because of an increase in demand, the customer is forced to pay the extra cost of waiting for delivery, and this inhibits consumption. A good which is customarily ordered for future delivery is priced on that basis, and a premium must be paid for expedited delivery. While expected delivery time may constitute a workable proxy for the future price of standardized goods, the heterogeneity of jobs and workers in the labor market brings in yet another issue, that of information. Neither future price nor orders for future delivery adequately reflect the search problem a worker faces in not knowing what jobs might be offered to *him,* personally, when, or at what wage rates. The future expenditure of time and anxiety in waiting, effort in searching, and the uncertain prospect of finding only inferior opportunities and wages must be weighed against any currently available job offer. The expectations of the individual worker with respect to his prospects should have an important influence on his labor market decisions. The same point, only on a somewhat more aggregate level, applies to the employer's decisions.

While relative wages influence decisions to offer and accept employ-ment and constitute a cheap means of economic communication, the complex influences of availability on these same decisions involve substantial real costs in terms of time, information, and uncertainty. The theory and estimates that will enable us to understand how both price and availability allocating mechanisms operate and interact both statically and dynamically must be developed. Finally, policies and programs to decrease the costs to both sides of the market of availability allocation and dynamic disequilibrium must be studied.

Allocation by availability also relates to the queuing hypothesis of labor markets in which the labor force is assumed to be "queued" in the order of workers' relative attractiveness to employers. Employers then begin at the head of the queue, hiring employees in the order of their perceived relative abilities. This hypothesis, in its strongest form, completely suppresses price allocation. The theory stated in this strong form also does not square with the incomplete knowledge and dynamic search processes of the labor market.

An illustration of availability allocation is found in Hall's cross-section study of wage and unemployment levels in cities (R.E. Hall, "Why is the Unemployment Rate So High at Full Employment?," *Brookings Papers on Economic Activity* 3, 1970: 369-410). H.C. White has developed a theoretical model of dynamic worker upgrading which is regulated by vacancy availability within the firm (Center for Human Resource Research, *The National Longitudinal Surveys Handbook*, The Ohio State University, December 1973).

3. C.D. MacRae and S.O. Schweitzer, "Wage Inflation and the Dispersion of Unemployment" (The Urban Institute Working Paper 350-50, June 1973).

4. C.D. MacRae and S.O. Schweitzer, "The Relation between Vacancies and Unemployment" (The Urban Institute Working Paper 350-42, June 1973).

5. R.E. Smith and C.C. Holt, "A Job Search-Turnover Analysis of the Black-White Unemployment Ratio," in *Proceedings of the Twenty-third Annual Winter Meeting*, Industrial Relations Research Association, pp. 76-86.

6. R.S. Toikka, "Supply Responses of the Unemployed: A Probability Model of Re-employment" (Ph.D. dissertation, University of Wisconsin, 1972).

7. W.J. Scanlon and C.C. Holt, "Demand for Labor in a Dynamic Theory of the Firm," mimeographed, 1974.

8. E.S. Phelps, ed., *Microeconomic Foundations of Employment and Inflation Theory* (New York: W.W. Norton Co., 1970), pp. 78-90.

9. R.S. Toikka and T. Tachibanaki, "The Economics of Human Capital and Labor Turnover," mimeographed, 1973.

10. H.M. Markowitz, B. Hausner, and H.W. Karr, *SIMSCRIPT: A Simulation Programming Language* (New York: Prentice-Hall, 1963).

11. G. Orcutt, S. Caldwell, H. Guthrie, G. Hendricks, G. Peabody, J. Smith, R. Wertheimer, *Microanalytic Simulation for Policy Exploration* (The Urban Institute Working Paper, January 1974).

12. For work by the former authors see D.A. Dawson and F.T. Denton, *Computer Models for Simulating the Canadian Manpower Training System* (Canada: Department of Manpower and Immigration, May 1973). For citations to the educational modeling work by Stone and others, see T. Thonstad, *Education and Manpower: Theoretical Models and Empirical Applications* (Toronto: University of Toronto Press, 1968), Part 1.

13. A type of model estimation pioneered by Jay Forrester (J.W. Forrester, *Industrial Dynamics*, Cambridge: The MIT Press, 1961) involves interviewing a sample of "actors" in the system under study, and translating an abstract version of their reported behavior into computable form, with "guesstimates" of the parameters. For validation, sensitivity tests are run on the parameters to obtain reasonable global behavior of the model when compared with empirical data on the system being modeled. This approach offers a useful tool for deductive logic, but the problems of statistical inference in the labor market are both subtle and difficult, and this approach to model construction would be vulnerable to serious errors. Even with much more data to work with, errors in inference pose serious problems. The risk of such errors are especially great when the prime objective is to reach conclusions about structural change.

14. J. Tobin, "Inflation and Unemployment," *American Economic Review*

62 (March 1972): 1-18. D. Nichols, "Simulating Labor Market Equilibrium," mimeographed (University of Wisconsin, September 14, 1973). B. Bergmann, "Labor Turnover, Segmentation, and Rates of Unemployment: Simulation-Theoretic Approach," mimeographed (University of Maryland, August 1973). B. Chinitz and L. Kadanoff, "The Job Market and Urban Poverty," mimeographed (Brown University, September 1973).

15. Because a group-transition model can be considered to be an aggregated version of a microanalytic model, it is useful to consider the conditions under which the grouped model would yield exactly equivalent results. See C.C. Holt, "The Solution of Micro Markov Process through Aggregation" (The Urban Institute Working Paper 350-61, November 1973). The most stringent conditions would require *all* of the individual workers, firms, vacancies, and so forth, in a group to have the same *attributes*. Thus, when these attributes are substituted in the behavioral functions, they yield the same results for all individuals either in terms of transition probabilities or in terms of changes in attributes. Because these probabilities reflect the presence of unobserved, omitted variables, which are treated as random, their effects must be equivalent, on the average. Finally, the behavioral responses to environmental variables must be the same. Under these conditions there is *no* loss in predicting the behavior of the group rather than the average behavior of its individual members. However, in a heterogeneous world it may take a very large number of different groups, defined in terms of their attributes and environmental responses, to accommodate every individual in a truly homogeneous group.

A weaker condition for aggregation would allow behaviorally equivalent individuals to be heterogeneous in terms of attributes. Many different combinations of attributes may be consistent with identical transition probabilities. Identical environmental responses would still be required. Even though this weaker condition preserves the accuracy of the model, it reduces the number of groups by allowing certain of the identical attribute groups to be combined. However, any attributes that change through the operation of the model must apply uniformly to all of the members of a group. Unfortunately, the equivalence of behavior is a stronger requirement than it initially appears to be, because it applies to the transition probabilities between *all* of the various states, such as employment and unemployment, through which the group passes. If changes in the attributes occur within the system to cause the behavior of individuals to change, and hence move from one behavioral group to another, then behavioral changes would need to be predicted. If this required recording the changing attributes of individuals, the model would be transformed into a microanalytic one.

Further grouping of behaviorally similar but nonidentical groups may be needed to obtain a manageable number of groups. This would erode somewhat, but perhaps not seriously, the accuracy of the model in simulating the system. Indeed, for many applications cruder but simpler models would be preferable, so the conditions for *perfect* aggregation need not become an overriding concern.

16. A recent BLS survey of vacancies has been discontinued partly for technical reasons. There is a critical need for such data. Canada's vacancy survey appears to be working well.

17. Y. Haitovsky, "Regression Analysis of Grouped Observations When the Cross Classifications are Unknown," *Review of Economic Studies* (January 1968): 77-90; F.J. Scheurem, "Ransacking CPS Tabulations: Applications of the Log Linear Model to Poverty Statistics," *Annals of Economic and Social Measurement* (April 1973).

18. D. McFadden, "Conditional Logit Analysis of Qualitative Choice Behavior," in *Frontiers in Econometrics*, P. Zarembha, ed. (New York: Academic Press, 1974); M. Nerlove and S.J. Press, *Univariate and Multivariate Log Linear and Logistic Models* (Santa Monica: RAND Corporation, 1973).

19. H. Theil, "A Multinomial Extension of the Linear Logit Model," *International Economic Review* (October 1969); H. Theil, *Statistical Decomposition Analysis* (New York: North-Holland Publishing Company, 1972); W.J. Scanlon, "Transition Probability Estimation for the Multinomial Case" (The Urban Institute Working Paper 350-64, August 1973).

20. Tests by G.C. Chow are relevant to empirical judgments on these questions. G.C. Chow, "Test of Equality Between Sets of Coefficients in Two Linear Regressions," *Econometrica* (July 1960).

21. Ralph E. Smith and Jean E. Vanski have conducted most of the research on this model. The labor market participation aspects of the model are discussed in the following: R.E. Smith, "The Discouraged Worker in a Full-Employment Economy," in *Proceedings of the American Statistical Association*, Business and Economics Section, 1973; R.E. Smith, "Dynamic Determinants of Labor Force Participation: Some Evidence from Gross Change Data" (The Urban Institute Working Paper 350-49, August 14, 1973).

22. In analyzing the gross flow data, it has been necessary to make adjustments in the model in order to achieve internal consistency within the CPS stock and flow data. However, these data are unadjusted.

23. These variables are the numbers of workers of a group who are in a particular labor market state, such as unemployment.

24. Smith, in working with the demographic model containing sixteen groups, observed the same phenomena. His results are discussed at length in the following work: R.E. Smith, "Dynamic Determinants of Labor Force Participation: Some Evidence from Gross Change Data" (The Urban Institute Working Paper 350-49, August 14, 1973).

Bibliography

Arrow, K.J. "Limited Knowledge and Economic Analysis." *American Economic Review* (March 1974): 1-10.

Auerbach Corporation. *The FAP Employability Model: A Description of Its Structure.* Vol. I. Philadelphia, September 1971.

Bergmann, B.R. "Labor Turnover, Segmentation, and Rates of Unemployment: Simulation-Theoretic Approach." Mimeographed. University of Maryland, August 1973.

Center for Human Resource Research. *The National Longitudinal Surveys Handbook.* The Ohio State University, December 1973.

Chinitz, B., and L. Kadanoff. "The Job Market and Urban Poverty." Mimeographed. Brown University, September 1973.

Chow, G.C. "Tests of Equality Between Sets of Coefficients in Two Linear Regressions." *Econometrica* (July 1960).

Dawson, D.A., and F.T. Denton. *Computer Models for Simulating the Canadian Manpower Training System.* Canada: Department of Manpower and Immigration, May 1973.

Forrester, J.W. *Industrial Dynamics.* Cambridge: The MIT Press, 1961.

Haitovsky, Y. "Regression Analysis of Grouped Observations When the Cross Classifications Are Unknown." *Review of Economic Studies* (January 1968): 77-90.

Hall, R.E. "Why is the Unemployment Rate So High at Full Employment?" *Brookings Papers on Economic Activity* 3 (1970): 369-410.

Hall, R.E., and R.A. Kasten. "The Relative Occupational Success of Blacks and Whites." *Brookings Papers on Economic Activity* 3 (1973): 781-798.

Holt, C.C. "The Potential Impact of the Employment Service on the Economy." In *Proceedings of the Fortieth Anniversary Symposium on the Changing Mission of the U.S. Employment Service: Increasing Productivity and Improving the Operation of the Labor Market*, 1974.

Holt, C.C. "The Solution Of Micro Markov Processes through Aggregation." The Urban Institute Working Paper 350-61, November 30, 1973.

Holt, C.C., and M.H. David. "The Concept of Job Vacancies in a Dynamic Theory of the Labor Market." In *The Measurement and Interpretation of Job Vacancies.* National Bureau of Economic Research Conference Report. New York, 1966.

Holt, C.C.; C.D. MacRae; S.O. Schweitzer; and R.E. Smith. "Manpower Programs to Reduce Inflation and Unemployment: Manpower Lyrics for Macro Music." The Urban Institute Paper 350-28, December 1971.

Ketron, Inc. "The Employability Model Data Base: A Discussion of Its Structure and Parameters." Final Report. Wayne, Pennsylvania, October 1972.

MacRae, C.D., and S.O. Schweitzer. "The Relation Between Vacancies and Unemployment." The Urban Institute Working Paper 350-42, June 1973.

MacRae, C.D., and S.O. Schweitzer. "Wage Inflation and the Dispersion of Unemployment." The Urban Institute Working Paper 350-50, June 1973.

Markowitz, H.M.; B. Hausner; and H.W. Karr. *SIMSCRIPT: A Simulation Programming Language.* New York: Prentice-Hall, 1963.

McFadden, D. "Conditional Logit Analysis of Qualitative Choice Behavior." In

Frontiers in Econometrics, P. Zarembha, ed. New York: Academic Press, 1974.

Morgan, J.N., and J.D. Smith. *A Panel Study of Income Dynamics.* Survey Research Center. University of Michigan, 1969.

Nerlove, M., and S.J. Press. *Univariate and Multivariate Log Linear and Logistic Models.* Santa Monica: RAND Corporation, 1973.

Nichols, D. "Simulating Labor Market Equilibrium." Mimeographed. University of Wisconsin, September 4, 1973.

Orcutt, G.; S. Caldwell; H. Guthrie; G. Hendricks; G. Peabody; J. Smith; and R. Wertheimer. *Microanalytic Simulation for Policy Exploration.* The Urban Institute Working Paper, January 1974.

Orcutt, G.; S. Caldwell; H. Guthrie; G. Hendricks; G. Peabody; and R. Wertheimer. *Microanalytic Simulation of American Family Behavior: A Tool for Policy Analysis.* The Urban Institute Working Paper, June 1973.

Orcutt, G.H.; M. Greenberger; J. Korbel; and A.M. Rivlin. *Microanalysis of Socioeconomic Systems: A Simulation Study.* New York: Harper and Brothers, 1961.

Phelps, E.S., ed. *Microeconomic Foundations of Employment and Inflation Theory.* New York: W.W. Norton Co., 1970.

Scanlon, W.J. "Transition Probability Estimation for the Multinomial Case." The Urban Institute Working Paper 350-64, August 1973.

Scanlon, W.J., and C.C. Holt. "Demand for Labor in a Dynamic Theory of the Firm." Mimeographed. The Urban Institute, 1974.

Scheurem, F.J. "Ransacking CPS Tabulations: Applications of the Log Linear Model to Poverty Statistics." *Annals of Economic and Social Measurement* (April 1973).

Smith, R.E. "The Discouraged Worker in a Full-Employment Economy." In *Proceedings of the American Statistical Association.* Business and Economics Section, 1973.

Smith, R.E. "Dynamic Determinants of Labor Force Participation: Some Evidence from Gross Change Data." The Urban Institute Working Paper 350-49, August 14, 1973.

Smith, R.E., and C.C. Holt. "A Job Search-Turnover Analysis of the Black-White Unemployment Ratio." In *Proceedings of the Twenty-third Annual Winter Meeting*, pp. 76-86. Industrial Relations Research Association.

Theil, H. "A Multinomial Extension of the Linear Logit Model." *International Economic Review* (October 1969).

Theil, H. *Statistical Decomposition Analysis.* New York: North-Holland Publishing Company, 1972.

Thonstad, T. *Education and Manpower: Theoretical Models and Empirical Applications.* Toronto: University of Toronto Press, 1968.

Tobin, J. "Inflation and Unemployment." *American Economic Review.* 62 (March 1972): 1-18.

Toikka, R.S. "Supply Responses of the Unemployed: A Probability Model of Re-employment." Ph.D. dissertation, University of Wisconsin, 1972.

Toikka, R.S., and T. Tachibanaki. "The Economics of Human Capital and Labor Turnover." Mimeographed. The Urban Institute, 1973.

Ulman, L., ed. *Manpower Programs in the Policy Mix.* Baltimore: The Johns Hopkins University Press, 1973.

Vanski, J.E. "Documentation of Demographic Model Program CHARLS, Version I." Mimeographed. The Urban Institute, 1974.

Vickery, C. "Why Unemployment Rates Differ by Race and Sex." Ph.D. dissertation, University of Maryland, 1973.

White, H.C. *Chains of Opportunity.* Cambridge, Mass.: Harvard University Press, 1970.

Comments

James E. Annable, Jr.

Charles Holt's paper is an imaginative attempt to model complex labor market processes. Holt's study is a craftsmanlike example of the rigorous analyses that are coming from a new breed of labor economists. It should be made clear at the outset that these comments emphasize reservations about Holt's model. Such an emphasis does not imply that the paper does not have many commendable aspects; a reading of it makes these good points evident. Less obvious are some of its limitations. These will be examined from the perspective of equal employment opportunity.

Because a reviewer must take care not to criticize a study for not doing what it was not intended to do, perhaps Holt's objectives should be reiterated. The paper discusses a simulation model of labor market adjustment processes constructed by Holt and his associates at The Urban Institute. The model, which is recursive and loosely linked through probability relationships, attempts to describe the interactive structure of the labor market. From the perspective of equal employment opportunity, there are two principal criteria with which to evaluate Holt's model: (1) the success with which it captures the structure of the labor market (generates realistic time paths of relevant variables); and (2) the contribution it makes to our knowledge of equal employment opportunity. Each of these will be considered in turn.

Comments on the first criterion will be cursory in nature and will concentrate on data limitations, model specification, estimation problems, and model completeness. The central difficulty with the model is its extensive data requirements. At the heart of the analysis are its several transformation matrices; there is little prospect of obtaining the necessary data to validate those that involve internal training. Further, in other model areas data are often absent or insufficiently detailed. The model structure presented in Table 6-3 could use more elaboration; the linkages between the conceptual framework and the specification of the structural equations need to be more explicit. The fitting of the simple model to the available data (Tables 6-4 and 6-5) is done through ordinary least squares. The nature of the estimation problem, however, suggests the use of simultaneous equation techniques. Finally, a systems analysis of labor market operations may legitimately be judged on its completeness. A noteworthy omission in the Holt model is a transformation function that shapes individual labor market expectations. The effect of this exclusion will be considered below.

Regarding the second criterion of what insights the model adds to our present understanding of equal employment opportunity, by Holt's own assessment, the model, if validated, could: (1) identify problem equal opportunity

120

areas in the economy; (2) predict, given constant structural parameters, the impact of various demographic groups; and (3) explore the effects of changing the parameters (especially labor market probabilities) for various demographic groups.

What the model cannot do is explain *why* differential labor market probabilities by groups exist. Thus, it cannot tell much about why unequal opportunity exists or how to design effective remedial programs.

Perhaps it would be useful to consider why it is difficult to analyze the causes of unequal employment opportunity within Holt's conceptual framework. Impediments to such equal opportunity result from a complex of dynamic forces. These barriers can be divided into two groups:

1. *External job-access barriers.* These impediments operate at the ports of entry to primary sector internal labor markets and manifest themselves in no-hire/last-to-be-hired decisions. Racial discrimination, inadequate transportation, poor education, low skill, and artificially high entry requirements are illustrative of such barriers.
2. *Internal job-access barriers.* These operate after the "disadvantaged" worker has been hired into a primary sector job and manifest themselves in voluntary turnover, absenteeism, tardiness, illness, lack of progress, and involuntary separation.

The latter set of impediments is not well understood and has, therefore, become a central focus of current research. Such research would take us inside Holt's transformation matrices. The reason Holt is unable to analyze the internal workings of his transformation functions is the same reason why his model cannot deal with the causes of job access barriers. This reason lies in an inadequate specification of the objective functions assigned to the actors in the labor market. Holt relies on simplistic neoclassical formulations. As a result, important factors are not considered; perhaps the most important of these is the formation of labor market expectations. Space is not sufficient here to permit an elaboration on the role of such expectations. (See, for example, Patricia Gurin's paper, "The Role of Worker Expectancies in the Study of Employment Discrimination," in this volume.) It is becoming clear that any model that relies wholly on a simple neoclassical specification of individual objective functions will be unable to explain the nature of or provide solutions to job access barriers.

While Holt hopes to contribute to our theoretical understanding of the operation of the labor market in validated quantitative terms by developing a sequence of group-transition simulation models, we may admit to having some reservations about the degree to which his hopes will be realized.

Comments

Bennet Harrison

Economic policy analysis is badly in need of a technique for "playing through" the consequences of changes in the values of variables and parameters in the complex real world. Conventional econometric estimations of mathematically "well-behaved" models are simply inadequate for this difficult task. What is needed is a tool that can cope with nonlinearity, indivisibility (especially threshold effects), feedback, and all manner of qualitative (yes-no or 0-1) phenomena. Most important of all for *policy* analysis purposes, the methodology must permit extensive *experimentation* by decision makers and their technicians so that learning can take place. The more unsatisfactory (or uncertain) the quality of the relevant data, the more urgent these remarks become.

Charles Holt has been one of the pioneers in developing heuristic simulation models applied to economic policy problems. Specifically, he has directed a major research project at The Urban Institute concerned with studying the processes by which workers flow through the various states of our labor markets, in order to improve the efficiency of the worker-job "match," thereby (according to one particular strand of neoclassical theory with which Holt is closely identified) improving the well-known "inflation-unemployment trade-off" (simultaneously reducing the severity of both conditions). The Holt paper describes the current status of this research.

Insofar as quantitative modeling is relevant to the concerns of those involved in fashioning equal employment opportunity policy, Holt's approach will probably be more useful for this purpose than further applications of the conventional econometric single-equation methodologies that have dominated past work on poverty and discrimination.[1] Computer simulation can be abused by modelers who are unable or unwilling to worry about the *social* science content of their science. Any quantitative technique is subject to misuse, to the extent that practitioners fail to bring to their lay audiences a clear understanding of the relationship between assumptions and outcomes. Holt and his associates are guilty of neither of these charges; they are first-rate social scientists, and sensitivity analysis (adjusting assumptions to examine the impact on model outcomes) plays a prominent role in shaping the advice they give to a government agency such as the Department of Labor.

However, one may question Holt with respect to foregone policy-relevant opportunities and basic choices about specification. Things that a labor market simulation model *could* be usefully studying are not being studied now by the Holt group, perhaps partly on ideological grounds. Moreover, some of the things that *are* being studied are not being formulated in ways calculated to tell what is necessary to know about labor market discrimination. Some of these gaps will be closed to some extent by the work of researchers who follow Holt's lead in this field.[2] Still, it seems useful to discuss these points.

First and foremost, the behavioral theory underlying the Holt model(s) may be unnecessarily naive. Even though demographic aggregates are created and analyzed as "groups," this is still a thoroughly utilitarian world of individualistic profit and utility maximizers. Interdependent preferences are ruled out, although the technique would permit their inclusion; that is, groups or classes of people are not permitted to respond to changes in one another's circumstances. This is a fundamental flaw in neoclassical economics as applied to problems of poverty and discrimination. Models of the black "suburbanization" process fail to allow for white "blacklash," as do forecasts from models of employment integration.[3] Forecasts of the black-white income "gap" amount to little more than intelligently constructed extrapolations (not necessarily linear), a procedure that again ignores feedback. In Holt's models, groups respond to one another only insofar as their particular statuses affect the price/wage or job vacancy signals to which each group is directly attentive; that is, there is no *direct* contact between sets of workers. Collective behavior (by producers as well as by consumer/workers) is a fact of economic life. The technique will permit its specification.

As in most poverty-discrimination literature, jobs here are characterized by the narrowest of descriptors, and the behavior of workers with respect to the network of jobs—staying, quitting, being fired, having one's wage increased, organizing into a union—is "caused" almost exclusively by characteristics of the workers themselves (age, sex, race, education, and experience). Possibly *the* major insight of institutional economics—from Marx to Veblen to Kerr to the modern "dual labor market theorist"—has been the central importance of labor *demand* variables (profits, market power, concentration, and so forth) on the ex post allocation of labor and distribution of income. A simulation model such as Holt's might beneficially give much more attention to the specification of such variables and the attendant relations. For example, it could be argued that a reduction in monopoly power in the American economy would, ceteris paribus also "shift in" the Phillips curve. Why not design models that allow for this possibility?

The Holt model pays little attention to the interactions between labor markets and other socioeconomic systems. In Karl Polanyi's terms, the model is not well "embedded." In particular, the flows between (and therefore the importance of) the relative "wages" and other price-type signals relating to labor markets, welfare dependency, criminal activity, or quasi-legal "hustling" are totally excluded.[4] Qualitative attitudes of workers toward participating in these other income-bearing activities (the stigma of welfare, the high risk of crime, and the high tolerance for crime in poverty areas) would seem to be important variables with which to experiment, if only to estimate less biased labor supply functions than those probably contained in a model such as Holt's.

Those criticisms are partly unfair, of course, in that Holt's major policy interest—the Phillips curve "dilemma"—is only tangentially related to the issue of employment discrimination. A model more explicitly concerned with the latter subject might look very different in terms of the modeler's decision on what and what not to include. Consider one example.

According to the "radical" theory of racial discrimination, capitalist control over the means of production requires a hierarchical organization of work in order to maintain order and keep workers divided against each other. Because human beings are (by assumption) *not* inherently (or are insufficiently) unequal in their potential skills, a hierarchy among workers must be created. In general, the system will use as allocative mechanisms the most efficient means available. These will generally include those allocators that are already socially sanctioned. Racism and sexism predate, and they generally exist independent of, capitalism. Thus, they are seized on by capitalists as efficient instruments for allocating relatively "equal" labor into the hierarchical job structure.[5] It follows that the practice of discrimination by individual employers must be made not only expensive (Lester Thurow recommends making it *prohibitively* expensive) but also less socially acceptable in *any* arena of American life.

If the radical view is correct, then blacks and at least some ("working class") whites are in a kind of zero-sum game in the labor market. If blacks gain from reduced discrimination or "affirmative action" by employers, it is likely to be at the expense of some whites.[6] Many people would question whether such gains by blacks or women are acceptable. Capitalists and upper-class white male workers must be made to share a greater part of the burden of eliminating discrimination.

In any case, these are issues (and relationships) that a computer simulation model designed to be relevant to equal employment opportunity concerns might well take into account. The Holt model is moving in this direction by representing the competition among different kinds of workers for scarce vacancies. Still, workers in the model are permitted only to relate to the *jobs*, not to one another. A more satisfying model would be one whose tone was dominated by conflict in the labor market between different groups (by zero-sum games and both worker and employer collusion).

Finally, a comment about methodology seems appropriate. It may be questioned whether the Holt model is already too big to "control"; that is, the process of learning about labor market structure from given runs, and embodying that knowledge by respecifying and reestimating new relationships, is very expensive. More seriously, the number of variables is so large that intuitive appreciation of what a good sensitivity analysis is designed to show—the dynamic relationships between assumptions and outcomes—is hard to achieve. The number of nonlinear econometric relations that had to be estimated in order to provide reasonable parameter values for so large a model is itself very large; yet Holt himself warns us eloquently of the limitations of econometric methodology in such a context (not to mention the prodigious data problems).

Perhaps it would be better to build simpler, more "stylized" models that—by virtue of their smaller size—could be used in a more deliberately experimental fashion. The ideal, of course, would be to construct models that policy makers could "play with" themselves. The techniques, although not necessarily the particular current models developed by Holt, should make this possible in the future.

Notes

1. See Lee Kadanoff, Bennett Harrison, and Benjamin Chinitz, "A Model of Job Distribution and Metropolitan Development," mimeographed (Providence, R.I.: Brown University, 1974).

2. Kadanoff et al., "A Model of Job Distribution"; Barbara Bergmann, "Combining Microsimulation and Regression: A Prepared Regression of Poverty Incidence on Unemployment and Growth," *Econometrica*, in press; Clare Vickery, "Why Unemployment Rates Differ by Race and Sex" (Ph.D. dissertation, University of Maryland, 1973).

3. One notable exception is Duran Bell. See Duran Bell, "Bonuses, Quotas, and the Employment of Black Workers," *Journal of Human Resources* (Summar 1971); "Occupational Discrimination as a Source of Income Differences: Lessons of the 1960s," *American Economic Review, Papers and Proceedings* (May 1972).

4. These flows are discussed in Bennett Harrison, *Education, Training, and the Urban Ghetto* (Baltimore: The Johns Hopkins University Press, 1972), Ch. 5. Their measurement is an important object of current research attention by economists and sociologists at M.I.T. and the New School of Social Research, including the author.

5. Richard Edwards, David Gordon, and Michael Reich, "Labor Market Segmentation," *American Economic Review, Papers and Proceedings* (May 1973).

6. This is a central theme in the work of Michael Reich; see Michael Reich, "The Economics of Racism," in *Problems in Political Economy: An Urban Perspective*, D.M. Gordon, ed. (Lexington, Mass.: D.C. Heath, 1971). There is some quantitative evidence in support of a zero-sum theory in the simulations of Barbara Bergmann, "The Effect on White Incomes of Discrimination in Employment," *Journal of Political Economy* (March/April 1971).

Bibliography

Bell, Duran. "Bonuses, Quotas, and the Employment of Black Workers." *Journal of Human Resources* (Summer 1971).

Bell, Duran. "Occupational Discrimination as a Source of Income Differences: Lessons of the 1960s." *American Economic Review, Papers and Proceedings* (May 1972).

Bergmann, Barbara. "The Effect on White Incomes of Discrimination in Employment." *Journal of Political Economy* (March/April 1971).

Bergmann, Barbara. "Combining Microsimulation and Regression: A Prepared Regression of Poverty Incidence on Unemployment and Growth," *Econometrica*, in press.

Edwards, Richard; David Gordon; and Michael Reich. "Labor Market Segmentation." *American Economic Review, Papers and Proceedings* (May 1973).

Harrison, Bennett. *Education, Training, and the Urban Ghetto*. Baltimore: The Johns Hopkins University Press, 1972.

Kadanoff, Lee; Bennett Harrison; and Benjamin Chinitz. "A Model of Job Distribution and Metropolitan Development." Mimeographed. Providence, R.I.: Brown University, 1974.

Reich, Michael. "The Economics of Racism." In *Problems in Political Economy: An Urban Perspective*, D.M. Gordon, ed. Lexington, Mass.: D.C. Heath, 1971.

Vickery, Claire. "Why Unemployment Rates Differ by Race and Sex." Ph.D. dissertation, University of Maryland, 1973.

7 Differences in Expected Post-School Investment as a Determinant of Market Wage Differentials

Solomon W. Polachek

Much of the recent literature on the distribution of income has centered not only on the distribution of earnings between the basic factors of production capital and labor, but also on the more narrow problem of the distribution of earnings within the labor sector. In this regard, labor is viewed as a heterogeneous group whose members have accumulated differing amounts of human capital. The problem of actually measuring human capital has proven to be a difficult task if only because some forms of human capital are not directly observable.

Early studies [2, 17, 8] have concentrated on measuring the effects of one form of human capital—namely that of education on earnings. However, even this concentration on schooling poses theoretical and empirical problems. First, as some [12, 28, 30] have argued, examining only levels of schooling accounts sufficiently neither for quality differences between schools nor for the interactive effects between schooling and individual ability. Second, since schooling does not represent the only form of investment, then neglecting other investments may bias measurements of the effects of education on earnings. A positive correlation between schooling level and other investments implies that the impact of schooling would be overestimated, while conversely a negative correlation implies an underestimate. Because of the importance of preventing such biases, a large portion of the research in human capital has been devoted to understanding nonschool investment. Although in part these investments consist of intergenerational transfers [27, 15] in the form of pre-school investment, the bulk of the research has centered on post-school investment (*PSI*) sometimes referred to as on-the-job training (*OJT*) [18, 4, 25, 13, 29, 11].

Post-school investment has not been directly observable. However, under two main assumptions, namely (1) that the marginal cost of human capital produced in a given period is upward sloping and (2) that an individual's labor force participation over his life cycle is non-increasing, *PSI* can be shown to decline monotonically with age. It is for this reason that *PSI* has been specified

The author is greatly indebted to Jacob Mincer, Robert Fearn, and Robert Strauss for their advice and comments, and to members of the Labor and Applications Workshops at Columbia University, the University of Chicago, and North Carolina State University at Raleigh. He gives special thanks to Gilbert Ghez and H. Greg Lewis for correcting several errors of an earlier draft of this paper, Ronald Oaxaca for commenting on a draft of this paper presented at the Equal Employment Opportunity Research Workshop at the Massachusetts Institute of Technology, as well as to the anonymous referees of this journal for their numerous suggestions. All remaining errors are the responsibility of the author.

as some function of age yielding a characteristically concave age-earnings profile. To date no one has questioned the validity of declining *PSI* with age. Instead, by analyzing the effects of ability and initial human capital endowment on the marginal cost of human capital investment, research has concentrated only on ascertaining the rate of decline of *PSI* over the life cycle [19, 4, 13, 29, 11]. This paper questions these results by illustrating that when the above second assumption (only implicit in past research) is violated, investment need not decline monotonically with age. Such non-monotonicity of investment becomes important in explaining the earnings behavior of secondary workers who tend to have more intermittent life cycle labor force participation (*LFP*) patterns than white married males to which most empirical studies apply.

Section 1 outlines the theory of life cycle human capital accumulation when expected labor force participation is intermittent; Section 2 applies this theory by developing a new technique for measuring expected human capital investment. These measurements are then used in Section 3 to explain male-female and married-single earnings differentials.

1. The Theory of Life Cycle Accumulation of Human Capital and Its Applicability to Those with Intermittent Labor Force Participation

For the most part, models in economics deal with the problem of allocation. The human capital model is no exception; it deals with the allocation of goods and time resources in the production of human capital. For the individual, the motivation behind such a choice is obvious. Higher stocks of human capital increase individual wages; yet the allocation of time and goods for such investment is costly. The individual must weigh the present value of these costs and benefits over the life cycle to determine an optimal path of human capital accumulation.

To analyze this problem we assume that an individual's objective is to maximize the present value of his earnings stream over a finite lifetime assumed to end with certainty at year T.[1] Such an objective function can be represented by maximizing a functional representing discounted lifetime earnings, and can be written as

$$\text{Max } J = \int_0^T [N_t - s_t] w(K_t) K_t e^{-rt} dt \tag{7.1a}$$

subject to the following constraint on the rate of change of capital stock

$$\dot{K} = Q_t - \delta(t, K) K_t \tag{7.1b}$$

$$= f[s_t, K_t, X_t] - \delta(t, K_t) K_t$$

$$= b_0 s_t^{b_1} K_t^{b_2} X_t^{b_3} - \delta K_t$$

where,

$K_t \equiv$ stock of human capital at time t,

$w(K_t) \equiv$ rental value (wage rate) per unit of human capital,

$s_t \equiv$ percent of total time available spent investing in period t,

$N_t \equiv$ percent of total time available spent in labor force participation (including the time devoted to investment),

$r \equiv r' + \delta$ the sum of the rate of discount and rate of depreciation of human capital stock,

$X_t \equiv$ goods used in the production of human capital, and

$\delta(t, K_t) \equiv$ the annual rate of depreciation of capital stock of age t.

The parameters b_0, b_1, b_2, and b_3 are parameters of the production function of human capital.

Since the latest studies discuss the effect of variation in the production function parameters b_1, b_2, and b_3 on the control variable s_t, we shall not deal with this problem. Instead we assume neutrality in the production function of human capital (i.e., $b_1 = b_2$) thereby guaranteeing that the marginal cost of investment does not shift as K_t changes over time.[2] Further, let us assume that the amount of investment in each period is invariant with the rental value of a unit of human capital ($b_3 = 0$), that the rate of depreciation is zero at all ages and levels of human capital stock ($\delta(t, K) = \delta = 0$), and finally that the wage rate per unit of human capital is constant and independent of total capital stock $[w(K_t) = w_0]$.[3]

The main point of departure of this model from its predecessors is that this model does not assume N_t to be a constant equal to one. Although such a hypothesis may be plausible for white married males who have a high and relatively constant commitment to the labor force over the life cycle, such an assumption is clearly not true for other groups such as single white males, blacks, or females all of whom have a lesser lifetime labor force commitment [7, 6].[4]

To solve the more traditional maximization for which it is assumed no corner solutions are binding and that N_t is constant over time but not equal to unity, the Hamiltonian[5]

$$H = w_0(N_t - s_t)e^{-rt}K_t + \lambda b_0 s_t^{b_1} K_t^{b_1}$$

is maximized with respect to the control variable s_t to obtain the following necessary conditions:

$$\frac{\partial H}{\partial s_t} = -w_0 K_t e^{-rt} + \lambda b_0 b_1 s_t^{b_1 - 1} K_t^{b_1} = 0, \tag{7.1}$$

$$\dot{\lambda} = -w_0(N_t - s_t)e^{-rt} - \lambda b_0 b_1 s_t^{b_1} K_t^{b_1 - 1}, \tag{7.2}$$

$$\dot{K} = Q_t = b_0 s_t^{b_1} K_t^{b_1}.$$

(7.3)

Equation (7.1), which implies that the quantity of investment in each period is obtained by equating its marginal costs and benefits may be solved for the costate variable, λ, representing marginal returns on human capital investment in terms of the production function parameters

$$\lambda = \left[\frac{w_0}{b_0 b_1}\right] K_t^{1-b_1} s_t^{1-b_1} e^{-rt}.$$

(7.1')

By substituting (7.1') into (7.2), $\dot{\lambda}$ can be expressed as:

$$\dot{\lambda} = -w_0 N_t e^{-rt} \leqslant 0$$

(7.2')

thereby illustrating that the marginal revenue of an incremental unit of human capital investment diminishes over the life cycle. Solving this differential equation for λ given the initial condition that

$$\lambda(t_0) = \int_0^T w_0 N_\tau e^{-r\tau} d\tau$$

yields the formula of marginal revenue per unit of investment

$$\lambda(t) = \int_t^T w_0 N_\tau e^{-r\tau} d\tau$$

(7.1'')

Further, (7.1) can be solved for $(s_t K_t)$—the amount of capital reinvested during each period:

$$s_t K_t = \left[\left(\frac{b_0 b_1}{w_0}\right) \Psi\right]^{1/(1-b_1)}$$

(7.4)

where Ψ equals λe^{rt} or the current dollar equivalent of marginal revenue. Taking the partial derivative of $s_t K_t$ with respect to time yields the yearly change in investment

$$\frac{\partial s_t K_t}{\partial t} = \left[\frac{1}{1-b_1}\right]\left[\frac{b_0 b_1}{w_0}\right]^{1/(1-b_1)} \Psi^{b_1/(1-b_1)} \leqslant 0$$

(7.5)

which, by being negative, illustrates that dollar investment declines with age.[6] Similarly, the percentage of one's available time devoted to investment $[\partial s_t/\partial t]$

is also declining.[7] To illustrate the effect on investment of an exogenous decrease in labor force participation (N_t), investment is differentiated with respect to N_t yielding

$$\frac{\partial}{\partial N_t} [s_t K_t] = \frac{1}{1 - b_1} (s_t K_t)^{b_1 /(1 - b_1)} \frac{\partial \dot{\Psi}}{\partial N_t} \leqslant 0$$

because $\partial \dot{\Psi}/\partial N_t \geqslant 0$. Thus an exogenous decrease of per period labor force participation decreases the amount of current investment in human capital, as well as decelerates the investment process. If this smaller labor force participation is sufficient to cause a decline in current marginal revenue of investment, by one percent, investment expenditures decrease by $(1 \div [1 - b_1])\%$, and the rate of decline of investment expenditure decreases by $(b_1 \div [1 - b_1])\%$.

Relaxing the assumption of constant per period LFP implies.[8]

$$\dot{\Psi} = -w_0 N(t) e^{(t-T)} + w_0 r e^{rt} \int_t^T [N(\tau) - N(t)] e^{-r\tau} d\tau. \qquad (7.7)$$

The first term represents the change in marginal revenue if labor force participation were constant. It is negative and identical to (7.6). The second represents the incremental change to marginal revenue when labor force participation is not constant over the life cycle. If labor force participation is rising then this second term is positive, and if sufficiently large in magnitude would cause the marginal revenue of investment to rise (i.e., $\dot{\Psi} > 0$), and hence investment $s_t K_t$ to rise too.[9] These results therefore illustrate that if one plans not to be in the labor force because of a greater degree of home specialization or unemployment, then marginal revenue of investment would be lower than it would otherwise be. Further, if the marginal cost function is unaffected by such an absence from the labor force, then human capital investment also would be lower thereby implying lower and flatter age-earnings profiles.

Whereas previous models deal only with differences in the rate of decline of $s_t K_t$ with respect to changes in the parameters of the human capital production function, this analysis shows that PSI crucially depends on expected life cycle LFP, and in fact need not decline monotonically with age. Similarly the level of PSI need not differ among individuals because of differences of initial human capital endowments or abilities, but instead may differ because of expectations of future labor force participation. For example, if females expect family, social, and maternal pressures to mold their work decisions during say only the child rearing period, then their investment patterns would be affected over their entire life history. If blacks are last hired and first fired, then expectations of greater unemployment also would affect their investment decisions. As a corollary, one may add that given the assumption of risk aversion, uncertainty with respect to one's expectations of future labor force participation would also result in less human capital investment.[10] It is for this reason, namely the failure to account for differing expectations and hence differing amounts of investment even while at work, that current studies of male-female wage differentials fail to explain more than fifty percent of the wage gap. In the remainder of this paper the theory developed in this section is applied to estimate the importance of differing life cycle labor force expectations on human capital investment and hence on the existing male-female and married-single wage gap.[11]

2. The Computation of Expected Post-School Investment

Assume that the human capital production function defined in Equation (7.1b) varies across schooling groups. It then follows that marginal cost of investment across individuals of the same level of education is identical, and that individual post-school investment in each time period is determined by the differing individual sets of marginal revenue (λ).[12] For such a determination of *PSI* (illustrated graphically in Figure 7-1), the marginal cost of investment (*MC*) is invariant over the life cycle, and *PSI* in each period t ($I_t = s_t K_t$) is determined by the intersection of *MC* and λ.[13] If labor force participation is continuous and constant over the life cycle, λ_t gradually shifts down and traces out an optimal path of diminishing gross investment:[14]

$$I = (I_1, I_2, \ldots, I_T) \text{ such that } I_1 > I_2 > \ldots > I_T.$$

On the other hand, if *LFP* is intermittent λ_t need not shift downward monotonically, and hence would generally result in a smaller lifetime investment

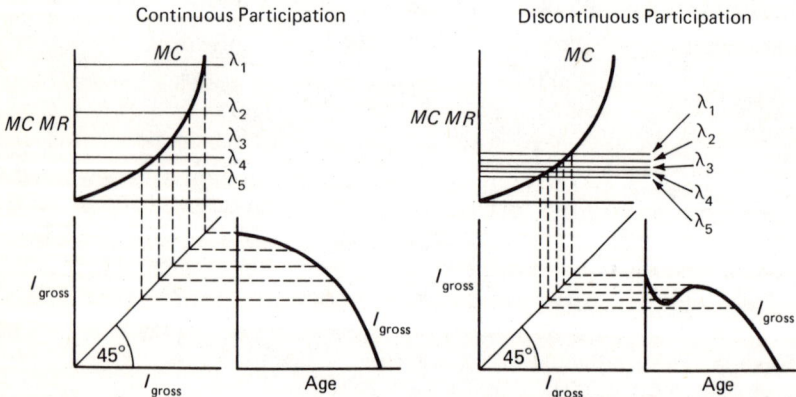

Figure 7-1. A Graphical Determination of Post-School Investment

(Figure 7-1). Based on these equilibrium conditions, this section is devoted to empirically measuring investment differences caused by differing *LFP* patterns.

To briefly outline the computational procedure,[15] note that if both the *MC* and $\lambda = (\lambda_1, \lambda_2, \ldots, \lambda_T)$ functions are known, then $\underline{I}$ can be estimated as the solution of the equation relating to *MC* to λ. Conversely, if given $\underline{I}$ and $\underline{\lambda}$, *MC* can be uniquely determined.[16] Since methods are available for determining the married male investment[17] [I (t; Male, Married, E) where $E = 1, \ldots, 5$ representing five levels of education] and the marginal revenue vectors λ [t; Male, Married, E][18], a unique *MC* can be determined for each level of education. When these marginal cost curves [$MC(E)$] are equated with single male as well as single and married female marginal revenue functions of comparable levels of education [$\lambda(S, N, E)$], estimates of each of these group's investment relative to that of married males are obtained.

As the theory developed in Section 1 predicts, both the quantity of investment as well as its rate of accumulation differs with the degree of labor force intermittency. For those groups with the least labor force commitment, investment is least monotonic and smallest in magnitude. Consequently, expected investment of married males exceeds that of single males, and expected investment of single females is greater than that of married females. Similarly, because of the greater labor force commitment of the more educated, expected gross investment rises consistently with education. However, because of the greater depreciation associated with higher levels of education, these patterns of rising investment need not hold for net investment. In fact, net *PSI* does not increase as continually by level of education as does gross *PSI*.

Consistent as these results are with respect to the human capital model, the assumptions explicit in the computation scheme no doubt bias these estimates of post-school investment. However, since each assumption has different and opposite effects, the net effect is impossible to determine. Assuming that each education group possesses the same production function for human capital may be unduly restrictive in the sense that differing labor market expectations may affect the quality of schooling in addition to the quantity of *PSI*. Hence if these differing labor force expectations affect the fields studied by each sex-marital status group such that investment in schooling is not Hicksian neutral with respect to home versus market production, then the assumption of invariance of marginal costs within education groups would cause an underestimate of the marginal cost function and hence *ceterus paribus*, an overestimate of expected investment. On the other hand, if the marginal cost curve of males is in reality rising over the life cycle [i.e., if $b_1 \neq b_2$ in Equation (7.1-7.6)] the outlined computation scheme would underestimate female investment.

Although these as well as certain other computational biases exist, this section has provided sufficiently robust evidence that post-school investment functions differ according to sex and marital status and further that behavior motivated by the maximization of discounted lifetime earnings is useful in understanding post-school investment behavior. The next section verifies the applicability of this investment process as an explanation for the intergroup wage differentials observed within the economy.

3. Differences in Expected Post-School Investment as a Determinant of Market Wage Differentials: An Application to Married Versus Single Males and Females

By applying the human capital model, a link has been established between life cycle *LFP* and *PSI*. As observed, *LFP* differs across demographic groups such that, on the average, females (especially married females) tend to have a smaller life time labor force commitment than single or married males. Regardless of the reasons why these differences in life cycle *LFP* exist, the expectation of such behavioral differences bring about systematic responses in the post-school investment process. Those with smaller expectations of life cycle *LFP* have been shown to invest less even while at work, and hence to have accumulated less human capital stock.[19] It is our purpose now to measure the importance of these differences in accumulated investment as a determinant of observed market wage differentials.

To perform such a test, wage differentials between the following four basic population strata are considered: (1) married males and married females, (2) single males and single females, (3) married and single males, and (4) married and single females. Earnings within these groups are viewed as functionally related to a set of independent variables. Because of the strong correlation between human capital, and education, potential labor market experience, occupation, and industry these latter variables are most widely chosen as determinants of earnings. Thus earnings may be specified[20] as:

$$Y = g(S, E, \underline{I}, \underline{O}, \underline{V}) + \epsilon \tag{7.8}$$

where

$S \equiv$ years of schooling
$E \equiv$ potential experience [age minus education minus six]
$\underline{I} \equiv$ industry (set of dummy variables)
$\underline{Q} \equiv$ occupation (set of dummy variables)
$\underline{V} \equiv$ set of other standardizing variables such as region, nativity, weeks and hours worked per year.

The rate of return to schooling can be measured by $\partial Ln Y/\partial S$, and when E is measured as a quadratic, the linear term is generally positive and the quadratic term negative, reflecting the concavity of the earnings function.

By adding a dummy variable representing group identification [(*SEX*) being one for females in the male-female stratum or a (*MS*) being one for those married-single stratum] , adjusted male-female and married-single wage differentials can be ascertained, so that $\partial Y/\partial SEX$ and $\partial Y/\partial MS$ in Equation (7.9) below

$$Y = g\left(S, E, \underline{I}, \underline{O}, \underline{V}, \left\{\frac{SEX}{MS}\right\}\right) + \epsilon \qquad (7.9)$$

would reflect adjusted within group differences in wages. If S, E, $\underline{I}$, $\underline{O}$ and $\underline{V}$ were omitted from the equation in a specification such as (7.10)

$$Y = \alpha_0 + \beta \left\{\frac{SEX}{MS}\right\} + \epsilon, \qquad (7.10)$$

$\partial Y/\partial SEX$ and $\partial Y/\partial MS$ would represent raw wage differentials. Such measures of wage differentials are given for each strata. As illustrated in Table 7-1 for the sample of both married and never married males and females absolute male-female wage differences are $3040.19 and decrease to $2491.31 when adjustments are made for schooling, experience (Age minus Education minus Sex), and hours worked per year. This decrease in the male-female wage differential, implies that by adjusting for human capital variables only 20% of the wage gap is explained. Similarly adjusting by occupation, industry, region, size of place and nativity yield equally poor explanatory power.

At least two reasons exist for such a poor performance of these human capital variables. First, experience measured as age minus education minus sex grossly overstates female experience, and second as illustrated in Section 1 the quantity of human capital investment per working year differs by sex according to expectations of life cycle labor force commitment. For this reason, namely to overcome these biases, independent measures of human capital were developed in the last section. These measures will now be employed in similar regression equations to ascertain their explanatory power in the determination of male-female wage differentials.

Since as is specified in objective Equation (7.1a), earnings at any given age are related to total human capital stock, the estimates of net investment per period (including the value of education) are summed to obtain the appropriate stock variable. Thus, expected capital stock at age t can be specified as:

$$K(t; S, M, E) = \sum_{i=1}^{t} I(t; S, M, E) \qquad (7.11)$$

where

$$I(t; S, M, E) = g[\lambda(t; S, M, E), MC] \qquad (7.12)$$
$$= f[N(1; S, M, E), N(2; S, M, E) \ldots N(T; S, M, E)]$$
$$= f[\underline{N}(S, M, E)]$$

Table 7-1

Earnings Equations for Married and Unmarried Males and Females (t-Values in Parentheses) N = 34,637

	[1]		[2]		[3]		[4]		[5]	
	Coef	t-value	Coef	t-value	Coef	t-value	Coef	t-value	Coef	t-value
Constant	144.70	8.34	5893.92	242.76	-3941.06	-39.98	2284.50	18.79	-1107.34	-8.59
Education					456.63	71.71				
Experience					198.15	39.37				
Experience²					-2.89	-27.80				
Hrs. worked/yr.					1.01	38.32	1.18	43.99	1.05	40.83
Region							696.52	16.93	593.52	15.14
Size							231.71	4.75	278.72	6.00
Nativity							24.02	0.32	-40.03	-0.56
Professional							1029.87	10.99	243.36	2.70
Farm							-2961.67	-11.72	-2441.36	-10.14
Managerial							1787.24	21.64	1497.34	19.00
Clerical							-918.97	-11.22	-713.26	-9.14
Craft							-976.64	-11.86	-458.60	-5.81
Operative							-1700.71	-21.63	-941.27	-12.39
Household							-1429.67	-5.84	-779.47	-3.34
Service							-1467.64	-13.90	-860.27	-8.52
Farm laborer							-2919.58	-10.33	-2126.49	-7.94
Laborer							-2121.57	-18.66	-1228.08	-11.24
Occup. N.R.							-901.40	-5.59	-510.09	-3.32
Agriculture							636.87	2.72	582.85	2.61
Mining							1750.01	10.92	1575.14	10.32
Construction							1495.07	16.75	1409.68	16.58
Manufac. durable							1650.58	25.16	1420.84	22.71
Manufac. non-durable							1572.81	23.18	1286.21	19.86
Public utility							1602.49	20.33	1381.40	18.38
Wholesale							1261.44	13.26	964.49	10.63

Variable	(1)		(2)		(3)		(4)		(5)	
Finance							1715.65	19.11	1236.12	14.39
Business service							765.16	6.82	570.03	5.33
Personal service							503.99	4.19	315.17	2.75
Entertainment/recreation							737.27	3.63	716.35	3.70
Professional services							1344.58	14.86	692.18	7.97
Industry N.R.							1461.39	8.59	1220.48	7.35
Sex	-3040.19	-65.95	-2491.31	-57.76			-2466.33	-43.88	-232.61	-3.56
Martial status							-1796.48	-30.87	-315.97	-3.21
Marital status × sex							1710.80	17.72	-971.03	-9.49
Exp. capital	0.1036	120.30							0.07	0.40
R^2	0.30		0.11		0.31		0.34		0.40	

Source: 1960 U.S. Census of Population and Housing (1/1000 sample)

Population: white married-once-spouse-present and single-never-been-married males and females at work and not employed by the government.

Dependent variable is earnings.

Variable Definitions:

constant

education ≡ years of schooling

experience ≡ age minus education minus six

experience² ≡ experience squared

hrs. worked/yr. ≡ hours worked per year measured as the product of hours worked in survey week and the number of weeks worked during the survey year (1959)

region ≡ dummy variable [1 = non-south]

size ≡ dummy variable [1 = size greater than 250,000]

nativity ≡ dummy variable [1 = native born]

sex ≡ dummy variable [1 = female]

marital status ≡ dummy variable [1 = married-once spouse present]

marital status × sex ≡ interaction of marital status and sex

exp. cap. ≡ expected capital stock accumulation as discussed in body of paper

Note that for the occupational and industrial dummy variables the missing category for occupations is sales; workers; for industry the missing category is retail sales.

as defined in Section 2. Earnings at each experience level are then linearly related to $K(t; S, M, E)$—the factor of proportionality being the average rate of return to human capital investment. Since expected capital stock is functionally related to the vector of group LFP rates $[\underline{N}(S, M, E)]$, expectations may differ across individuals within the same sex-age-marital status-education group. To account for these individual deviations from the norm the vector $\underline{V}$ of individual, standardization variables is added. Thus in Equation (7.13),

$$Y = a + bK + \underline{c}\underline{V} + d \left\{ \frac{SEX}{MS} \right\} + \epsilon \qquad (7.13)$$

the b coefficient can be interpreted as the rate of return of net capital, and the $\underline{c}$ coefficient as a measure of individual deviations from expectations. Again, as in Equations (7.9) and (7.10) the coefficient d would represent the male-female or married-single wage differential adjusted by K and $\underline{V}$. Note that in Equation (7.13) adjustments are not made for schooling and experience. These variables are not included because they already are implicitly used in the computation of K [Equations (7.11) and (7.12)].

Examining Table 7-1 reveals that when measuring human capital as we have by accounting for expected life cycle labor force participation paths, most of the wage differential by sex and marital status is explained. The male-female earnings gap is reduced from over $3000 to about $230, and although the single male-female wage is increased,[21] the marital status earnings gap is reduced from $1796 to $315.

Taken at face value, these results have important implications with respect to the hypotheses generated in Section 1. The findings are consistent with the fact that the bulk of wage differentials can be explained by differences in human capital stock. However, to present further evidence regarding the importance of life cycle labor force participation patterns, we apply this technique to each of the four groups separately. These results, a summary of which is presented in Tables 7-2, 7-3, and 7-4, again indicate that the wage gap for each group (except perhaps the wage gap between single males and single females) can be explained by expected differences in human capital accumulation. Rather than belabor the point let us just note that, in the case of married males and females, over 90% of the gap is explained. For the cases in which the data are stratified by marital status, differences in the single-married human capital investment paths explain between 75 and 83 percent of the wage gap. For single males and single females (Table 7-3) differences in human capital accumulation paths had little explanatory power. Perhaps this existing $486 differential may better approximate a measure of market discrimination against women.

Summary and Conclusions

In this paper it was hypothesized that there exists a relation between one's life cycle labor force participation, post-school investment, and wage rate. This

Table 7-2
Earnings Equations for Married Males and Females

	[1] Coef	[1] t-value	[2] Coef	[2] t-value	[3] Coef	[3] t-value	[4] Coef	[4] t-value	[5]a Coef	[5]a t-value	[6]a Coef	[6]a t-value
Constant	406	8.5	662.9	9.4	-578.8	-4.5	-3620.5	-25.95	-1988.15	-12.42	1577.67	10.28
Education					65.28	7.0	476.47	60.84				
Experience					29.78	4.2	175.19	23.88				
Experience^2					-.26	-1.93	2.80	-21.42				
Hrs. worked/yr.							0.89	27.66	1.027	32.57	1.15	36.64
Region									637.70	14.17	751.30	15.90
Size									214.16	3.78	173.85	2.92
Nativity									22.24	0.27	76.92	0.89
Sex			-324.7	-5.07			-3032.0	-54.87	-80.30	-1.07	-2533.35	-40.36
Yrs. married							23.57	5.76	25.73	11.90	28.89	12.71
NCH 6									87.58	3.47	-3.39	-.13
NCH < 6-11									70.34	2.89	242.50	9.56
NCH 12-17									31.59	1.14	206.49	7.15
NCH >18									-26.47	-.42	-21.58	-.33
Exp. capital	0.106	108.5	0.102	80.7	0.1004	78.92			0.076	54.30		
$\bar{R}^2$	0.30		0.30		0.30		0.29		0.38		0.32	

Dependent variable: earnings–2nd value in column is t-statistic. Population: white married-once-spouse-present males and females not employed by the government. No. obs. = 28,065; see Table 7-1 for variables definitions.

Additional variables are as follows:
Yrs. married ≡ number of years since marriage
NCH < 6 ≡ number of children less than six years
NCH 6-11 ≡ number of children between 6 and 11 years of age
NCH 12-17 ≡ number of children between 12 and 17 years of age
NCH > 18 ≡ the existence of children over 18 in the household

aAdjustment made for occupation and industry.

Table 7-3
Earnings Equations for Single Males and Females Using Modified Measure of Expected Human Capital Stock

	[1]		[2]		[3]		[4][a]		[5][a]	
	Coef	t-value	Coef	t-value	Coef	t-value	Coef	t-value	Coef	t-value
Constant	986.27	13.22	1127.02	14.73	-2193.9	-17.99	-919.13	-8.00	208.35	1.15
Education					253.73	25.75				
Experience					139.23	19.00				
Experience²					-2.23	-13.28				
Hrs. worked/yr.					0.96	25.87	1.16	33.99	1.29	36.46
Region							340.99	5.12	375.85	5.48
Size							549.33	9.43	598.46	9.14
Sex			-473.80	-7.67	-671.17	-11.90	-486.41	-7.70	-507.71	-7.80
Exp. capital	0.0645	30.41	0.0659	30.77			0.0444	20.22		
R²	0.12		0.13		0.29		0.36		0.32	

See Tables 7-1 and 7-2 for variable definitions.
Population: Single (never-been married, white, nongovernmental) males and females
Dependent Variable: Earnings (wage, salary, and self-employment income)
Exp. Capital is defined to account for the probability of becoming married.
Second value in each column is the t-statistic; no. observations: 6572.
[a]Adjusted by occupation, industry, and nativity.

Table 7-4
Earnings Equations Stratified by Sex

			Males			
Constant	3467.39	18.56	386.55	2.09	156.47	0.77
Mar Stat	3001.82	14.71			534.65	2.64
Exp Cap			0.1102	32.51	0.1059	28.20
R^2	0.0640		0.2503		0.2520	
No. Obs.	3167		3167		3167	
			Females			
Constant	1796.61	23.38	1956.56	16.18	3142.69	50.31
Mar Stat	−624.73	−8.03			−148.26	−1.71
Exp Cap			0.0388	13.92	0.0362	11.35
R^2	0.0627		0.0762		0.0774	
No. Obs.	2350		2350		2350	

Key
Dependent Variable: Earnings (wage, salary, and self-employment income)
Mar Stat: dummy variable (1 ≡ married, 0 ≡ single)
Exp Cap ≡ expected capital stock
Second value in each column is *t*-statistic.

relationship derived theoretically by maximizing expected earnings over the life cycle was implemented empirically by determining the extent to which differing male-female (married-single) life cycle labor force participation explains male-female (married-single) wage differentials. Since these measures were obtained by assuming the same costs of investment for all groups, the differences in human capital investments can be attributed to differences in life cycle labor force participation. When these derived rates of investment were used in regressions on wages, much of the original intergroup wage differentials were explained. This result is consistent with the hypothesis that differences in wages can largely be attributable to differences in expected labor force participation over the entire life cycle.

In existing studies of intergroup wage differentials these differing expectations have been largely ignored. For example, to explain the male-female wage gap it is not sufficient to account only for quantity differences in labor force experience. Instead, quality defined to be the difference in the rate of *PSI* even while at work is important. Therefore empirical studies should account for the interaction of differing experience patterns and their associated rates of *PSI*. The methods devised in this paper account for such interactions.

Although the estimation procedures of capital stock are by no means beyond reproach because of the problems discussed throughout this paper, nevertheless the hypotheses generated seem to yield suggestive results such that refinements should be carried out to further substantiate the role of expected life cycle labor force participation behavior in the determination of both male-female and married-single wage differentials.

Table 7-5

Computed Gross and Net Investment at Five-Year Intervals by Education, Sex, and Marital Status (in dollars)

Education	Age	Expected Gross Investment				Expected Net Investment			
		Male		Female		Male		Female	
		Single	Married	Single	Married	Single	Married	Single	Married
8 or less	15	630	1533	180	243	217	1120	−232	−169
	20	1010	1691	306	306	548	1141	−85	−88
	25	824	1756	435	306	309	1073	49	−78
	30	824	1744	500	306	279	940	111	−69
	35	630	1651	435	306	69	743	35	−63
	40	630	1479	500	306	60	494	95	−55
	45	565	1239	500	243	−11	209	84	−110
	50	500	949	370	119	−74	−91	−48	−217
	55	370	630	243	58	−190	−385	−163	−252
	60	180	306	119	0	−350	−650	−260	−280
	65	0	0	0	0	−482	−868	−344	−248
9-12	20	2035	2976	966	577	948	1860	−76	−454
	25	2035	3272	1505	577	781	1813	422	−376
	30	1905	3391	2284	577	540	1609	1069	−311
	35	1505	3301	2161	704	70	1247	778	−149
	40	1369	3001	2161	704	−71	751	619	−123
	45	1234	2518	1773	577	−189	171	157	−220
	50	1099	1905	1369	454	−277	−428	−264	−296
	55	704	1234	834	218	−600	−973	−715	−460
	60	334	577	334	0	−849	−1419	−1060	−591
	65	0	0	0	0	−1010	−1711	−1188	−490
13-15	25	2654	4153	2056	679	1249	2556	809	−481
	30	2654	4528	2056	865	1031	2451	529	−210
	35	2457	4595	3706	1057	681	2077	1921	17
	40	2258	4315	2654	1057	384	1447	543	14
	45	1854	3706	3033	1057	−57	624	760	11
	50	1451	2846	2056	679	−421	−285	−231	−333
	55	1252	1854	865	499	−538	−1155	−1295	−441
	60	679	865	679	158	−988	−1867	−1260	−673
	65	0	0	0	0	−1443	−2339	−1649	−698
16	25	5190	6418	4825	1159	2646	3792	2542	−958
	30	5190	7531	5190	1159	1950	3773	2104	−706
	35	4452	8047	7045	1490	740	3223	3210	−244
	40	3311	7800	5881	1835	−553	2138	1537	144
	45	4074	5788	7276	1835	207	661	2360	106
	50	3692	5190	5881	1490	−229	−941	623	−246
	55	2192	3311	3311	843	−1460	−2365	−1817	−773
	60	843	1490	1490	262	−2305	−3355	−2992	−1100
	65	0	0	0	0	−2476	−3787	−3569	−1058

Table 7-5 (cont.)

| Education | Age | Expected Gross Investment | | | | Expected Net Investment | | | |
| | | Male | | Female | | Male | | Female | |
		Single	Married	Single	Married	Single	Married	Single	Married
Greater	25	4883	5634	5263	2478	2999	3750	3378	594
than 16	30	5263	7111	7139	2879	2716	4241	4198	844
	35	5628	7896	6883	3284	2483	4088	3076	1025
	40	5263	7933	7896	3690	1653	3145	3313	1130
	45	4094	7139	6608	3284	208	1716	1869	512
	50	4094	5628	5263	2085	180	−43	−106	−724
	55	2085	3690	2879	970	−1740	−1796	−2198	−1558
	60	1700	1700	970	304	−1774	−3204	−3425	−1803
	65	0	0	0	0	−2904	−4034	−3578	−1656

Notes

1. Such an objective function is not the most general. However, as was pointed out by a reviewer of this paper, if the individual's utility function in each period is a monotonic transformation of earnings, and the market and subjective discount rates are equal, then both the more general model of utility maximization and the simplified model of maximization of discounted lifetime earnings yield the same results.

2. For discussion of the cases for which $b_1 \neq b_2$ see Becker [3], Ben-Porath [4, 5] and Ghez [10].

3. The assumption that $\delta = 0$ is relaxed in the empirical implementation of the model. It is used here to simplify the notation.

4. It is beyond the scope of this paper to postulate reasons for life cycle differences in labor force participation across groups. Rather, our point of view is to ascertain what if any effect such differences in labor force participation have on one's human capital investment stream.

5. The Hamiltonian is defined on the basis of assuming that no corner solutions are binding. An interior solution is guaranteed because H is concave in N_t and s_t for a given K and t. See [1, Proposition 5, lecture 1].

6. This result holds because:

$$
\begin{aligned}
\dot{\Psi} &= \lambda r e^{rt} + \dot{\lambda} e^{rt} \\
&= N_t e^{rt} \left[r \int_t^T w_0 e^{-r\tau} d\tau - w_0 e^{-rt} \right] \\
&= N_t e^{rt} \left[-w_0 e^{rT} + w_0 e^{-rt} - w_0 e^{-rt} \right] \\
&= -w_0 N_t e^{r(t-T)} \leqslant 0.
\end{aligned}
\tag{7.6}
$$

7. Because $(b_1 - 1) \leqslant 0$ and $\dot{\Psi} \leqslant 0$

$$\frac{\partial s_t}{\partial t} = \frac{\partial}{\partial t} \left[\frac{b_0 b_1}{w_0} \Psi K^{b_1 - 1} \right]^{1 - (1 - b_1)}$$

$$= \left[\frac{b_1}{(1 - b_1)} \right] \left[\frac{b_0 b_1}{w_0} \right]^{1 - (1 - b_1)} [\Psi K_t^{b_1} - 1]^{b_1 - (1 - b_1)}$$

$$= [(b_1 - 1) \Psi \dot{K} + K_t^{b_1 - 1} \dot{\Psi}] \leqslant 0.$$

8. This result can be derived from Equation (7.6):

$$\dot{\Psi} = \lambda r e^{rt} + \dot{\lambda} e^{rt}$$

$$= r e^{rt} \int_0^T w_0 N(\tau) e^{-r\tau} d\tau - w_0 N(t) e^{-rt} e^{rt}.$$

Adding and subtracting

$$w_0 e^{rt} \int_t^T N(\tau) e^{-r\tau} d\tau,$$

we obtain

$$\dot{\Psi} = w_0 e^{rt} \int_t^T N(\tau) e^{-r\tau} - w_0 N(t) e^{-rt} e^{rt}$$

$$+ r e^{rt} \int_t^T w_0 N(\tau) e^{-r\tau} d\tau - w_0 e^{rt} \int_t^T N(\tau) e^{-r\tau} d\tau,$$

which upon simplification yields Equation (7.7)

9. For the special case when *LFP* is constant

$$N(\tau) = N(t) \text{ for all } t \leqslant \tau \leqslant T$$

then the second term becomes zero and (7.7) reduces to (7.6).

10. Such a conclusion can be derived by attaching probabilities on the degree of per period labor force participation $[N(t)]$.

11. The exact groups on which we concentrate are: (1) married-once-spouse-present males compared to married-once-spouse-present females, (2) single-never-been married males compared to single-never-been married females,

(3) married-once-spouse-present males compared to married-once-spouse-present females, and (4) single-never-been-married males compared to single-never-been married females.

12. According to the model presented, differences in the wage rate (w_0) per unit of embodied human capital would not affect the amount or rate of *PSI* because b_3 of Equation (7.1b) is assumed equal to zero. Such an assumption is made so as to isolate the implicit discrimination effect of differing wages for the same stock of human capital.

13. *MC* is invariant over the life cycle because the specification of the production of human capital assumes $b_1 = b_2$ in Equation (7.1b).

14. We specify "gross" investment because in the process of simplifying the notation of the theoretical model, the assumption $\delta = 0$, (Equation (7.1b) was made. If, as is more realistic, $\delta \neq 0$, depreciation must be subtracted out to obtain "net" or "observed" investment. In the empirical computation of investment depreciation of existing capital stock was computed, and subtracted from gross investment.

15. A more detailed explanation of the estimation method as well as sets of tables containing the precise data are available upon request to the interested reader.

16. If *MC* is identical across individuals of given levels of education regardless of sex and marital status, then the solution of

$$\lambda(t; 1, 1, E) = I(t; 1, 1, E) \qquad \text{for } E = 1, 2, \ldots, 5 \text{ representing}$$
$$8, 12, 14, 16 \text{ and } 18 \text{ years}$$
$$\text{of schooling}$$

yields *MC*, such that

$$MC(S, M, E) = MC(E) \qquad \text{for } S = \text{male (1), female (2)}$$
$$M = \text{Married (1), single (2)}$$
$$E = 1, \ldots, 5.$$

17. Married male investment for each level of education can be computed from age-earnings profiles fit according to the following specification:

$$LnY_t = LnE_0 + r \int_0^t S(\tau)d\tau + \epsilon$$

where

$Y_t \equiv$ earnings at period t

$E_0 \equiv$ initial earnings capacity

$r \equiv$ rate of return to *PSI*

$s(t) \equiv$ net time equivalent *PSI* in year t specified as a linear function of experience in the labor force (t).

Thus net *PSI* in time equivalent terms (S_t) can be computed as

$$S_t = \frac{1}{r} \frac{\partial LnY_t}{\partial_t} = \frac{1}{r} (\alpha_0 - \beta t).$$

Net *PSI* in dollar terms would be:

$$I_N = \frac{1}{r} \frac{\partial Y_t}{\partial_t} = S_t Y_t = (\alpha_0 - \beta t) Y_t$$

$$= (\alpha_0 - \beta t) \exp \left[LnE_0 + \alpha_0 t - \frac{1}{2} \beta t^2 \right].$$

In principle net investment of the other groups can also be determined by such methods. However, since only cross sectional data is available, biases of measurement exist because of these groups' labor force intermittency. Further, we wish to obtain independent measures of the *PSI* of these groups so as to enable their use in Section 3 as a determinant of own wage rate.

18. Marginal revenue $\lambda(S, M, E)$ is computed for all groups using a discrete form of (7.1″). Cross Sectional Data on labor force participation by age and education were computed from the *1960 U.S. Census of Population and Housing*, (1/1000) sample. The *LFP* rates of single females used in Table 7-3 were adjusted by the probability of becoming married. Rates of discount were assumed equal to the rate of return from education for each sex—marital status category.

19. No doubt more explicit forms of market discrimination would probably strengthen these differences. However, in our model direct market discrimination in terms of differing wages across groups need not imply differing investment paths. Because we assumed $b_3 = 0$ in Equation (7.1b), differing wages (w_0) across groups would shift *MC* and λ in the same proportion, causing no differences in time allocated to investment. On the other hand, if in reality $b_3 \neq 0$, differing wages w_0 would imply differing investments.

20. The function g is usually taken as exponential. However, because the estimates of expected capital stock to be used in Equation (7.13) are dollar estimates and not time equivalent measures as are S and E, a linear functional form is used.

21. In the table the single male-female wage gap may be misleading because

the single *LFP* rates were not adjusted by the probability of marriage. This problem is alleviated in the remainder of the tables.

Bibliography

[1] Arrow, Kenneth, "Applications of Control Theory to Economic Growth," *Mathematics of Decision Sciences, Part 2* (Providence, Rhode Island: 1968).

[2] Becker, Gary S., *Human Capital; A Theoretical and Empirical Analysis, with Special Reference to Education*, National Bureau of Economic Research (New York: Columbia University Press, 1964).

[3] _____ , "Human Capital and the Personal Distribution of Income," W.S. Waytinsky Lecture No. 1 (Department of Economics, Institute of Public Administration, The University of Michigan, 1967).

[4] Ben-Porath, Yoram, "The Production of Human Capital and the Life Cycle of Earnings," *Journal of Political Economy*, LXXV (August 1967), 352-365.

[5] _____ , "The Production of Human Capital Over Time," in W. Lee Hansen, ed., *Education, Income, and Human Capital* (New York: Columbia University Press, 1970), 129-147.

[6] Bowen, William, and T. Aldrich Finegan, *The Economics of Labor Force Participation* (Princeton: Princeton University Press, 1969).

[7] Cain, Glen G., *Married Women in the Labor Force; An Economic Analysis* (Chicago and London: The University of Chicago Press, 1966).

[8] Chiswick, Barry, "An Inter-regional Analysis of Schooling and the Skewness of Income," in Lee Hansen, ed., *Education, Income and Human Capital* (New York: National Bureau of Economic Research, 1970).

[9] Fuchs, Victor, "Male-Female Differentials in Hourly Earnings," *Monthly Labor Review*, XCIV (May 1971) 9-15.

[10] Ghez, Gilbert, "A Note on the Earnings Function when Human Capital is Biased Towards Earnings" (University of Chicago, Mimeographed, 1973).

[11] Haley, William J., "Human Capital: The Choice Between Investment and Income," *American Economic Review* LXIII (December 1973), 929-944.

[12] Hause, John, "Earnings Profile: Ability and Schooling," *Journal of Political Economy*, LXXX (May/June, 1972), S108-138.

[13] Johnson, George, and Frank Stafford, "The Earnings and Promotion of Women Faculty," *American Economic Review*, forthcoming.

[14] Johnson, Thomas, "Returns from Investment-Human Capital," *American Economic Review*, LX (September 1970), 546-560.

[15] Leibowitz, Arlene, "Education and Home Production," American Economic Association *Papers and Proceedings of the 86th Annual Meeting*, LXIV (May 1974), 243-250.

[16] Malkiel, Burton, and Judith Malkiel, "Male-Female Pay Differences in Professional Employment," *American Economic Review*, LXIII (September 1973), 693-705.

[17] Mincer, Jacob, "Investment in Human Capital and Personal Income Distribution," *Journal of Political Economy*, LXVI (August 1958), 281-302.

[18] _____, "On-the-Job Training: Costs, Returns, and Some Implications," *Journal of Political Economy*, LXX (October 1962, Supplement), 50-79.

[19] _____, "The Distribution of Labor Incomes: A Survey with Special Reference to the Human Capital Approach," *Journal of Economic Literature*, VIII (March 1970) 1-26.

[20] _____, *Schooling, Experience, and Earnings* (New York: Columbia University Press for the National Bureau of Economic Research, 1974).

[21] _____ and Solomon Polachek, "Family Investment in Human Capital: Earnings of Women," *Journal of Political Economy*, LXXXII (March/April 1974), S76-S108.

[22] Oaxaca, Ronald, "Male-Female Wage Differentials in Urban Labor Markets," *International Economic Review*, XIV (October 1973), 693-709.

[23] Polachek, Solomon William, "Work Experience and the Difference Between Male and Female Wages," unpublished Ph.D. dissertation, Columbia University (1973).

[24] Rahm, Carl M., "Human Capital and the Occupational Wage Structure," unpublished Ph.D. dissertation, Columbia University (1971).

[25] Sheshinski, Eytan, "On the Individual's Lifetime Allocation Between Education and Work," *Metroeconomica*, XX (January, 1968), 42-49.

[26] Suter, L., and H. Miller, "Components of Income Differences Between Men and Career Women," (Paper presented at the American Sociological Association Meetings, Colorado, September 1971).

[27] Swift, William, and Burton Weisbrod, "On the Monetary Value of Education's Intergenerational Effects," *Journal of Political Economy*, LXXIII (December 1965), 643-649.

[28] Taubman, Paul, and Terrence Wales, "Mental Ability and Higher Educational Attainment in the 20th Century," National Bureau of Research, Occasional Paper 118, 1972.

[29] Weiss, Yoram, "Ability and the Investment in Schooling: A Theoretical Note on J. Mincer's Distribution of Labor Income," *Journal of Economic Literature*, IX (June 1971), 459-461.

[30] Welch, Finis, "Black-White Differences in Returns to Schooling," *American Economic Review*, LXIII (December 1973), 893-907.

Comments

Ronald L. Oaxaca

In "Differences in Expected Post-School Investment as a Determinant of Market Wage Differentials," Solomon Polachek attempts to redress a methodological imbalance in the economics literature on discrimination and wage differentials— namely, the total concentration on the demand side rather than the supply side of labor. To do this, he adopts a human capital production function approach. In a departure from previous studies of post-schooling investment, Polachek examines the implications for age earnings profiles when labor force participation over the life cycle is expected to be intermittent. When he abandons the assumption that labor force participation is nonincreasing over the life cycle, he shows that post-schooling investment does not necessarily decline monotonically with age.

Under Polachek's assumptions, the services of the human capital stock serve as a single input in the formation of additional human capital (that is, time does not enter as a separate input). This implies that the long marginal cost curve does not shift over the life cycle as changes in capital stock occur. Another assumption made is that individuals with the same level of schooling face identical marginal cost curves. Further, Polachek assumes that post-schooling investments do not require market inputs (that is, all costs consist of foregone earnings). In view of the fact that on-the-job training (OJT) is the major component of post-schooling investment, this assumption is quite reasonable. This assumption also implies that changes in the market rental value of human capital would not lead to changes in post-schooling investment, other things being equal. In particular, this assumption disposes of the problem of different market rental values for the services of human capital leading to differential investments between males and females; marginal revenue and marginal cost curves are merely shifted by offsetting amounts. Any observed differences in investment among individuals with the same level of schooling would have to be the result of differences in marginal revenues which vary with labor force participation, which, in turn, varies by age, sex, and marital status.

Polachek's hypothesis is that expected differences in labor force attachment lead to male-female and married-single differences in post-schooling investments which, in turn, lead to wage differentials. As Polachek points out, studies that follow the conventional approach of controlling for characteristics such as schooling, experience, marital status, region, occupation, and industry can account for only 50 percent to 54 percent of the male-female wage differential. By calculating an expected capital stock variable and entering it in an earnings regression, Polachek finds that 90 percent of the male-female earnings differentials can be explained away. His implied policy recommendation for narrowing

149

the earnings differential is that women should be encouraged to form stronger attachments to the labor force.

The increasing labor force participation of females combined with the declining labor force participation of males, has made for dramatic changes in relative labor force attachments. Yet there has been no dramatic narrowing of male-female earnings differentials among year-round, full-time workers. Over the period from 1955 to 1971 the labor force participation rate increased about 8 percentage points for females and decreased by 6 percentage points for males. Thus, the male-female difference in labor force participation rates narrowed by 14 percentage points. There has been a narrowing of male-female earnings differentials among nonwhites, but the differential among whites actually increased over the period, even after adjustments for changes in relative labor quality. Around 1966, the widening of the sex earnings differential among whites ceased and the differential began to narrow somewhat; however, the period ended with the differential remaining much higher than it was in 1955.

If Polachek's approach is applied to racial earnings differentials, race differences in expected human investment would undoubtedly explain away much of the differential. Yet, labor force participation rates do not differ all that much between white and nonwhite males. Because the labor force participation rates of nonwhite males have decreased more rapidly than that for white males over the period from 1955 to 1971, a gap of 5 percentage points existed at the end of the period. Nonwhites do experience more unemployment and, hence, less exposure to OJT, but it is hardly likely that this is voluntary in the sense of their desiring to substitute leisure for income. Nonwhite females have traditionally participated in the labor force to a greater extent than white females, yet an earnings disparity in favor of white females has long existed. Although this disparity has been diminishing in recent years, it has done so over a period in which white females have narrowed the gap between their labor force participation and that of nonwhite females. From the standpoint of Polachek's policy recommendation, these are unusual circumstances in which to find nonwhite females gaining relative to white females.

How can the above facts be reconciled with Polachek's approach? I certainly do not dispute the suggestion that there are race and sex differences in OJT and that these differences result in race and sex earnings differentials. The interesting question is why such differences in OJT exist. For example, if males and females are viewed as essentially noncompeting groups, it is not hard to imagine that occupational barriers deny women access to OJT. Consequently, women would find it virtually impossible to match male investment even if they had identical commitments to the length of stay in the labor force over the life cycle. The anticipation of discrimination in acquiring OJT would be reason enough to produce lower wages to compensate the employer for foregone output during the investment acquisition stage. Women seem to be caught short on two counts—they receive the low wages but receive no significant OJT comparable to that received by males in male-dominated jobs. The narrowing of the earnings differential between white and nonwhite females can be explained as the result of a trend in which nonwhite females are experiencing a dropping of barriers to white female jobs at a rate faster than white females are experiencing a dropping of barriers to white male jobs.

Although Polachek has not explicitly stated that he regards differences in the post-schooling investment among males and females as mainly voluntary in the absence of discrimination, his policy recommendation would not make much sense unless this were assumed. To exhort women to increase their labor force participation as a means of reducing the sex earnings differentials would generate false hopes if in fact there are widespread entry barriers to jobs offering OJT opportunities.

Turning to more technical matters, the use of cross-section data to approximate time-series relationships involves problems well known to economists. Significant changes in the labor force participation rates of various age, sex, and marital status groups cannot be captured by cross-section data. The estimated parameters of a cross-section post-schooling investment model merely reflect the state of affairs that would exist in a stationary economy.

Polachek's procedure for estimating net post-schooling investments is based on a relationship between gross earnings (earnings capacity) and experience. Unfortunately, we do not observe gross earnings. Under Polachek's assumptions, observed earnings are equivalent to net earnings (that is, earnings net of opportunity costs). The use of observed earnings to infer changes in earnings capacity leads to estimation bias. In other words, net earnings data are used to estimate a gross earnings relationship, and this affects the estimates of net investment.

In conclusion, this paper opens up a fruitful line of inquiry into wage differentials and is suggestive of the direction new research should take. The empirical results offer striking confirmation of the role differential post-schooling investment plays in determining wage differentials. Polachek has been innovative in his development and testing of a model of human capital formation. However, why males and females have radically different expectations about labor force attachment is a question left unresolved. Presently it is not known to what extent preferences are identical, but preferences differ. The papers in this volume by Patricia Gurin and Judith Long Laws suggest that in these matters the psychologist's trail begins where that of the economist leaves off.

8 A Dynamic Theory of Racial Income Differences

Glenn C. Loury

Introduction

The conventional wisdom regarding equal opportunity policy is that the elimination of racial discrimination will result in the eventual elimination of racial economic inequality. This view derives from traditional economic analyses of labor markets and racial income differences. The thesis of this paper is that traditional theory does not adequately reflect the impact of an individual's family and community background on his or her acquisition of labor market skills. Racial income differences will persist to the extent that the low level of education and earnings of blacks in today's labor market inhibit their children's ability to convert natural abilities into skills valued by employers.

The second section of this paper briefly examines the traditional economic analysis of labor markets and racial income differences. In the third section, the traditional theory is extended through analytical recognition of the effects of an individual's family and community background. This approach differs from the standard one in its treatment of the process by which workers acquire skills in that it considers the effect of parental economic status on a child's opportunity to acquire marketable skills as an intergenerational external economy.[1] The fourth section demonstrates that this classical market failure not only vitiates the efficiency properties of equilibrium in a competitive labor market, but may also render equal opportunity policy an ineffective tool for assuring equality in the long run. The final section assesses the implications of this analysis for public policy in regard to racial income differentials.

Conventional Theory and Its Problems

Conventional economic analysis has attempted to explain black-white income disparities by appealing to supply and demand factors. Arguments focusing on the supply side of the labor market center on the characteristics of black workers (that is, poor quality and limited quantity of education and work experience) which, on the average, are below those of white workers. Thus, even in the absence of discrimination, black earnings would be lower as a result of a lower investment in human capital. These factors, however, are not sufficient to account for the entire differential. When the quality and quantity of human capital are controlled, blacks still earn considerably less than whites.[2] To explain

153

this differential, economists have hypothesized that white employers or workers may harbor a distaste for association with blacks. The market implications of these tastes can be differential returns to otherwise identical black and white workers.[3] Racial differences in incomes may thus be attributed to differences in the supply of market-valued characteristics (human capital) or to differences in the demand for workers due to a "taste for discrimination" against blacks.

Traditional economics suggests that two approaches can be taken to attack racial income differences. The first is to close the earnings gap by prohibiting the expression of discriminatory tastes, or at least, to neutralize the deleterious effects of discriminatory preferences. The second looks to the racial differences in the acquisition of market-valued characteristics. If these differences can be narrowed,[4] further progress would be made toward the elimination of income disparity.

Important steps in both of these directions have been taken in recent years. Particularly noteworthy are the Supreme Court's interpretation of the Fourteenth Amendment's "equal protection" clause and the enactment of the Civil Rights Act of 1964.[5] Together, these judicial and legislative actions embody the view that the expression of discriminatory preferences, whether private or public, cannot be permitted if the consequence is to limit the educational or employment opportunity of minorities.

Equal opportunity laws attempt to assure each individual the opportunity to develop his or her abilities to the fullest. If effectively enforced, equal opportunity would eliminate the expression of discriminatory preferences as a factor in generating racial income differences. Assuming that the distribution of ability among blacks and whites is the same, racial differences in the supply of market-valued characteristics would be expected to diminish over time. The traditional analysis suggests that, once established, equal opportunity would lead to the eventual elimination of racial income differences. This notion has gained widespread acceptance in the social sciences community.[6]

The complex problem of differences in the acquisition of market-valued characteristics, however, is not recognized in the traditional analysis. While economists have analyzed the impact of investment in human capital on earnings, the socioeconomic process underlying its acquisition has generally been ignored.[7] Understanding this process is fundamental to understanding the persistence of racial inequality. As long as the social class and racial background of an individual influence the process by which he or she acquires marketable skills, group differences in the supply of market-valued characteristics will tend to persist. These socioeconomic effects are likely to be evident even in the presence of equal opportunity. Thus, the ability of the equal opportunity laws to guarantee (eventual) racial economic justice must be questioned.

The growing sociological literature on occupational mobility sheds some light on this issue.[8] Of particular interest is the development of recursive, life-cycle models of individual achievement. These models enable the analyst to focus successively on (1) the impact of family background variables (usually father's occupation and education) on educational achievement; (2) the effect of background and education on occupation; and (3) the combined effect of background, education, and occupation on income.[9] Empirical tests have revealed several important relationships. They have shown that family background has a significant direct effect on the educational and occupational achievement of both blacks and whites. Yet, the effect of a father's occupation and educational attainment on his children's occupation and earnings differs appreciably between blacks and whites.[10] Blacks suffer a relative disadvantage in occupational achievement even where their social background is favorable. Moreover, they tend to earn less than whites in the same occupations.[11]

Fully effective enforcement of equal opportunity laws would lead to a world in which occupational achievement is determined solely by the ability of the worker. Similarly, earning differentials between equally well-educated blacks and whites in the same occupation would be eliminated. However, the influence of lower educational and occupational achievement of black parents on the opportunities of black children, relative to those of white children, implies a more subtle racial bias than that which equal opportunity laws are intended to eradicate.

In a racially stratified society where individuals place themselves in social groups along racial lines, the intergenerational influences for families of different racial groups can be expected to differ. However, racial differences of this sort are not recognized in the traditional economic explanation of discrimination on the basis of individual "tastes for discrimination."[12]

The conventional analytical framework used to study racial income differences is thus inadequate for forecasting the long-term consequences of particular policy alternatives. First, the traditional theory does not take into account the intertemporal consequences of racial discrimination which stem from the effect of parental economic status on opportunities available to offspring. Second, the theory is an individualistic one, ignoring group processes, that is, it conceives of discrimination as an act perpetrated by one individual against another. As such, the traditional theory views race relations in individual terms rather than social group interactions.

There are many reasons why a child's opportunities to acquire skills vary with the economic success of his or her parents. For example, the quality of schooling any child receives varies considerably across communities and tends to be higher in the suburbs than in the central city.[13] Where there is housing segregation based on income, and the quality of neighborhood schools shows a positive correlation with the community's wealth,[14] a child's educational opportunities can be expected to vary directly with parental economic achievement. Further, the absence of a perfect capital market for educational loans means that the opportunity for higher education and the quality of that education will be sensitive to an individual's socioeconomic background.[15]

The information about career opportunities and job requirements available to young people also depends on the socioeconomic status of their parents.[16] Word-of-mouth referrals and informal contacts have always played an important role in the job allocation process. Prospective workers from high-income families are no doubt "better connected" than their low-income counterparts. Thus, the quality of career information, as well as the quality of education, varies with parental status for both blacks and whites.

Considerations such as these indicate that a careful analysis of racial economic differences must recognize both the ongoing effects of past discrimination and the role played by group processes in the perpetuation of black-white economic differences. The traditional theory of racial income differences is a theory of flow equilibrium.[17] It determines income differences in the market today, given the existing stock of inequality. No attempt is made to explain the evolution of the stock over time, or to understand how a change in the stock might affect the flow equilibrium. Hence, the traditional view does not provide an adequate framework for the evaluation of long-run policy.

A number of writers have considered the possibility that whites might find it in their economic interest to act collectively against blacks.[18] Where group behavior has been considered, it has been viewed as the outcome of rational coalition formation by individuals. However, this approach cannot explain why coalitions form along racial dimensions rather than some other lines. If collusive behavior for group gain were the only motive for discrimination, many possible criteria could be used to partition society into competing groups.

Social relations between racial groups thus have not been explicitly recognized by neoclassical economists. Yet, the social setting in which economic activity takes place has an obvious influence on market processes and outcomes. For example, Samuel Bowles argues that "[t]he legitimation of the hierarchical division of labor, as well as the smooth day-to-day control over the work process, requires the authority structure of the enterprise . . . [to] respect the wider society's ascriptive and symbolic distinctions. In particular, socially acceptable relations of domination and subordination must be respected: white over black; male over female; old over young; and schooled over unschooled."[19] Such social distinctions are pervasive in our society. Their economic consequences cannot be adequately accounted for by the presence or absence of a "taste for discrimination" on the part of individual economic agents.

It is the thesis of this paper that a careful analysis of racial income differences must consider the effects of both parental economic status and social relations between racial groups on individual achievement. A simplified model of income determination which incorporates these effects is presented in the following section. Analysis of the model reveals that equal opportunity laws cannot be relied on to eliminate economic differences between the races, even over the long run.

A Socioeconomic Model of Income Determination

Preliminaries

The model of income determination developed here abstracts from all but the essentials of the problem. As such, it should not be viewed as an attempt to describe realistically the job allocation process. By removing complicating real-world factors, the roles of the basic forces that determine the evolution of income differences can be brought into focus.

An individual's economic life is assumed to consist of three stages: a primary socialization phase where the principal interactions occur within the family; the acquisition of educational characteristics and behavioral traits necessary for productive and satisfying employment; and, finally, the employment stage when the individual is involved in productive activity.[20] The hypothetical economic agent is assumed to possess innate capabilities, such as intelligence, as well as certain physical characteristics. Socioeconomic background is determined by race (black or white) and parental income. Thus, in the model an individual is completely characterized at the beginning of life by his or her innate endowment, race, and parental income.

Temporally speaking, it is assumed that life occurs in two equal time periods, youth and maturity. The initial period, youth, encompasses the first two stages of the life cycle—socialization and education—while maturity is characterized by employment activity. The demographic structure of the model assumes that the population size is stationary, that only men participate in economic activity,[21] that each family consists of two parents (but only one breadwinner) and two children (one male and one female), and that mating occurs randomly among the young at the end of the first period of life[22]; the offspring of a couple are assumed to "appear" after mating (at the onset of maturity). These assumptions are designed for simplicity and play no substantive role in the model. Two other assumptions are also made. First, there is no interracial marriage, a phenomenon of minute empirical significance.[23] Second, and more crucial, the socioeconomic background of an individual depends only on the income of the breadwinner of his or her family. This assumption is strong, but is necessary for simplicity.

The acquisition of productive characteristics by a young person is modeled as a social process; that is, interactions of home, community environment, and an educational institution convert a young person's innate capabilities into marketable characteristics. The employment opportunities of a mature individual are determined by the characteristics acquired through this social process during youth. This specification recognizes that an individual's opportunities for achievement depend on his or her socioeconomic background.

The social structure of this economy may exhibit both racial and income stratification, given the assumption that mature individuals tend to group themselves along these lines, both residentially and in terms of their informal social contacts. (Such groupings will be referred to hereafter as "communities."[24]) Young individuals belonging to the same community will tend to have similar socioeconomic backgrounds to the extent that society is stratified along racial and income lines. They will attend the same educational institution provided by the mature individuals of that community, and the maintenance of this institution will be paid for by the levying of a poll tax on all parents in each period.

Equal Opportunity and Racialism

Because society is composed of people with different innate capabilities, individuals will not offer equal qualifications for all jobs. The differences in qualifications or characteristics that justify differences in individual opportunity are termed "critical characteristics." The situation where any two individuals with identical holdings of critical characteristics are faced with the same set of employment possibilities is described as equality of opportunity.

Let "α" denote a young individual's innate capabilities and "x" the bundle of productive characteristics possessed by a mature individual. A young individual is assumed to exercise some discretion in choosing the productive characteristics actually acquired, though in general the array of possibilities from which he can choose depends on his innate capabilities or endowment, home, and community environment. Conceptually, genetic (that is, innate) influences are distinguished from environmental ones in individual achievement, though empirically this separation remains a serious problem.

Equal opportunity characteristics, innate or productive, may be conceptualized in two distinct ways, depending on whether α or x are considered to be critical characteristics. In the first case, equal opportunity exists if any two people with the same innate endowment face the same set of possible productive characteristics and the reward structure for these productive characteristics is identical for all individuals. With this definition, equal opportunity does not permit socioeconomic background (that is, family and community environment) to affect achievement independently of innate ability.

In the second case, productive characteristics are assumed to be critical. Here equal opportunity implies that individuals with the same characteristics should have the same employment opportunities and be entitled to the same rewards in the labor market. This definition of equal opportunity is consistent with, but does not imply, the first one; that is, equal opportunity with critical characteristics, x, allows family background to affect earnings through the skill acquisition process rather than in the labor market.

Current equal opportunity policy is characterized by the second of the two definitions. The legislative mandate of the Equal Employment Opportunity Commission is limited to enforcing the laws against employment discrimination. While there has been much discussion of equal educational opportunity, the varying quality of public education across communities is widely acknowledged.[25] Further, as long as parents have the ability to allocate resources (including their time) and thereby affect the quality of both the home and the community environment, parental income and education can be expected to condition the opportunities of children of both racial groups. For these reasons the definition of equal opportunity in this model takes productive characteristics, x, as critical.

The quality of home (family) environment is indexed by parental income. If there is social stratification by income, parental income may serve as a proxy for the quality of the community environment as well. Now suppose that there is also social stratification by race. In this instance the racial composition of communities, while not necessarily completely homogeneous, will tend to be somewhat concentrated. Hence, the community environment of an individual will depend on the economic position of his or her racial group as well as that of his or her family. Here again, a history of discrimination against a particular group will impact the earning opportunities of young people in that group. Note that in this situation every person in the group will be affected, not just those from low-income families. This is because if a person belongs to a racial group that has been discriminated against, even though *his* or *her* parents may have been successful, the average income of the community to which he or she belongs is lowered by the past discrimination.[26]

Racialism may be said to exist whenever the community environment of individuals with equivalent family environments but of different racial groups differs. No normative connotation is intended by use of the word "racialism." It simply means that people tend to group themselves socially along racial lines, a tendency that affects the opportunities of their offspring. It should be noted that equal opportunity, as interpreted here, is perfectly consistent with the notion of racialism. However, it will be demonstrated that the long-run success of equal opportunity laws in eliminating group economic differences depends on whether racialism prevails.

Market-Valued Characteristics and Earnings

The following provides a more detailed specification of how an individual's earnings are determined.[27] It is assumed that innate capability, α, may be measured as a non-negative number. This capability will vary among individuals, one person being "more able" than another if his or her innate endowment is greater. The distribution of innate capabilities among the young people of each generation is also assumed to be identical to, though independent of, that which prevailed in the previous generation. A third assumption is that the distribution of innate capability is the same for each racial group.[28] Thus, the innate endowment of an individual is independent of his or her socioeconomic background.

For simplicity, the market-valued characteristics that an individual acquires in the first period of life is represented by a pair of non-negative numbers, $x = (x_1, x_2)$. As such, there are effectively only two types of characteristics, and the quantities of these characteristics acquired are represented by x_1 and x_2. The acquisition of characteristics during youth may be described as an abstract interactive process involving the home, community, and social environments. The young individual decides the outcome of this process, within limits determined by his or her innate endowment and social and educational environments.

These constraints may be expressed by a set of attainable characteristic bundles from which the individual chooses. Two sets, representing the opportunities of two different individuals, are illustrated in Figure 8-1. The first individual, A, may choose among all characteristic pairs (x_1, x_2) that lie on or below the locus AB. The other individual, A', can select any pair that does not lie above $A'B'$. It is apparent that the opportunities of A' are broader than those of A. This may occur for several reasons. First, A and A', though facing identical social environments and educational institutions, may differ in their innate capabilities (that is, $\alpha_{A'} > \alpha_A$). A more favorable innate endowment means that

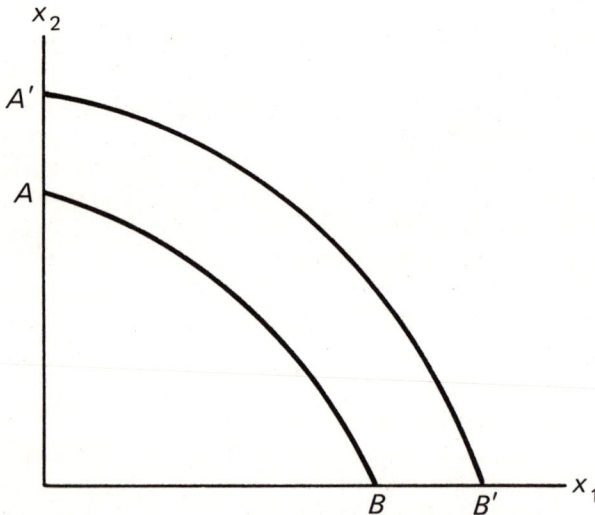

Figure 8-1. Characteristic Opportunity Sets

an individual has wider latitude in choosing the benefits he will derive from the education-socialization process. In addition, even if A and A' have the same innate endowment and are part of the same community, A' may have a "better" home environment than A (that is, a higher family income). Finally, opportunities may vary for otherwise identical young individuals living in different communities; that is, A' may come from a community with a higher quality educational institution or more favorable environmental influences than A.

The last effect assumes that social stratification exists. In the absence of stratification the composition of each community would mirror the composition of the population as a whole. Social stratification by income implies that families with similar incomes will gravitate to the same communities. This reinforces the influence of parental income on the child's opportunities (a greater family income would tend to be associated with a more favorable community environment as well as a better home environment). If social stratification also occurs on the basis of race, the community environment would depend on the average income of an individual's racial group as well as his parental income. Accordingly, two individuals—one black and one white—who are otherwise identical would face different opportunities, unless the economic positions of their respective groups were the same.[29] The extent to which these opportunities diverge, as measured by the "distance" between AB and $A'B'$ in Figure 8-1, would depend directly on the magnitude of existing racial income differences. The extent of racial income differences is indexed by the ratio, r, of mean black income to mean white income; r is assumed to lie between zero and one.

The demand side of the labor market is specified as follows. A large number of identical competitive firms are assumed to produce a homogeneous output under conditions of constant returns to scale and diminishing returns to inputs. Firms employ only skilled and unskilled labor. Output is perishable so that there is no accumulation of capital in the model.[30] The set of characteristic bundles that enables an individual to obtain employment as a skilled worker is called the *acceptance set*, and is denoted by A. The acceptance set functions as a rule that enables employers to determine whether or not a given employee can perform skilled tasks. If the employee has characteristics in the set A, $x \in$ A, he or she qualifies as a skilled worker. On the other hand, if that person does not possess such characteristics, $x \notin$ A, he or she can find only unskilled employment. The acceptance set is assumed to be time invariant and known to all firms and workers.

Factor markets are assumed to be competitive with workers receiving their marginal products. Skilled employees earn more than unskilled employees, but wages are the same for all workers within a given occupational class. $\overline{w}$ denotes the wage of a skilled worker and w the wage of an unskilled employee. $w = \overline{w} - w$ represents the wage differential. In Figure 8-2 the acceptance set A is given by the collection of characteristic pairs on or below the locus BC. As can

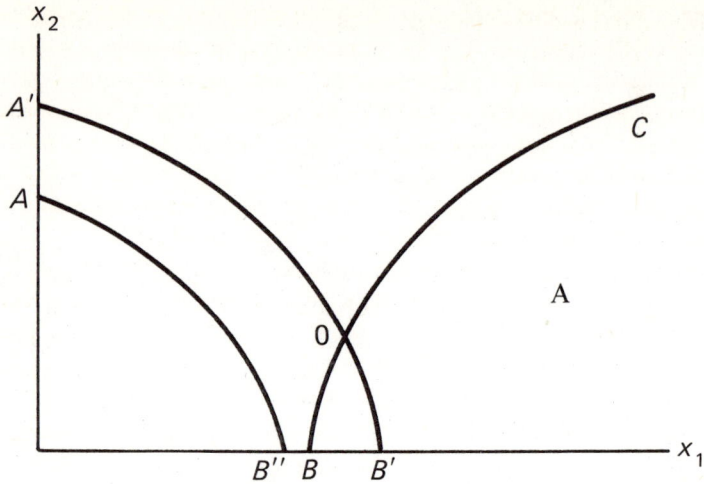

Figure 8-2. Individual Opportunities and the Acceptance Set

be seen, firms consider x_1 to be a positive characteristic for skilled work and x_2 a negative one. This may be inferred from the fact that the minimal level of the first characteristic necessary to qualify for skilled employment is an increasing function of the quantity of the second characteristic possessed by the worker.

Whether an individual obtains skilled employment depends on the characteristics acquired during youth. Figure 8-2 illustrates a case where an individual with possibilities AB'' cannot obtain acceptable characteristics for skilled employment, while the person with opportunities $A'B'$ can acquire the requisite skills by choosing a pair in the "triangle" BOB'. Because the array of possible characteristics varies with an individual's innate capabilities and socioeconomic background, these factors affect his or her chances of becoming a skilled worker, and hence earnings. To determine which people become skilled workers requires a consideration of the criterion used by young individuals in selecting characteristics. This is facilitated by assuming that only two occupational categories exist. Because an individual's socioeconomic background is defined by his or her parents' income and race, only four different backgrounds are possible for the members of a given generation. This permits an analysis of how the distribution of economic advantages evolves over time.[31]

Each individual is assumed to possess a set of preferences by which he or she evaluates his state of well-being. It is further assumed that these preferences are identical for all individuals.[32] A person's well-being is determined by two factors: the bundle of characteristics acquired in the first period of life, and the level of income obtained in the second period. Each characteristic bundle may be assigned a value that represents its dollar equivalent to all individuals. An individual's well-being may then be measured in dollar terms as the sum of the value of characteristics acquired during youth plus the wages earned in employment during maturity. An individual chooses a bundle of characteristics that will maximize his or her state of well-being, given the bundles attainable.

This choice is illustrated in Figure 8-3 for an individual with a set of attainable characteristic pairs given by all points on or below the locus $A'B'$. The acceptance set A is bounded from above by the curve BC. The individual's preferences among characteristics are depicted by a collection of indifference curves. The locus UU is a representative indifference curve. Characteristic pairs on an indifference curve have the same value to an individual. Characteristic bundles on an indifference curve that lies above another are more valuable than bundles on lower curves. A young individual thus makes his choice in two stages. First, he or she decides whether or not to become skilled. Second, given the decision, he or she chooses an appropriate bundle of characteristics. The second choice will be discussed first.

Given the set of attainable characteristics, the individual considers the bundle of characteristics whose dollar value is the greatest of all attainable bundles. For example, $x*$ in Figure 8-3 lies on the highest indifference curve,

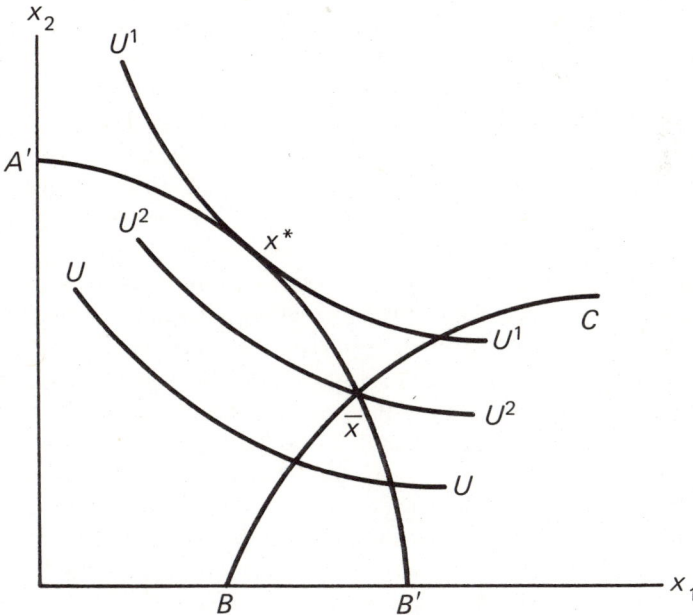

Figure 8-3. Selection of Optimal Characteristics

$U^1 U^1$, attainable to the individual (that is, it intersects the set of points on or below $A'B'$). If x^* is in A, the individual will select x^*, because this characteristic bundle gives the greatest income during maturity as well as the greatest value during youth. In general, however, these characteristics will be insufficient to qualify him or her for skilled employment. In this instance the individual will select x^* only if he or she decides to enter unskilled employment.

Next, the individual will consider the most desirable characteristic bundle that is both attainable and consistent with becoming a skilled worker. This assumes, of course, that such points exist. If not, the individual has no occupational decision to make. The set of all such points for the hypothetical individual in Figure 8-3 is bounded by the curve $B \bar{x} B'$. $U^2 U^2$ is the highest indifference curve that intersects this set and the most desirable bundle is $\bar{x}$. Thus, if the individual decides to become skilled, $\bar{x}$ will be the chosen bundle. The difference between the value of the bundle x^* and the bundle $\bar{x}$ is the cost of skill acquisition. If x^* is in A, this cost is zero. On the other hand, if an individual has no feasible points in A, the cost is infinite.

It is apparent from this analysis that the cost to a young person of becoming skilled depends only on his or her attainable set of characteristic bundles and preferences for characteristics during youth. Preferences are identical across individuals. However, the cost of acquiring skills varies with individual opportunities for acquiring characteristics. These opportunities depend on the innate endowment of the individual, α, and his or her socioeconomic background. It is natural to assume that the cost of becoming skilled will decline as α increases. Further, a more favorable socioeconomic background should also lead to a lower cost of acquiring skilled employment. Hence, higher parental income, with other things being equal, implies lower costs. Moreover, a given increase in parental income will reduce the cost to a young person of gaining skilled employment by more, the greater the degree of social stratification by income. This is because with greater stratification the community environment will change sharply with a change in parental income. Further, when there is racialism blacks will generally have higher costs than equally able whites with the same family income. The magnitude of this difference will increase with an increase in the degree of racial economic differences among mature workers (that is, with a decrease in r) as long as there is social stratification by race. Indeed, the greater the degree of racialism, the more the cost of becoming skilled increases for a black worker with a given decrease in r.

Figure 8-4 depicts the cost of acquiring skills as a function of innate capabilities for individuals of two different socioeconomic backgrounds. Each curve holds socioeconomic background constant and considers the effect of α on costs. The diagram illustrates that more capable individuals may acquire the characteristics of skilled workers at a lower expense than less capable individuals. As can be seen, the socioeconomic background corresponding to curve C^1 is more favorable for young people than that associated with C^2. Holding the

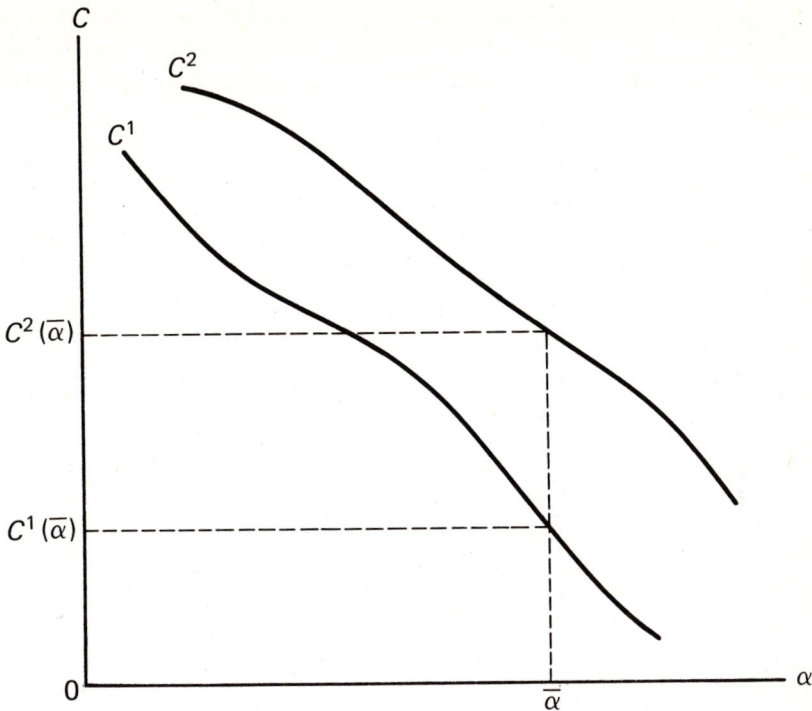

Figure 8-4. Cost of Becoming Skilled

degree of social stratification constant, this difference may reflect (1) the advantage of having greater parental income; (2) the advantage of being white rather than black in an environment where whites earn higher average incomes and racialism exists; or (3) the relative advantage of being black in a racist society when the extent of racial income differences has been lessened (that is, r has increased). In any event, a more favorable socioeconomic background will imply a decrease in cost for equally capable individuals. This is shown in Figure 8-4 by $C^1(\alpha) < C^2(\alpha)$.

It is now possible to determine when an individual will choose to become a skilled worker. As noted above, an individual with infinite costs cannot qualify for skilled employment while someone with zero costs will always be employed as a skilled worker. These cases, however, are not the norm.[33] Most people may obtain skilled employment if they are willing to make the necessary sacrifice during their youth. This necessary sacrifice depends on the individual's innate endowment and socioeconomic background, and is measured in monetary terms by the cost of becoming skilled. Suppose that at the beginning of each time period firms announce the wages they will pay to skilled and unskilled workers, $\bar{w}$ and $\underline{w}$, respectively, in the subsequent period. The wage differential, w, is the payoff to a young person for incurring the cost of becoming skilled. Because people choose characteristics to maximize their well-being, they will become skilled workers if and only if the payoff exceeds the cost.

A young person's choice of characteristics involves the following. First, that person considers the most valuable of all his or her attainable characteristic bundles, and then considers the best bundle he or she can acquire that also qualifies him or her for skilled employment. The cost of becoming skilled is represented by the difference between the values of these two bundles. Only if the extra wages the person could earn by becoming skilled exceed this cost will he or she choose the bundle qualifying him or her for skilled employment. This situation is illustrated in Figure 8-5 where cost is measured on the vertical axis and capability on the horizontal axis. Figure 8-5 depicts cost curves that are representative of two distinct socioeconomic backgrounds. The wage differential announced by firms for next period's employment is given as w. Because cost declines with increasing innate capability, each socioeconomic background has a corresponding critical level of innate ability. Anyone of that background with a capability greater than this critical level will become skilled.

Obviously, this critical level of capability is determined by the requirement that the cost of becoming skilled to a person of the given socioeconomic background endowed with the critical level of innate capability be equal to the wage differential offered by firms. α^1 and α^2 satisfy this requirement for the socioeconomic backgrounds represented by cost functions C^1 and C^2, respectively, in Figure 8-5. Hence, given an offered wage differential, in each generation young individuals with the same socioeconomic background (that is, race and parental income) will or will not become skilled on the basis of innate endowment. The dividing point—or critical level of capability—is determined once the cost function for this group and the wage differential are known. Because the distribution of innate capabilities in the population is identical for each generation, race, and social class, the number of individuals from this group who will become skilled workers can be determined.

This process is also illustrated in Figure 8-5. If $F(\alpha)$ is the cumulative distribution function of innate capability, then $1-F(\alpha)$, measured on the downward vertical axis, represents the fraction of the population with innate capability greater than α. Given the independence assumptions, this will also be the fraction of young individuals from a particular socioeconomic background with an innate endowment greater than α. Thus, for the socioeconomic backgrounds represented by C^1 and C^2, the fractions of these groups that acquire skilled characteristics depend on w, the skilled/unskilled wage differential. These fractions are depicted by $V^1(w)$ and $V^2(w)$ in Figure 8-5. It is clear from the figure that V^1 and V^2 are increasing functions of w, and that for every w, $V^1(w) > V^2(w)$; that is, higher wage differentials for skilled workers will

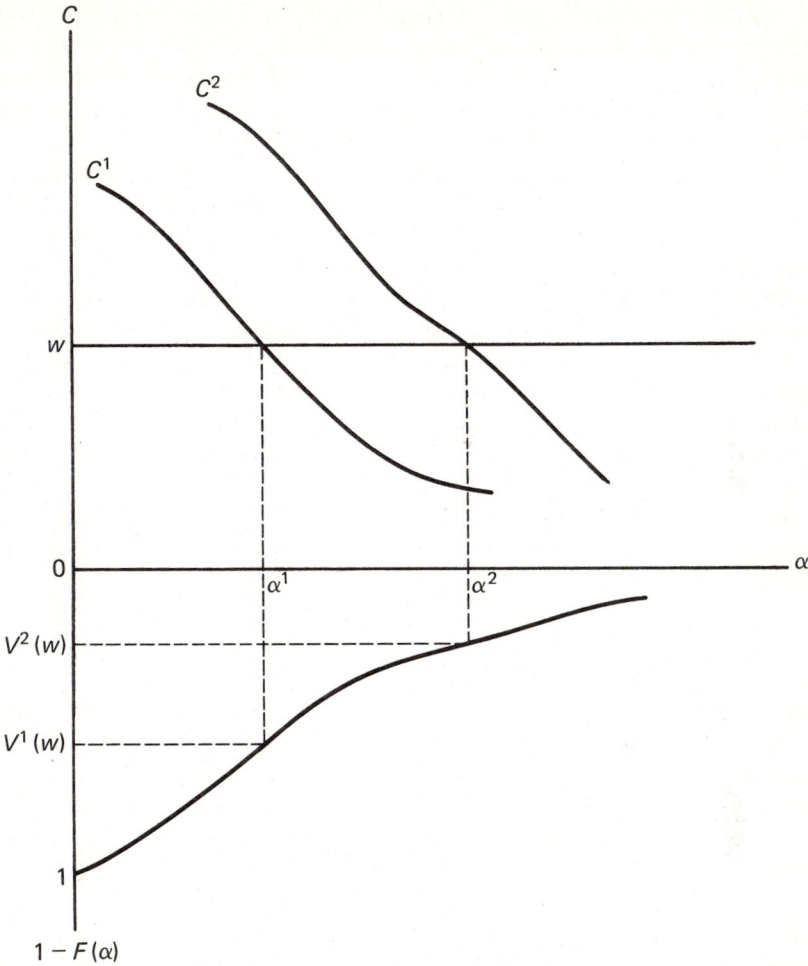

Figure 8-5. Critical Capability Levels

induce more young people to acquire the characteristics of skilled employees. Further, a group with a more favorable socioeconomic background than another will always have a larger fraction of its young people qualified for skilled employment.

Static Equilibrium

It is now possible to describe the static labor market equilibrium for a given generation. Equilibrium occurs when the supply of and demand for both skilled and unskilled workers is equal. Although two kinds of labor are involved, the assumptions made earlier permit the equilibrium in the simple supply-demand framework pictured in Figure 8-6 to be analyzed. In Figure 8-6 the wage differential between skilled and unskilled workers is measured on the vertical axis while the aggregate ratio of skilled to unskilled employment, denoted by l, is given on the horizontal axis. The assumptions of competitive factor markets and constant returns to scale imply a downward sloping demand curve D. Firms can be on their demand curves for both types of labor if and only if the corresponding wage differential and employment ratio is on the curve D.[34]

Because the decision of an individual to acquire skilled characteristics depends on his or her socioeconomic background, it is apparent that the supply of skilled workers will depend on the labor market equilibrium established during the previous period.[35] This is the result of the intergenerational externalities in the model. Accordingly, the static labor market equilibrium for any generation will always be conditional on the equilibrium obtained for the

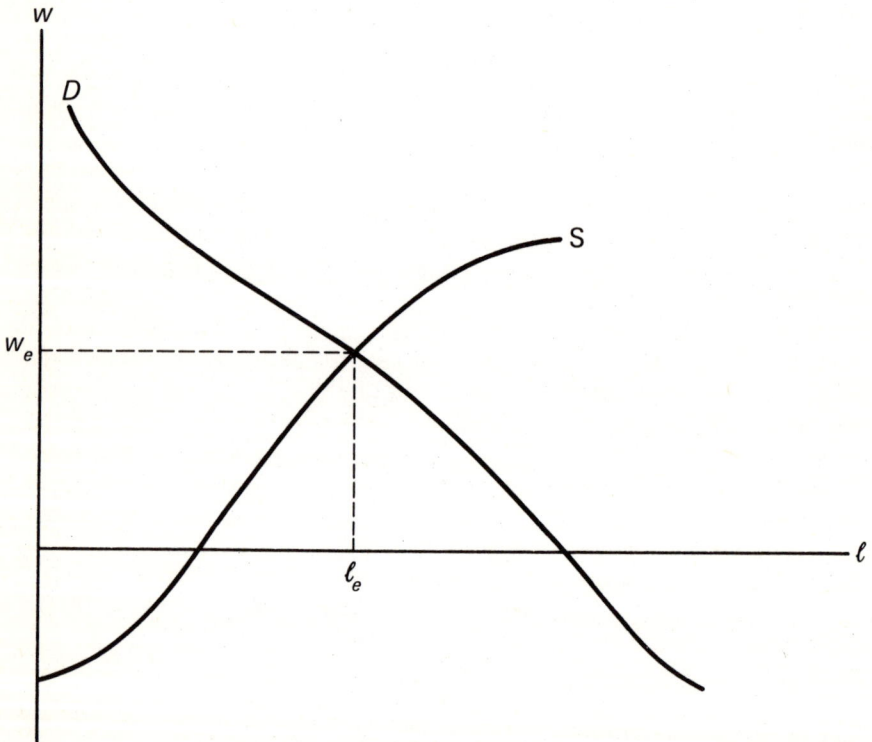

Figure 8-6. Labor Market Equilibrium

preceding period. The path that these equilibria follow over time is analyzed in the fourth section of this paper. However, the supply of skilled workers as a function of the wage differential (the S curve in Figure 8-6) can be specified, given the fractions of black and white workers who acquired skilled characteristics during the previous period. This information is sufficient to determine the socioeconomic backgrounds of all young individuals in the economy.[36]

Assume that the extent of social stratification by income and race remains unchanged over time. The cost of becoming skilled can then be determined as a function of innate ability for individuals of the four possible socioeconomic backgrounds. Again, for whites this cost function depends only on parental income, while for blacks it depends on both parental income and the degree of racial income differences. The locus S shown in Figure 8-6 may be constructed. This supply curve may be traced given the fraction of young people from the four socioeconomic backgrounds who will acquire skilled characteristics at various wage differentials.[37]

Equilibrium holds at the intersection of the demand and supply curves in Figure 8-6. Here the fraction of young people who want to become skilled equals the fraction of skilled employees to all employees required by each firm at a given wage differential.[38] Given the equilibrium wage differential, the fractions of black and white youths who will be employed in skilled occupations in the subsequent period can be determined. Knowledge of these fractions, in turn, enables the labor market equilibrium in the next generation to be determined. In this way a sequence of market equilibria and associated income distribution can be generated, starting from any initial situation.

In summary, this section has presented an economic model of individual earnings determination in which the social structure directly affects economic outcome. In preparing for employment, individuals weigh the costs and benefits of alternative actions, choosing the one that maximizes their well-being. Costs are directly influenced by an individual's innate capability and socioeconomic background. The impact of socioeconomic background on achievement is strongly conditioned by the degree of income and racial stratification in the society. If community associations tend to divide sharply along these lines, the relative lack of economic success by a young person's parents and/or racial group becomes a serious liability to that individual's own achievement. The more representative the composition of a community, the greater the importance of an individual's innate capabilities in determining his or her success. In any event, the distribution of economic advantage within any generation depends on the distribution that prevailed in the preceding generation. The dynamic implications of these observations are analyzed in the following section.

Dynamic Analysis of the Model

Equal Opportunity and Racial Income Equality

The determination of equilibrium wages and employment levels of skilled and unskilled workers of any generation was described above. Equilibrium is determined by the fractions of black and white workers employed in skilled occupations in the previous generation. Analysis of equilibrium where equal opportunity prevails reveals a dynamic relation determining the fractions of blacks and whites in skilled employment in subsequent generations, knowing only the state in which the economy started.[39]

The current observed earning differential between the races may be represented in the model in terms of a smaller initial fraction of blacks than of whites employed in skilled occupations. Accordingly, the future path of the black and white economic position can be traced. In each subsequent generation (the tth), the index of racial income differences takes on a value ($r^t \cdot r^t$ represents the ratio of the average income of blacks to the average earnings of whites in the tth generation). This ratio may be determined once the fractions of blacks and whites employed in skilled occupations in that generation are known.[40] Because blacks have been discriminated against in the past, r^o will be less than one. As r^t approaches one, racial economic differences become negligible for t sufficiently large.

This analysis is illustrated by Figure 8-7, which summarizes the dynamic relation of labor market equilibria across generations. The horizontal axis represents the index of racial income differences in an arbitrary generation, t. The vertical axis measures the degree of racial economic disparity in the succeeding generation, $t + 1$. The locus AB summarizes the relationship between these indices. However, in order for this graphical analysis to be valid, this relationship must not change over time. This reflects the assumption that the social structure (that is, extent of income and racial stratification) remains unchanged over time. The analysis thus focuses on the impact of a *given* set of social relations on the evolution of racial economic positions.

Suppose that the current racial income differential is represented by the point r^o on the horizontal axis in Figure 8-7. Following a vertical line from r^o to the curve AB, it can be seen that r^1 indexes racial differences in the following generation. Similarly, the horizontal line from the point r^1 on the vertical axis to the $45°$ line determines the extent of racial income differences, r^2, in two generations. The path of future relative economic positions may be determined in this manner. The path in the figure leads to the eventual elimination of racial income differences since r^t will eventually become only negligibly different from one. Moreover, inspection of the diagram shows that *any* initial position will determine a path with the same long-run consequence; that is, no matter how great the initial disadvantage of the black population, the dynamic process of income determination will lead to an eventual equalization of racial economic positions.

Another possibility is illustrated in Figure 8-8. Here the intergenerational relation of relative economic positions is depicted by the locus AD. Inspection of the diagram reveals that the long-run evolution of racial income differences critically depends on the starting position. If past discrimination has not been too severe, so that the initial index of racial earnings disparity is greater than $\bar{r}$,

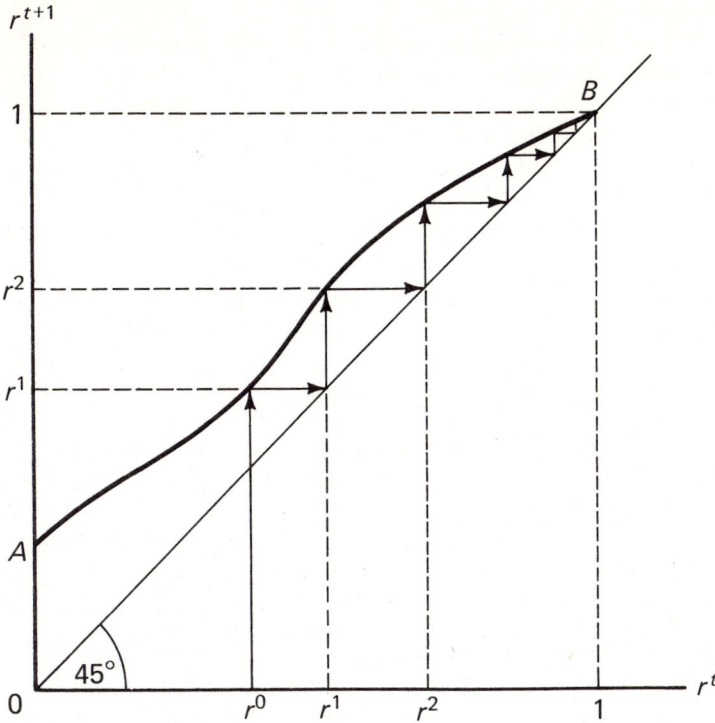

Figure 8-7. Long-Run Income Equality

eventual equality may be expected. A representative path, beginning at r_b^o in the figure, illustrates this point. However, if the initial earnings gap is represented by r_a^o, black-white income differences will persist indefinitely and may even increase over time. As can be seen, an initial earnings ratio less than $\bar{r}$, in the long run, will lead to the ratio r_I, which represents permanent inequality.

An extreme example of the failure of the equal opportunity to eliminate racial income differences is illustrated in Figure 8-9. If the locus AC characterizes the relation of relative economic positions across a generation, the slightest degree of initial inequality is sufficient to guarantee a permanent earnings gap. The social structure underlying the relationship depicted in the figure exhibits an inherent tendency toward inequality.

The Limits of Equal Opportunity

What are the reasons for these drastic differences in the long-run performance of a laissez-faire economy with no racial discrimination? What factors determine

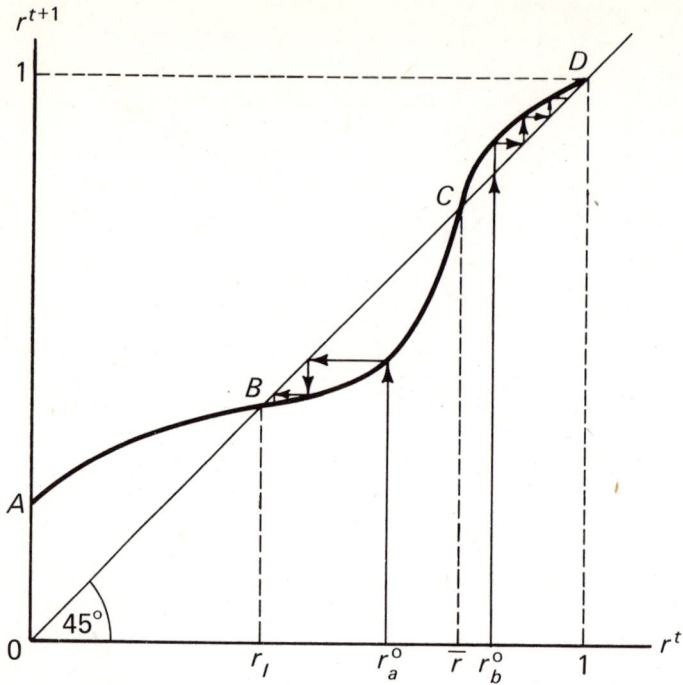

Figure 8-8. Long-Run Income Equality or Inequality Dependent on Initial
Position

whether a benign structure such as that illustrated in Figure 8-7, or an
inequality-preserving relation as in Figure 8-9, will hold? These questions are
answered in the propositions presented below. Before discussing these, however,
it is possible to gain some insight into the forces at work. Recall that there are
three major influences that determine whether a young person can become a
skilled worker—family background, community environment, and endowment of
innate capabilities. Innate ability has been assumed to be identically distributed
among blacks and whites. Hence, any persistence of racial income differences in
the face of equal opportunity must result from family background and the
community environment.

Given the effect of family background on achievement, the fact that more
black than white youngsters inherit poor family backgrounds due to past
discrimination against their parents means that fewer blacks than whites will
achieve skilled occupational status in the next generation. However, each
generation's advancement, if indeed there is advancement, enables the next
generation to start with a smaller relative disadvantage. The cumulative effect of
this process could eventually eliminate differences in the average earnings of the
two groups.

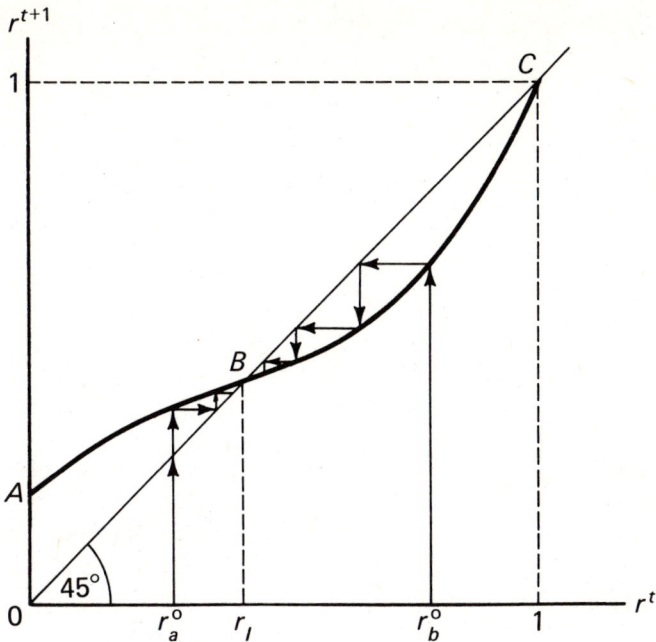

Figure 8-9. Long-Run Income Inequality

Community effects are important when there is some degree of social stratification. With stratification by income, a poor family background represents an even greater handicap than that discussed above. Moreover, historical discrimination implies that blacks will face this impediment more frequently than whites.

Social stratification by race leads to racially homogeneous communities. In this case if there has been discrimination, the community effects for blacks and white youngsters, even with the same parental income, will differ. Consequently, black parents who have succeeded will be less able than white parents to assure the success of their children. Again, however, if the racial earnings gap continues to narrow under equal opportunity laws, this effect will diminish over time.

Thus, there seem to be two separate though related elements that work to distinguish the dynamic relations of earnings over generations. The first is the extent of social stratification by income and race, determining the strength of the bond between parental socioeconomic status and offspring achievement. The other element is the ability of each generation of black workers to make progress with respect to the position of the preceding generation, allowing a diminution of the handicap of historical discrimination over time. The significance of the social structure is illustrated in the following proposition:[41]

PROPOSITION I: Suppose there is no racialism in the society, so that social stratification occurs only along income lines. Assume that whenever a parent's income is increased by one dollar, the cost to his or her offspring of acquiring skilled characteristics is reduced by less than one dollar. Assume further that the greater a parent's income, the less a dollar increment to that income will reduce the offspring's cost of becoming skilled. Under these conditions enforcement of equal opportunity laws means that historical differences in earnings between blacks and whites will diminish and tend to zero over time.

The implication of this proposition is that in a society where one's race is socially irrelevant, and where the practice of racial discrimination in the labor market is prohibited, differences in racial economic positions cannot persist. This proposition is not transparent. Note the conditions under which it is true. First, it is required that parental economic position not be so important that a given increase in parental earnings leads to an even greater ultimate monetary benefit to the offspring. This would be a weak requirement if family environment were the only vehicle for the intergenerational external effect. If an increase in parental income is accompanied by a shift in community income and society is stratified by income, this condition could be violated.

The second condition requires that the marginal benefit to young people of parental income does not increase as parental earnings increase. This is a stronger condition and there is some evidence that it may not hold.[42]

These conditions are sufficient, but not necessary, for long-run equality. However, even if they do not hold, in the absence of racialism, it is likely that equal opportunity will lead to the elimination of racial income differences. Faith in the free market is not without foundation.

Proposition I also addresses the question raised in the sociology literature of the late 1960s—specifically, whether the "inheritance of poverty," which blacks face more frequently than whites, could cause persistent racial inequality. By considering linear models in which the assumptions of Proposition I are constrained to hold, the writers of this period answered with an unqualified "no."[43] As stated, Proposition I gives a precise set of conditions under which this answer is correct.

The assumption of no racialism in Proposition I is very strong. However, racial stratification is widespread in our society. The true test of the efficacy of equal opportunity laws is how they stand up in the presence of antagonistic social relations among racial groups. In order to isolate the impact of racialism, the following proposition considers an economy without income stratification. Moreover, family background is assumed not to affect an offspring's opportunities; only community effects are assumed to be operative. As demonstrated above, under certain conditions parental income effects alone cannot sustain racial economic differences. Unfortunately, the consequences of racialism are not so benign. This is demonstrated by Proposition II:

PROPOSITION II: Suppose there is no social stratification by income, and that family environment does not affect a young person's opportunities. Imagine, however, that social stratification by race is prevalent and that community external influences are present. In such a situation, equal opportunity laws need not ensure that any initial difference in group earnings will eventually become negligible. Further, eventual equality will result from establishing equal opportunity only if the relative economic position of blacks improves continually over time.

The first result of Proposition II is a negative one. It states that the presence of racialism implies that equal opportunity (as defined in this paper) will not necessarily lead to eventual equality for blacks. While the possibility that the favorable situation of Figure 8-7 obtains cannot be ruled out, no assurance can be given when there is racialism. What ultimately happens will depend on the strength of community external effects (the importance of school quality and job market information) and the extent of social stratification by race.

The final statement in the proposition yields further insights. It gives a specific test of whether racial income differences will eventually be eliminated in a given economy. If, through normal operation of the competitive labor market under equal opportunity, a worsening of the relative economic position of blacks should occur, there exists an historical disparity of sufficient magnitude that blacks will never gain equality if they start at any greater disadvantage. Given the simplicity of the model, however, this result is only suggestive of the more complex conditions under which equal opportunity laws may fail in reality. Particularly troublesome is the absence of unemployment and cyclical effects in the model. The comfortable long-run conclusions of the traditional liberal view may thus be called fundamentally into question.

Conclusion

Several preliminary conclusions about the process of personal income determination and related public policy may be drawn from this socioeconomic analysis. This discussion has considered the problem of income distribution in an explicitly intertemporal framework. By doing so it has shown that, even in the absence of transfers of physical wealth within families, the economic achievement of an individual will only partially reflect his or her innate productive capabilities. The overlapping of generations and the influences of the prevailing external environment on individual development mean that the present pattern of ownership of resources will influence the distribution of productive capabilities among succeeding generations of workers.

It thus follows that the creation of a skilled work force is a social process.

The merit notion, that in a free society each individual will rise to the level justified by his or her competence, conflicts with the observation that no one travels that road entirely alone. The social context within which individual maturation occurs strongly conditions what otherwise equally competent individuals can achieve. This implies that absolute equality of opportunity, where an individual's chance to succeed depends only on his or her innate capabilities, is an ideal that cannot be achieved. It has been shown here that the limited version of equal opportunity that *is* attainable does not have the desirable properties of the impossible ideal.

Traditional economic theory teaches that earnings differentials among workers may be understood on the basis of individual differences in amounts of education and work experience. The notion of "human capital" has been used to describe these investments in individuals. This focus on objective determinants of earnings disparities, while providing a convenient rationale for existing inequalities, ignores the process by which such investments are made. Thus, human capital theorists can accurately predict the consequence that an individual's dropping out of high school will have on his or her lifetime earnings, but such theorists have not analyzed *why* a given per capita expenditure yields a lower quality education in the ghetto than in more affluent communities of the same school district.

An individual's social origin has an obvious and important effect on the amount of resources that is ultimately invested in his or her development. It may thus be useful to employ a concept of "social capital" to represent the consequences of social position in facilitating acquisition of the standard human capital characteristics. While measurement problems abound, this idea does have the advantage of forcing the analyst to consider the extent to which individual earnings are accounted for by social forces outside an individual's control. However, for precisely this reason such analysis is unlikely to develop within the confines of traditional neoclassical theory.

Notes

1. Intergeneration externalities have been studied in a partial equilibrium context in T. Ishikawa, "Family Structure and Family Values in the Theory of Income Distribution," *Journal of Political Economy* 83 (1975): 987-1008; and E. Lazear, "Intergenerational Externalities," mimeographed (Chicago: The University of Chicago, February 1976). The distributional implications of these effects, however, have not been investigated.

2. See, for example, F. Welch, "Labor Market Discrimination: An Interpretation of Income Differences in the Rural South," *Journal of Political Economy* 75 (1967): 225-241; and R.D. Weiss, "The Effect of Education on the Earnings of Blacks and Whites," *Review of Economics and Statistics* 52 (1970): 150-159.

3. This is, of course, Becker's idea, G.S. Becker, *The Economics of Discrimination* (Chicago: The University of Chicago Press, 1971). Whether or not differential returns will actually occur depends on how costly it is for employers to turn over their work force (K. Arrow, "Models of Job Discrimination," "Some Mathematical Models of Race in the Labor Market," in *Racial Discrimination in Economic Life*, A. Pascal, ed. (Lexington, Mass.: D.C. Heath-Lexington Books, 1972) and on the ability of nondiscriminating entrepreneurs to expand their numbers and scale of production (as emphasized by R.B. Freeman, "Labor Market Discrimination: Analysis, Findings, and Problems," in *Frontiers of Quantitative Economics*, M.D. Intriligator and D.A. Kendricks, eds. (New York: North-Holland Publishing Company, 1974). To the extent that labor turnover costs are high, or growth of the nondiscriminating sector is limited, the theory predicts protracted black-white wage differentials.

4. The term "market-valued characteristics" is used interchangeably with the more common term "human capital." This is done to avoid the possibly erroneous association of these characteristics with some objective notion of productivity. The empirical results of human capital theory are apparently consistent with the assumption that education per se does not appreciably affect job performance. See, for example, L. Thurow, *Poverty and Discrimination* (Washington: The Brookings Institution, 1969).

5. The development of this policy since 1964 has been summarized in P.A. Wallace, "A Decade of Policy Developments in Equal Opportunities in Employment and Housing," in *A Decade of Federal Antipoverty Policy: Achievement, Failure and Lessons*, R. Haverman, ed. (New York: Academic Press, forthcoming).

6. Consider: "... it appears that the absence of racial discrimination in the job market would not eliminate racial differences in occupations immediately, since there are broad societal processes operating to the disadvantage of Negroes. ... Several generations would be necessary before parity was reached" (S. Lieberson and G. Fuguitt, "Negro-White Occupational Differences in the Absence of Discrimination," *American Journal of Sociology* 73, 1967: 188); or "But if there were remedies for all these forms of discrimination, so that the only handicap of family background remained, that handicap would be materially diminished in the next generation. It would be further attenuated in successive generations ... and ... *would tend to disappear of its own accord*" (O.D. Duncan, "Inheritance of Poverty or Inheritance of Race?" in *On Understanding Poverty*, D. Moynihan, ed., New York: Basic Books, 1968, p. 102), (emphasis added); or finally, "In other words, if we could eliminate the inheritance of race, in the sense of the exposure to discrimination experienced by Negroes, the inheritance of poverty in this group would take care of itself (Duncan, "Inheritance of Poverty," p. 103).

7. Possible exceptions to this statement are the recent literature on job market signaling. See M. Spence, "Job Market Signaling," *Quarterly Journal of Economics* 87 (1973): 355-374; D. Starrett, "Social Institutions and the

Distribution of Income: A Neoclassical Defense of Radical Positions," Technical Report #117 (Institute for Mathematical Studies in the Social Sciences: Stanford University, December 1973); and J. Stiglitz, "The Theory of 'Screening' Education and the Distribution of Income," *American Economic Review* 65 (June 1975): 283-300. The "radical" literature on education provides a totally different perspective. See, for example, S. Bowles and H. Gintis, "The Problem with Human Capital Theory: A Marxian Critique," *American Economic Review* 65 (1975): 74-82, and S. Bowles and H. Gintis, *Schooling in Capitalist America* (New York: Basic Books, 1976).

8. See especially, P. Blau and O.D. Duncan, *The American Occupational Structure* (New York: John Wiley and Sons, 1967); or O.D. Duncan et al., *Socioeconomic Background and Achievement* (New York: Seminar Press, 1972); or Duncan, "Inheritance of Poverty"; or Lieberson and Fuguitt, "Negro-White Differences." For a review of the intragenerational mobility literature, see D. McFarland, "Intragenerational Social Mobility as a Markov Process," *American Sociological Review* 35 (1970): 463-476. An interesting analysis of the intergenerational dynamic interplay of social mobility and educational opportunity is provided by R. Boudon, *Education, Opportunity and Social Inequality* (New York: John Wiley and Sons, 1973). A recent comparative study of intragenerational occupational mobility among young black and white males is R. Hall and R. Kasten, "The Relative Occupational Success of Blacks and Whites," *Brookings Papers on Economic Activity* 3 (1973): 781-798.

9. This is the analytic method of path analysis applied to life-cycle models of socioeconomic achievement. For a discussion of the development of this methodology, see Duncan et al., *Socioeconomic Background*, especially Chapters 1 and 2.

10. This was established early in the development of this research by sociologists. See Duncan, "Inheritance of Poverty" or Duncan et al., *Socioeconomic Background*, pp. 95-96, ". . . the (relatively few) Negroes who do have favorable social origins cannot, as readily as whites, convert this advantage into occupational achievement and monetary returns . . . (The Negro Family) is relatively less able than the white to pass on to the next generation any advantage that may accrue to substantial status achievement in the present generation."

11. This effect may be an artifact of the broad definition of occupation used in these studies. A more recent study of occupational achievement by R.M. Stolzenberg, "Education, Occupation, and Wage Differences between White and Black Men," *American Journal of Sociology* 81 (1975): 299-323, using much finer occupational categories, finds negligible intraoccupational earnings differences between blacks and whites, once education is controlled. However, he also finds that blacks tend to be concentrated in the lower paying occupations of each broad occupational category.

12. The term is Becker's, *Economics of Discrimination*, p. 6.

13. See, for example, U.S. Commission on Civil Rights, *Racial Isolation in the Public Schools* (Washington: U.S. Government Printing Office, 1967), Vols. I-II.

14. That this is the case has been firmly established. See, for example, M. Feldstein, "Wealth Neutrality and Local Choice in Public Education," *American Economic Review* 65 (1975): 82, Table 1; or A.E. Wise, *Rich Schools, Poor Schools: The Promise of Equal Educational Opportunity* (Chicago: The University of Chicago Press, 1968), p. 125, Table 2.

15. In their provocative book, Bowles and Gintis give data that support this argument. For example, in 1971 the ratio of the number of students with family income over $20,000 to the number of students with family income under $8,000 was nine times greater in private universities than in public two-year colleges, p. 210, Fig. 8-1.

16. The importance of imperfect information in determining the distribution of income is also emphasized by Starret, "Neoclassical Defense of Radical Positions."

17. It has recently been argued that this very omission in macroeconomics lies at the heart of the differences between Monetarists and Kenesians over the long-term effects of fiscal policy. See A. Blinder and R.M. Solow, "Does Fiscal Policy Matter?," *Journal of Public Economics* 2 (1973): 319-337.

18. See, for example, Arrow, *Racial Discrimination in Economic Life*, pp. 98-100; Freeman, "Labor Market Discrimination," pp. 525-529; or R. Marshall, "The Economics of Racial Discrimination: A Survey," *Journal of Economic Literature* (September 1974): 849-871.

19. Samuel Bowles, "Understanding Unequal Economic Opportunity," *American Economic Review* 63 (May 1973): 352.

20. This temporal sequence is merely Duncan's socioeconomic life cycle mentioned earlier. See Duncan et al., *Socioeconomic Background.*

21. In order to consider the dynamic implications of racial discrimination we must (regrettably) neglect the problems of sexism. The economic consequences of the interaction of these two important social forces provide a formidable agenda for future research.

22. The possibility of assortative mating, which could slow considerably the convergence of black and white incomes, is not analyzed here.

23. There are not national estimates of the frequency of interracial marriage. Casual empiricism suggests that the incidence of the phenomenon, while limited, has been increasing in recent years.

24. The term "community" is used here in a generalized sense. Its connotation is intended to be broader than the oridinary notion of the residential neighborhood.

25. See note 22, supra. It must be acknowledged that recent judicial efforts toward school desegregation exemplify how the equal opportunity law might be used to limit *some* of the effects of social stratification by race on young people's opportunities. Note, however, the hesitancy of the courts to consider this issue along class as well as racial lines.

26. One instance of this phenomenon is that in many large cities the residential areas of middle- and lower-class blacks are contiguous, with the obvious spill-over effects.

27. For ease and clarity of exposition, many technical details of the specification of the theory are omitted here. Further, no attempt is made at mathematical rigor in the arguments. Readers interested in a more general and completely rigorous derivation of results cited here are referred to G.C. Loury, "Essays in the Theory of the Distribution of Income" (Ph.D. dissertation, Massachusetts Institute of Technology, May 1976).

28. This analysis thus explicitly disregards the arguments of Hernstein, Jensen et al. that the heritability of IQ has a major role in sustaining racial income differences. This omission may be justified on two grounds. First, nearly all of the racial differences in performance on IQ tests may be accounted for by the difference in family environments (R.H. Gordon, "The Influence of a Father's Education and Occupation on his Offspring's IQ Score," mimeographed (Cambridge, Mass.: Massachusetts Institute of Technology, 1975) and hence are already considered here. Second, the relationship between IQ and earnings is extremely tenuous at best (see Bowles and Gintis, *Capitalist America*, Chapter 4), and thus could hardly explain the magnitude of observed racial earnings differences.

29. A subtle point is that the equal opportunity does not imply complete racial equality of opportunity unless either (1) an individual's ability to acquire characteristics is independent of his or her community environment; or (2) the economic status of blacks and whites is on the whole equalized. Apparently, condition (1) requires a great deal more than integrated education.

30. The model abstracts from physical capital and the existence of a propertied class. Racial income inequality derives primarily from the relatively poor position of the black worker. Consequently, nothing fundamental is lost by our assumption. A full investigation of the determination of the social relations that obtain among various groups must incorporate this factor.

31. The method employed here could be used as the basis for a large-scale simulation effort with considerably more detail in the characterization of the occupational structure and the family and community background. The simple framework, however, lends insight into the qualitative properties of the system. Such insight should be useful in the formulation of policy, and in the eventual construction of more elaborate empirically based models.

32. Thus, Moynihan-Banfield "culture of poverty" effects are neglected to

the extent that they require the poor to have a greater preference for leisure, or to be more "present oriented." Hence the assumption is made here because we seek to show that even under the most favorable of conditions, the equal opportunity may fail to achieve its goal.

33. If almost all people had zero costs, nearly everyone would become skilled. If both types of labor were necessary to production, diminished marginal productivity would eventually lead to the unskilled wage rising relative to the skilled wage. Because the initial designation of occupational categories as "skilled" and "unskilled" was arbitrary, this assumption is effectively innocuous.

34. Let $F(L_1, L_2)$ be the production function of a representative firm where L_1 (L_2) is the number of skilled (unskilled) employees. Let Y denote output. Then constant returns to scale imply:

$$Y = L_2 \left(\frac{Y}{L_2}\right) = L_2 \left(\frac{1}{L_2} F\right) (L_1, L_2) = L_2 F \left(\frac{L_1}{L_2}, 1\right) = F_2 (F(l)).$$

35. This analysis is based on the implicit assumption that jobs and wages are settled in the labor market for any generation in the period before these agents become employed.

36. Let M_B (M_W) denote the fraction of the black (white) mature population with skilled characteristics in the previous period. Let b denote the constant fraction of the population that is black. Then the socioeconomic backgrounds of the t-generation young people are determined as follows:

$$l^{t-1} = \frac{bm_B^{t-1} + (1-b)m_W^{t-1}}{1 - [bm_B^{t-1} + (1-b)m_W^{t-1}]} \tag{8.1}$$

gives the ratio of skilled to unskilled mature workers. Thus, by the analysis of note 34 above (assuming equilibrium in the previous period),

$$\overline{w}^{t-1} = f^1 (l^{t-1}), \underline{w}^{t-1} = f(l^{t-1}) - l^{t-1} f^1 (l^{t-1})$$

and

$$w^{t-1} = \overline{w}^{t-1} - \underline{w}^{t-1} \tag{8.2}$$

may be determined from the technology of production. The degree of racial income differences may also be determined.

$$r^{t-1} = \frac{\overline{w}^{t-1} m_B^{t-1} + \underline{w}^{t-1}}{\overline{w}^{t-1} m_W^{t-1} + \underline{w}^{t-1}}. \tag{8.3}$$

37. Let $C\,(\alpha, y, r)$ represent the cost of becoming skilled for a black with parental income y, and $C\,(\alpha, y, 1)$ be the similar function for whites. Note that when $r = 1$ there are no racial income differences and the cost function is the same for blacks and whites. This is also true if there is no social stratification by race, since in that case

$$\frac{\partial c}{\partial r} = 0.$$

Now, let $v\,(w, y, r)$ be the fraction of individuals with socioeconomic background (y, r) who acquired skilled characteristics in the tth generation when the offered wage differential is w. From Figure 8-5 and note 36 we have that if (m_B^{t-1}, m_w^{t-1}) are given in the mature population, then the fraction of young blacks who would want to acquire skilled characteristics at the offered wage differential w is simply

$$m_B^t\,(w) = m_B^{t-1} V\,(w; \overline{w}^{t-1}, 1) + (1 - m_W^{t-1})\,V\,(w; \overline{w}^{t-1}, r^{t-1}). \qquad (8.4)$$

Similarly, the fraction of whites who will desire to qualify for skilled employment is

$$m_w^t\,(w) = m_w^{t-1}\,V\,(w; \overline{w}^{t-1}, 1) + (1 - m_w^{t-1})\,V\,(w; \overline{w}^{t-1}, 1). \qquad (8.5)$$

Now the supply curve S is given by

$$S(w) = \frac{b m_B^t\,(w) + (1 - b)\,m_w^t\,(w)}{1 - [b m_B^t\,(w) + (1 - b)\,m_W^t\,(w)]}. \qquad (8.6)$$

The t-generation supply curve (and hence equilibrium) depends upon the $(t - 1)$-generation equilibrium

$$(mt_B - 1, mt_w - 1).$$

38. In the language developed in the last few footnotes, the equilibrium (l_e, w_e) must satisfy

$$w_e = (1 + S\,(w_e))\,f'\,(S\,(w_e)) - f\,(S\,(w_e)), \text{ and} \qquad (8.7)$$

$$l_e = S\,(w_e).$$

The fractions of black and white young people who become skilled are then determined (using the notation of note 37):

$$m^t_B = m^t_B\,(w_e) = m^{t-1}_b\,V\,(w_e;\overline{w}^{t-1},r^t) + (1-m^{t-1})V\,(w;\underline{w}^{t-1},r^{t-1}) \quad (8.8)$$

and

$$m^t_w = m^t_w\,(w_e) = m^{t-1}_w\,V\,(w_e;\overline{w}^{t-1},1) + (1-m^{t-1}_w)\,V\,(w_e;\underline{w}^{t-1},1). \quad (8.9)$$

39. Mathematically, this relation is obtained by combining Equations (8.1), (8.2), and (8.4)-(8.9) of notes 36, 37, and 38 above.

40. To do so one need only combine Equations (8.1), (8.2), and (8.3) of note 36.

41. While logically valid under the assumptions already made, these proposition proofs involve mathematical techniques beyond the scope of the present work. The interested reader is referred to Loury, "Theory of the Distribution of Income."

42. Consider the analysis of the Survey of Educational Opportunity data conducted by the United States Civil Rights Commission in the late 1960s (*Racial Isolation*, Vol. 1, pp. 80-85). The commission found that grade-level performance of twelfth-grade students varied significantly by the individual student's social class, as well as by the average social class attending the school. Middle- and upper-class students did consistently better than lower-class students. However, there were some interesting differences in the patterns between blacks and whites. While white gains from increasing student's social class diminished as one moved first from lower to middle, and then from middle to upper class (Figure 1, p. 80), blacks gained little in moving from lower to middle class but made quite significant gains when background was advanced to upper class (Figure 1, p. 80 and Figure 3, p. 85). Similar nonconvexities for blacks in the effect of social class on achievement on IQ tests have been uncovered by Gordon, "Influence of a Father's Education." In his work, piecewise linear regression of IQ performance on socioeconomic background variables reveals significantly greater marginal effects for parent's income in the range $7,500 to $10,000 than for either lower- or higher-income classes.

43. See Duncan, "Inheritance of Poverty" and Lieberson and Fuguitt "Negro-White Differences." See also the passages from these works quoted in note 6.

Bibliography

Arrow, K. "Models of Job Discrimination." In *Racial Discrimination in Economic Life*, A. Pascal, ed. Lexington, Mass.: D.C. Heath-Lexington Books, 1972.

Arrow, K. "Some Mathematical Models of Race in the Labor Market." In *Racial Discrimination*, A. Pascal, ed.

184

Ashenfelter, O., and Heckman, J. *Measuring the Effect of an Antidiscrimination Program.* Industrial Relations Section, Princeton University, Working Paper No. 52, 1974.

Beaza, M.L. "Efficiency, Equality and Justice in Admissions Procedures to Higher Education: A Constitutional Model for Resolving Conflicting Goals and Competing Claims." *The Black Law Journal* (1974): 132-161.

Becker, G.S. *The Economics of Discrimination.* Chicago: The University of Chicago Press, 1957.

Blau, P., and O.D. Duncan. *The American Occupational Structure.* New York: John Wiley and Sons, 1967.

Blinder, A., and R.M. Solow, "Does Fiscal Policy Matter?" *Journal of Public Economics* 2 (1973): 319-337.

Bloom, L. *The Social Psychology of Race Relations.* London: George Allen and Unwin, 1971.

Blumen, H. "Race Prejudice as a Sense of Group Position." *Pacific Sociological Review* 1 (Spring 1958): 3-7.

Boudon, R. *Education, Opportunity and Social Inequality.* New York: John Wiley and Sons, 1973.

Bowles, S. "Understanding Unequal Economic Opportunity." *American Economic Review Papers and Proceedings* 63 (1973): 346-355.

Bowles, S., and H. Gintis. "The Problem with Human Capital Theory: A Marxian Critique." *American Economic Review* 65 (1975): 74-82.

Bowles, S., and H. Gintis. *Schooling in Capitalist America.* New York: Basic Books, 1976.

Cox, O.C. *Caste, Class, and Race: A Study in Social Dynamics.* New York: Doubleday, 1948.

Darity, W. "Economic Theory and Racial Economic Inequality." *The Review of Black Political Economy* 5 (Spring 1975): 225-249.

Doeringer, P., and M. Piore. *Internal Labor Markets and Manpower Analysis.* Lexington, Mass.: D.C. Heath, 1971.

Duncan, O.D., and R.W. Hodge. "Education and Occupational Mobility." *American Journal of Sociology* 67 (1963): 629-644.

Duncan, O.D. "Inheritance of Poverty or Inheritance of Race?" In *On Understanding Poverty*, D. Moynihan, ed. New York: Basic Books, 1968.

Duncan, O.D., D.K. Featherman, and B. Duncan. *Socioeconomic Background and Achievement.* New York: Seminar Press, 1972.

Feldstein, M. "Wealth Neutrality and Local Choice in Public Education." *American Economic Review* 65 (1975): 75-89.

Freeman, R.B. "Changes in the Labor Market for Black Americans, 1948-72." *Brookings Papers on Economic Activity*, I (1973): 67-131.

Freeman, R.B. "Labor Market Discrimination: Analysis, Findings, and Problems." In *Frontiers of Quantitative Economics*, M.D. Intriligator and D.A. Kendricks, eds. New York: North-Holland Publishing Company, 1974.

Gordon, R.H. "The Influence of a Father's Education and Occupation on his Offspring's IQ Score." Mimeographed. Cambridge, Mass.: Massachusetts Institute of Technology, 1975.

Hall, R., and R. Kasten. "The Relative Occupational Success of Blacks and Whites." *Brookings Papers on Economic Activity*, 3 (1973): 781-798.

Ishikawa, T. "Family Structure and Family Values in the Theory of Income Distribution." *Journal of Political Economy* 83 (1975): 987-1008.

Jencks, C. et al. *Inequality, A Reassessment of the Effect of Family and Schooling in America.* New York: Basic Books, 1972.

Lazear, E. "Intergenerational Externalities." Mimeographed. Chicago: The University of Chicago, February 1976.

Lieberson, S., and G. Fuguitt. "Negro-White Occupational Difference in the Absence of Discrimination." *American Journal of Sociology* 73 (1967): 188-200.

Loury, G.C. "Essays in the Theory of the Distribution of Income." Ph.D. dissertation, Massachusetts Institute of Technology, May 1976.

McFarland, D. "Intragenerational Social Mobility as a Markov Process." *American Sociological Review* 35 (1970): 463-476.

Manpower Policy Task Force. "The Status of Black Employment." Position Paper, Washington, D.C., January 1975.

Marshall, R. "The Economics of Racial Discrimination: A Survey." *Journal of Economic Literature* (September 1974): 849-871.

Metzger, L.P. "American Sociology and Black Assimilation: Conflicting Perspectives." *American Journal of Sociology* 76, (1971): 627-647.

Spence, M. "Job Market Signaling." *Quarterly Journal of Economics* 87 (1973): 355-374.

Starrett, D. "Social Institutions and the Distribution of Income: A Neoclassical Defense of Radical Positions." Technical Report #117. Institute for Mathematical Studies in the Social Sciences, Stanford University, December 1973.

Stiglitz, J. "The Theory of 'Screening,' Education and the Distribution of Income." *American Economic Review* 65: 283-300.

Stolzenberg, R.M. "Education, Occupation, and Wage Differences between White and Black Men." *American Journal of Sociology* 81 (1975): 299-323.

Thurow, L. *Poverty and Discrimination.* Washington: The Brookings Institution, 1969.

Thurow, L. *Generating Inequality.* New York: Basic Books, 1975.

U.S. Commission on Civil Rights. *Racial Isolation in the Public Schools*, Vols. I and II. Washington: U.S. Government Printing Office, 1967.

van der Berghe, P. *Race and Racism: A Comparative Perspective.* New York: John Wiley and Sons, 1967.

Vroman, W. "Changes in the Labor Market Position of Black Men Since 1964." *Proceedings of the Twenty-Seventh Annual Winter Meeting.* Industrial Relations Research Association, 1974: 294-306.

Wallace, P.A. "A Decade of Policy Developments in Equal Opportunities in Employment and Housing." In *A Decade of Federal Antipoverty Policy: Achievement, Failure and Lessons*, R. Haveman, ed. New York: Academic Press, forthcoming, 1976.

Wallace, P.A., and B. Anderson. "Public Policy and Black Economic Progress: A Review of the Evidence." *American Economic Review* 65 (1975): 43-52.

Weiss, R.D. "The Effect of Education on the Earnings of Blacks and Whites." *Review of Economics and Statistics* 52 (1970): 150-159.

Welch, F. "Labor Market Discrimination: An Interpretation of Income Differences in the Rural South." *Journal of Political Economy* 75 (1967): 225-241.

Wilson, W.J. *Power, Racism, and Privilege.* New York: Macmillan Company, 1973.

Wise, A.E. *Rich Schools, Poor Schools: The Promise of Equal Educational Opportunity.* Chicago: The University of Chicago Press, 1968.

Comments

Lester C. Thurow

These comments are not so much a critique of what Glenn Loury has done as they are suggestions for various ways in which the paper could be extended. The thesis of the paper is that economic equality cannot be achieved unless the social context as well as the economic context is free of racism. "Equal opportunity" in the economic sphere alone will not solve the problem, even over time.

This conclusion is even stronger than the powerful case presented by Loury. Imagine for the moment an atrophied market for human capital loans where each person or family must internally generate all of the funds necessary for his or her or its human capital investments. In this case, each person invests in his or her own human capital to the point where the marginal rate of return on human capital investments is equal to his or her own marginal rate of time preference instead of some common market rate of interest.

Marginal rates of time preferences decline with rising income levels. The man on the edge of starvation has a rate of time preference approaching infinity; the millionaire has a rate of time preference approaching zero. Thus, high-income individuals will rationally accept investment projects that would be rejected by low-income individuals. Further, human capital goods are joint products—partially investment goods and partially superior consumption goods with a high income elasticity of demand. Once again the high-income individual or family will rationally purchase more human capital goods than a low-income family or individual.

In this imaginary world an unequal start with respect to budget constraints can perpetuate itself indefinitely, even though each individual has identical preferences and there is no racism—economic or social—in the system. As a result, any low incomes produced by discrimination will tend to be perpetuated, even though discrimination has ended.

If this conclusion holds in our imaginary world, the real question is the extent to which the real world is like this imaginary world. To what extent are educational investments joint products with important high-income elasticity of demand consumption elements? It would appear that they have this aspect to a great extent. To what extent is the human capital market atrophied so that individuals must internally generate their own funds for human capital investments? A few years ago human capital loans were very limited. With government loans they are now more available, but it would be interesting to investigate the extent to which government loan policies have improved the human capital funds market. Even if these two factors are not at the extreme levels where they would prevent an eventual equalization of incomes at infinity, they could easily be in a range where the time necessary to achieve equality becomes so long as to be infinity for all practical purposes.

187

Loury analyzes the impact of "social" human capital investments in individuals, but the concept of "social" human capital investments is greater than this. Analysis indicates that a substantial fraction of all human capital investments are made on the job rather than in some formal educational institution. This immediately raises the question of how these private human capital investments are allocated. Does the individual allocate investments to himself or herself by being willing to pay for them? Or does the employer allocate investments to those individuals he or she thinks will make the "best" employees. If the latter is the case, a much larger fraction of the total human capital stock than a simple analysis of public education would indicate is out from under the control of the individuals who receive it.

While this is not the place to argue whether employees could really be implicitly paying for their on-the-job human capital investments, it is clear that they do not explicitly pay for them in a bidding market where they can signify their willingness to make human capital investments by accepting wages below that of other employees who are not making human capital investments. The lack of an explicit market means that the allocation process, at the very least, is rather inefficient. Thus, some substantial fraction of on-the-job investments are not being made in accordance with the personal tastes of the work force. Employers are doing some of the allocation, and the Loury proposition with respect to "social capital" applies to private firms as well as to public agencies.

9

Recommendations from Research Workshops on Equal Employment Opportunity

Phyllis A. Wallace

In 1974 the Industrial Relations Section of the Alfred P. Sloan School of Management at M.I.T. received a grant from the National Science Foundation, Research Applied to National Needs (RANN),[1] to conduct three research workshops on equal employment opportunity. A number of individuals representing different perspectives participated in these sessions which were held during the period January through June 1974. The objectives of these workshops were: (1) to evaluate the status of research on equal employment opportunity in all of its ramifications—race, ethnicity, sex, and religion; (2) to define research needs and to assess their scope and deficiencies; (3) to develop a comprehensive research agenda specifying the kinds of research required to develop appropriate strategies to reduce job discrimination; and (4) to identify effective techniques of increasing the utilization of employment opportunity research results.

The workshops brought together academic researchers from several social science disciplines, public officials, business managers, and practitioners from nonprofit agencies. Within a neutral academic setting, such a highly diversified group could examine equal employment opportunity issues and recommend research priorities for improving our knowledge of the barriers to occupational and employment mobility. The highlights of the workshop proceedings are reported below, followed by a review of the common themes expressed in all of the sessions.

Public Sector Workshops

The participants of the workshop on equal employment opportunity in the public sector agreed that careful research was needed on the types of jobs held by minorities and women at the various levels of federal, state, and local government. An accurate statistical portrait of the employment of these groups in the public sector would permit an assessment of past programs as well as a strong foundation for the formulation of future equal employment strategy.

Analysis of differences among public agencies in their responses to affirmative action directives and the identification of factors accounting for such differences was also recommended. What, for example, have been the characteristics of successful programs in the public sphere? Do such programs make any difference in the speed with which equal employment is advanced or are

189

penetration rates determined by the nature of the organization? The rate of progress toward equal employment opportunity in both the public and private sector should be compared.

In the 1960s, substantial increases in the numbers of minorities in public employment were directly attributable to federal agencies that focused on social and communal problems. With the transition to the "New Federalism," important research and policy questions arose concerning the shifts in employment that might accompany the shift from federal to more local administrative centers for dealing with some of these issues.

The workshop participants also examined the question of unionization in the public sector. What, for example, will be the impact of public employee unionism on the hiring and advancement of minorities and women? In reviewing past experience, could we also seek to relate variations in experience in the public sector as between craft and industrial unions? What sorts of union structures might be most effective in encouraging minority employment in the public sector?

The participants then discussed how informal organizational groups may nurture and maintain job discrimination. Despite commitment to affirmative action at the top of an organization, and even with threat of sanctions, the informal and incidental learning networks of an organization exclude women and minorities. The group agreed that more research was needed on organizational socialization processes if minorities and women were not to be excluded from the informal networks. What has been the character and effectiveness of the organizational socialization process where affirmative employment action has been attempted and succeeds?

Many questions were raised regarding the selection of public sector employees. For example, what is the effect of either an absolute or a point system of veterans' preference on public employment of minorities and women? Who should bear the cost of "gambling" on a variety of statistical predictors with people hired on non-Civil Service or merit basis? Is valid statistical discrimination acceptable? Who suffers because of statistical discrimination and what is the real cost to the taxpayer of adopting statistical predictors as guides in the selection of employees? Finally, are selection tests for public employment valid in the sense that they have a clear relationship to subsequent performance on the job?

Private Sector Workshop

The workshop on equal employment opportunity in the private sector was attended mainly by representatives from private employers. As such the workshop's proceedings were of interest not only as an expression of research needs but also as a reading of private sector sentiment toward affirmative action. The participants approached the issue of equal employment opportunity in the private sector from a tactical point of view. Among the important influences mentioned in the development of affirmative action programs were: commitment on the part of top management; pressure from various government agencies; the work force already on the job in a firm; and community pressures. The group agreed that these factors should be studied on a case-by-case basis so that conditions facilitating progress toward equal employment opportunity might be better understood. For example, is it the social climate, the money sanction, the legal sanction, or leadership, that makes a particular institution more receptive to the changes required? It is important to undertake longitudinal studies that examine the response of the different firms and industries, the backlashes that are developed behind the public stance, and the dynamics of the internal labor market. It was felt that research into the results of consent agreements between private firms and government agencies was especially needed.

If the regulatory agencies provided researchers with data on two sets of firms—those that used innovative and successful methods of achieving targets and those that have been less successful—the experience in these two groups could be compared without identifying specific firms. Research could then focus on the organizational factors that explain the difference between the two groups of firms. The advantage of this type of research is that it is not subject to problems of confidence on the part of firms fearful of publicity or further litigation.

The group expressed concern with respect to the issue of winning private sector acceptance of equal employment opportunity research. For example, confusion was often said to result from a misunderstanding of terminology. Consequently the workshop recommended that there be an effort made to standardize definitions, guide lines, and measurement criteria among the private, public, and educational spheres.[2]

The participants also noted the divergence between the researcher's approach to equal employment opportunity and the realities of the decision-making process in large firms. The workshop's recommendation was that researchers bring the constraints facing the line manager with responsibility for implementing affirmative action programs explicitly into the analysis. Research was called for in the area of incentives for instituting meaningful affirmative action programs.

The participants also argued that the business community needs to be involved in the affirmative action process. The government should seek to bring private sector employers into active policy consultation. It was felt that if private sector input is considered in the formulation of government programs, such programs will be more workable and meet less resistance at the company level. Exchange and consultation was seen as a means of gaining a greater commitment to affirmative action. In addition, a need was seen for more equal employment research sponsored by the firm itself. If private sector confidence is gained, perhaps the initiative for affirmative action will come from the private sector and the government.

Human Resources Workshop

The recommendations of the workshop on equal employment opportunity and human resources fell into three general areas:

Manpower and public policy—How can we improve the operation of the labor market?

Labor market regulation—What rules and information are needed?

Analysis of the relationship between the equal employment opportunity and other programs for the development and management of human resources—How effective are government and private employment programs?

As the workshop was attended by a broad cross-section of social scientists, the research agenda stressed interdisciplinary team research, experimentation, and assistance to equal employment opportunity administrators.

Segmentation of the labor market was associated with barriers to employment as the way in which social institutions and labor markets channel minorities and women down separate career paths with negative consequences on earnings. Drawing a distinction between career employment and dead-end employment patterns, the participants placed the following questions on the research agenda:

What are the market and institutional influences shaping observed career patterns in the labor market? What factors account for persistence or change in the different career patterns? More specifically, to what extent do family, school system, formal and informal labor market information systems, or employer practices create separate channels in the labor market? At what point is such channeling critical to career formation, and at what point or points in the channeling process should policy intervention occur?

To what extent are careers formed through external labor market mobility, and to what extent through internal labor market mobility? Furthermore, what does work experience mean? Is it possible to achieve a fuller understanding of how factors such as job content, supervisory behavior, personnel policies, and coworker attitudes are likely to affect career development in the work place?

Finally, can the career paths characterizing the dominant section of the American work force—better educated, white males—be reproduced for women and minorities? On the one hand, to what extent must traditional attitudes and expectations held by minorities and women be changed, and on the other, what modifications should be made in traditional male career routes?

A second area of research discussed by the participants involved the possibility of "rehabilitating" some of the lower paying or dead-end labor markets within which women and minorities are crowded. For example, could intervention in such markets improve the career and earnings potential of sectors where workers facing discrimination are traditionally employed?

The participants also recommended the development of programs for the assessment and evaluation of regulatory activities in the labor market so that the consequences of labor market regulation might be better understood. Examples mentioned included the follow-up of affirmative action enforcement activities of government agencies, the effect of minimum wage legislation, compliance activities including court action, voluntary affirmative action programs, and training programs directly related to equal employment opportunity activities.

Research analyzing the pressure for equal employment opportunity on manpower development and personnel assessment with the firm was also recommended. To what extent is the manpower development and utilization system within the firm altered as a result of equal employment opportunity programs? Have there been unintended effects of equal employment opportunity activities not contemplated at the time of the initial compliance activity?

The group recommended that research be followed up by carefully designed social science experimentation in public policy areas related to equal employment opportunity. Among the candidates nominated for such experimentation were: the effect of various day-care arrangements upon the labor force participation of women, testing alternative placement mechanisms, and the restructuring of procedures and incentives for personnel development within the firm.

Finally, the workshop participants considered a variety of follow-up research activities that would provide technical assistance to government administrators of equal employment opportunity laws. Among these were technical issues such as criteria and standards for compliance, projections of supply and demand by occupation, and development and validation of improved testing procedures. Case studies of firms and unions summarizing "best practice" experience with employment programs for minorities and women were also recommended. These research activities, it was suggested, might be offered by university-based groups providing various kinds of manpower and equal employment opportunity services to manpower agencies and small business concerns.

Longitudinal Studies Workshop[3]

At the second research workshop on equal employment opportunity, Dr. Herbert Parnes, Director of the Center for Human Resources Research, Ohio State University, described his unique longitudinal data on different groups in the labor force and its applications in employment discrimination research. In 1965, the Center for Human Resources Research at Ohio State University undertook a five-year longitudinal study of four groups in the labor market: middle-aged men—30 to 44 years old; middle-aged women—30 to 44 years old; young men—14 to 24 years old; and young women—14 to 24 years old. The study focused on work experience and factors affecting work experience. Other factors affecting productivity on the job were also measured, including amount and quality of education, extent of training outside of formal education networks, ability measures from high school aptitude tests for the two younger groups, health, and various social-psychological variables that might proxy for motivation. It was thought that knowledge of this kind would make an important contribution to understanding how labor markets operated and would be useful for the development and implementation of labor market policies.

Parnes noted that the oversampling of blacks in his studies ensured that racial discrimination in employment will be readable from statistically reliable data. Second, the four age-sex cohorts, with data available for the two youth groups, permit a clear focus on sex discrimination. Third, the study included variables, such as quality of education, which, although they have an important influence on productivity differentials and should therefore be controlled for, are not commonly found in micro data. Finally, the longitudinal nature of the study will for the first time allow analyses of the trends in racial and sexual discrimination in employment based on one sample observed over time.

In sum, Parnes addressed the following research problems in employment discrimination. 1. How do you control for different variables that affect rewards other than discrimination? 2. How do you measure productivity? What factors need one control for? Some might be quantity of education, quality of education, work experience and on-the-job training, health, innate ability, and motivation. Refined measures for these factors are needed. 3. What part of the difference between favored and nonfavored groups is attributable to occupational advantages, and what part is due to better wages within given structures? 4. To what extent are limitations of groups in certain occupations a result of poor access to the area, and to what extent are they a cultural role phenomenon? Parnes noted that these factors make empirical work difficult, but argued that such difficulties should not hold up the formulation of policy solutions. An example of this is discrimination against blacks. What part of this is past discrimination, and what part is present discrimination is not as critical as eliminating both (a policy decision). Policy choices need not wait for final understanding of these issues.

Research Strategies Workshop

The major focus of this final workshop was on alternative strategies for achieving better utilization of minorities and women and how research might facilitate the achievement of this objective. A very lively discussion followed a suggestion that "People who are supportive of equal employment opportunity should now begin to consider when to stop using numerical standards for enhancing minority employment opportunity." Participants responded by noting that:

Where any group is a subcritical mass, it will always require special protection.

Sex discrimination is far more complicated than race discrimination.

Where quotas are established, an index of available supply is a function of discrimination.

White males assume that they will always automatically have the leadership positions.

Participants at the workshops were concerned about the limited information available on the labor market experiences of minority groups other than black workers. From 1965 to 1969, primary emphasis was placed on understanding the racial aspects of employment discrimination. Beginning in 1970, sex discrimination received wide attention. A broader research effort would increase our knowledge of the impact of employment discrimination against the Hispanic population and other ethnic groups. Religion, age, and other conditions that constrain the structure of job opportunities might also be included on future research agenda.[4]

Since much of the future research that was suggested is longitudinal in nature and by definition costly, it was recommended that a special coordinating agency be established through which the major funding for research on equal employment opportunity could be channeled. Such an organization might reduce duplication of efforts, narrow the gap between academic research and more program-oriented efforts, concentrate on broader issues, "develop and try out new analytic tools, and help to assure greater overall payoff from the research."

Workshop Themes

While the recommendations from the three workshops reflect both the variety of perspectives represented and the wide range of debate that took place, they also reveal a number of common themes. The need for formulation and implementation of affirmative action goals and strategy was articulated again and again by the conference participants. There was broad agreement that the dynamics of the labor market both internal and external to the firm must be studied in greater depth so that strategies might be improved. With a better understanding of the peculiar demand and supply phenomena associated with racial and sexual discrimination, it was felt that forces inhibiting or actually resisting change may be more easily overcome. For example, if the role of unions, public and private, in employment discrimination is better understood, the barriers unions pose to affirmative action may be lowered.

Although the participants generally focused their comments on the particular labor market sector they knew by experience, the strategic policy questions raised were similar. Some debated intensely as to whether legislation vigorously pressed by government agencies is the critical factor in achieving equal employment opportunity, or whether strong leadership and enthusiasm on the part of a few key people within an organization are the determining ingredients in a successful affirmative action policy. Others saw the force of community pressure as a necessary condition for change. Although opinion as to the relative importance of these factors was divided, the participants urged support of studies of affirmative action programs that would weigh the characteristics distinguishing the successful from the less successful ones.

Beyond these tangible features of affirmative action strategy, the participants uniformly called for more research into the psychological dimensions of equal employment opportunity intervention. It was noted that informal meeting patterns and learning networks within an organization may nurture and maintain subtle forms of job discrimination. Subtle forms of discrimination pose barriers not only to entry into an organization but also to career advancement once on the job. Much interest was expressed in studies of interpersonal relations, group dynamics and social-psychological systems within organizations. Recognition of these factors, it was pointed out, may make the difference in successful affirmative action planning.

Participants from all sectors argued that the business community should become more involved in strategic planning for affirmative action, consulting with government agencies and academic researchers. While it was felt that more initiative must come from the business sector in this regard, it was agreed that if input from companies is considered, government programs will be viewed as being more workable and thus meet less resistance.

Finally, many of the conference participants addressed the question of affirmative action goals and strategy in relation to the economic environment. Indeed, the participants proved themselves to be farsighted in anticipating the problems which later confronted affirmative action policy as a result of the downturn in business activity in 1974/1975. There was general agreement that the implications of the zero-sum game should be examined with respect to competition among white males, minorities, and females for scarce jobs, particularly in relatively attractive areas. If affirmative action is easier under conditions of strong demand and rising employment, what progress toward equal employment goals can be expected in a recessionary period? When total employment is falling, effective affirmative action for minorities and women will have a direct correlation with a relative loss of opportunity for traditionally privileged groups in the labor market. Should affirmative action goals be sacrificed, the position of minorities and women will once again suffer.

That affirmative action goals have been accorded a low rung on the scale of priorities by employers faced with these questions is demonstrated by the layoff process that the economy recently experienced. Employers appealed to the last in, first out principle as minorities and women holding newly won positions were the first laid off.[5] Beyond the immediate damage to the affirmative action progress of minorities and women that has been done during the economic downswing, there was a noticeable increase in the resistance of both white- and blue-collar workers to programs that threatened the seniority principle. Given the fact that unacceptable levels of unemployment are likely to be with us for several years, what effects may we expect on the employment and income positions of minorities and women? As the federal compliance agencies for equal employment have negotiated settlements covering significant segments of American industry, the transitional costs of achieving a new equilibrium in the labor market are clearly specified.[6] Indeed, should the U.S. economy sustain only a moderate level of growth, affirmative action goals conceived in the expansive period of the 1960s may be seriously challenged.

Notes

1. NSF Contract No. GI-3980.

2. A session on employment discrimination in institutions of higher education produced similar recommendations.

3. Herbert S. Parnes, "The National Longitudinal Surveys: Lessons for Human Resource Policy," in *Current Issues in the Relationship Between Manpower Research and Policy*, National Commission for Manpower Policy, Special Report No. 7 (March 1976).

4. During one of the workshops, Walter Fogel discussed research on the labor market experience of Mexican-American workers. Fogel commented on issues related to accurate enumeration of the Hispanic population, labor force participation, income status, occupational groups, and immigration policies.

5. See *Franks et al. v. Bowman Transportation Company Inc., et al.*, 12 FEP Cases, 549-569.

6. See Phyllis A. Wallace, editor, *Equal Employment Opportunity and the AT&T Case*, MIT Press, 1976.

Index

Adolescence, 46, 50, 157-158
Affirmative action programs, 7, 49, 54, 124, 189-197. *See also* Equal Employment opportunity
AFL-CIO, 67, 68
Age factor, 102-112 *passim,* 127-128
Aggregation and disaggregation, 102, 115
Agriculture, 65, 71-72, 76
Alexis, Marcus, 2
American Telephone and Telegraph, 28
Antidiscrimination laws, 75, 77, 78. *See also* Equal opportunity laws; Regulatory agencies
Arrow, Kenneth, 4-5, 58, 59, 60, 112
Ashenfelter, Orley, 15, 17
Astin, Alexander W., 21

"Backlash," 45, 123
Bargaining model, 7-8, 64, 65-66
Becker, Gary, 1-8, 58, 177, 179
Behavioral model, 62-63, 70-71
Behavioral probabilities, 87-89, 90, 97, 115
Bell Telephone System, 54
Bergmann, Barbara, 3, 58-59, 94, 125
Bias, computational, 133, 135, 151
Blacks: career aspirations, 19, 23, 87; education, 23, 58, 69-72, 75; employment patterns, 57-78, 82; government employment, 74, 76-77; income, 71, 73, 76; men, 24, 70, 73; political power, 73; private employment, 77-78; rural, 71-73, 76; Southern, 71-75; and unions, 61, 66-68; urban, 70, 73; women, 24-27, 33, 70, 73
Blue-collar workers, 61, 63, 73
Bohn, M.J., 50
Bowles, Samuel, 156, 179
Bureau of Labor Statistics, 97, 116
Bureau of the Census, 97

Cade, Toni, 27
Canada, 116
Capitalism, 7, 61
Career aspirations, 19, 21-23, 25-26, 27, 28, 39, 46, 50
Career commitment, 16
Career development, 42-43, 192
Chinitz, B., 94
Chow, G.C., 116
Cities, 73, 90-91, 155, 180
Civil Rights Act of 1964, 154
Civil rights movement, 68, 69
Civil Service Commission, 77

Class consciousness, 7, 61
Colleges, 19, 21-22, 25-26, 40, 197
Community, defined, 158, 179
Community background, 155, 157-169 *passim,* 172, 173, 174, 175
Community pressure, 65, 66, 68, 71
Competition factors, 3, 6, 27, 58, 59, 60, 64, 65, 72, 153. *See also* Equilibrium factors
Concerted Services in Training and Education, 72-73, 76
Consent agreements, 191
Construction industry, 64, 67
Cost minimization, 3, 58
Courts, 154, 180
Crowley, J., 22
"Culture of poverty" (Moynihan-Banfield), 180
Current Population Survey (CPS), 95, 96, 97, 98, 116

Data, 54, 95-98, 120, 146, 151
Decision-making, 39, 45
Demographic model, 102-112
Discrimination, 124, 195; past, 159, 170, 172; status vs. physical phenomenon, 3, 61, 62; types, 5, 49, 61, 155; and wage differentials, 138, 149
"Discrimination coefficient," 58, 59
Divorce, 46
Doeringer, Peter, 6
Dual labor market, 6-7, 14, 60-61, 65, 123, 192, 195
Duncan, Otis Dudley, 18, 177, 178, 179
Dunlop, John, 62

Econometric methodology, 97-99, 122, 124-125
Econometric models, 91-93
Economic conditions, 69, 196-197
Economic development, 72-73
Economic research, 53-54
Economics of Discrimination (Becker), 1
Education, 70, 87, 187; equal opportunity policy, 159, 180; quality of, 69, 133, 155, 159, 175
Educational aspirations, 21, 23, 25-26, 27, 69
Educational attainment, 133, 149, 155, 177; blacks, 58, 69-72, 75; sex differentials, 17-18, 21, 23
Educational loans, 155, 179, 187
Empirical models, 59-60

United States Department of Labor, 76, 95, 96, 97
United States Office of Federal Contract Compliance, 77
United States Supreme Court, 154
University of Michigan Survey Research Center, 20
Urban Institute, 83-112 *passim*
Utility maximation, 59, 123, 128, 133-134, 143

Vacancy data, 90, 96, 97, 113, 116
Value factors, measure of, 20-21
Vanski, Jean E., 116
"Victim deficit" model, 13, 24

Wage differentials: and human capital investment, 127-147; intergroup, 132, 134-138, 144, 146, 149-151; racial, 3,

4-5, 58, 59, 62, 66, 177
Wallace, Phyllis A., 18, 177
Welch, Finis, 3, 58, 78
White, H.C., 113
White-collar jobs, 63, 72, 73, 74, 75, 77
White workers, 3, 58-71 *passim*
Women: adolescence, 46, 50; boyfriends, 46, 50; education, 17-18, 21, 23, 25-26, 40; family care, 25, 46, 50; fear of success, 25, 47; life cycle and labor force participation, 16, 45-50, 131; role models, 46-47, 50; tokenism, 47, 48-49
Work ethic values, measure of, 20-21
Work experience, 72, 96, 97, 191, 194
Worker-job pairing, 87, 88
Workers, substitute and complementary, 3, 58

Zero-sum game, 7, 124, 125, 196

List of Contributors

James E. Annable, Jr.
Senior Labor Economist, Board of Governors
Federal Reserve System

Lotte Bailyn
Associate Professor of Organizational Psychology and Management
Massachusetts Institute of Technology

Carolyn Shaw Bell
Katharine Coman Professor of Economics
Wellesley College

Barbara R. Bergmann
Professor of Economics, and Director of the Project on the Economics of
Discrimination
University of Maryland

Patricia Gurin
Professor of Psychology
University of Michigan

Bennett Harrison
Associate Professor of Economics and Urban Studies
Massachusetts Institute of Technology

Charles C. Holt
Director, Inflation/Unemployment Research
The Urban Institute

Judith Long Laws
Assistant Professor of Sociology
Cornell University

Glenn C. Loury
Assistant Professor of Economics
Northwestern University

Ray Marshall
Professor of Economics and Director of the Center for the Study of Human
Resources
The University of Texas at Austin

Ronald L. Oaxaca
Associate Professor of Economics
University of Arizona

Michael Piore
Professor of Economics
Massachusetts Institute of Technology

Solomon W. Polachek
Assistant Professor of Economics
The University of North Carolina at Chapel Hill

Lester C. Thurow
Professor of Economics
Massachusetts Institute of Technology

About the Editors

Phyllis A. Wallace is Professor of Management at the Alfred P. Sloan School of Management at the Massachusetts Institute of Technology. Dr. Wallace has been actively engaged as a researcher, teacher, and consultant on problems concerning the development and management of human resources with special emphasis on employment discrimination. She is the author of *Pathways to Work* (Lexington Books, 1974) and the co-author and editor of *Equal Employment Opportunity and the AT&T Case* (Cambridge: M.I.T. Press, 1976). Her other works have been published in collections and specialized journals.

Annette M. La Mond is a Ph.D. candidate in Economics at Yale University. She received the B.A. in Economics from Wellesley College and the M.S. from the Alfred P. Sloan School of Management. She has lectured in Economics at Wellesley College and consulted on a variety of projects in the fields of transportation and labor economics.